ILLEGAL ALIENS IN THE WESTERN HEMISPHERE

ILLEGAL ALIENS IN THE WESTERN HEMISPHERE

Political and Economic Factors

Kenneth F. Johnson
Miles W. Williams

EPILOGUE by
STEPHEN P. MUMME

PRAEGER SPECIAL STUDIES • PRAEGER SCIENTIFIC

Library of Congress Cataloging in Publication Data

Johnson, Kenneth F.
    Illegal aliens in the Western Hemisphere.

    Bibliography: p.
    Includes index.
    1. Aliens, Illegal. I. Williams, Miles. II. Title.
JV6271.J64   325.6'31'091812   81-2729
ISBN 0-03-052461-X   AACR2

Published in 1981 by Praeger Publishers
CBS Educational and Professional Publishing
A Division of CBS, Inc.
521 Fifth Avenue, New York, New York 10175 U.S.A.

© 1981 by Praeger Publishers

123456789   145   987654321

Printed in the United States of America

To Nina Maria Johnson
for her love and
support

and

Ted and Reah Carnes,
esteemed foster parents

Kenneth F. Johnson
October, 1980

To Helen M. Williams
and the memory of
Claude W. Williams

Miles W. Williams
October, 1980

CONTENTS

LIST OF TABLES

ILLEGAL ALIENS IN THE WESTERN HEMISPHERE

INTRODUCTION

When the twentieth century ends, there may be no room left for human cultures to survive as we now know them. Thorny questions of survival for ethnic subgroups may well have been submerged in the broader crisis of saving the planet. While the affluent First World societies consume an acutely disproportionate share of the planet's riches, the impoverished Third World societies are exhausting both their resources and their space. This is partly because Third World resources are drained off to sustain First World enterprises. There seem to be no viable frontiers left for human expansion, other than going underground, into the sea, or into outer space. Since World War II demographic pressures for people to migrate in search of a better life have grown to proportions that now greatly concern governments in the receiving countries. North America — Canada and the United States — is one of the most attractive target areas for would-be migrants.

Not all immigrants receive joyous official welcomes. As some governments have responded to population pressure with more restrictive immigration regulations, the option of clandestine or illegal migration has been taken by more migrants. Countries that once prided themselves on being "immigrant nations" now feel demands from within to stop the "angry Third World horde."

In the Western Hemisphere, the focal area of this book, illegal immigration (including clandestine, unsanctioned, fraudulent, and/or undocumented entry) is reaching crisis proportions for some governments. In this study we consider the ideal of creating a hemispheric community-of-nations government as one approach to handling what is clearly a hemispheric dilemma. We devote the majority of our attention to analysis of the causes and consequences of the illegal migration in its various stages and locations. As to the size of the movement, that is a difficult question. How does one study an illegal and/or clandestine population? Surely not by conducting a census. The U.S. census of 1980 was challenged in court on the ground that counting illegal aliens would give representational advantages to those districts having the greatest concentrations of them (such as California, Illinois, New Jersey, New York, and Texas). The Supreme Court, in refusing the challenge, held that the Constitution is silent on the alienage of those who are to be represented in Congress. So the census was taken, the illegals were counted, and their alienage went unquestioned. But the issue will not be dropped there. The south-to-north hemispheric trend in illegal migration continues full speed as of this writing, and voices are rising both for and against it.

The unsanctioned migration of Cubans and Haitians into the United States almost forced its way into the 1980 presidential campaign. Odds are that illegal

1

aliens will be a full-blown issue in 1984. When a West German newspaper takes notice of the growing "Latinization of America," it may be safe to assume that the south-to-north migration of people is causing hemispheric change that has worldwide meaning.[1] For one thing, it means that Latins have replaced Europeans as the principal group asking to be let into North America. The brunt of this is now felt in the United States. Hispanics (those who maintain the cultural practice of speaking Spanish at least in the family setting) have become large minorities in most of the larger American cities. They now constitute a political majority in San Antonio, Texas. The entire American Southwest has been given the name Atzlán, which signifies, for some Mexican Americans, a geographically defined zone of political solidarity. There has been open talk of the secession of Atzlán, as if it were a "Chicano Quebec." It is claimed that what the United States took from Mexico by conquest in 1848 will be repatriated to Mexico via the seeping wave of clandestine immigrants, perhaps by the century's end.

In southern Florida the invasion of Cubans and other Caribbean peoples has created strains with the black citizen community; it is alleged that some 30,000 "Anglos" have left the Miami area as a result of Cuban pressures during recent years. It is also estimated that by 1990, Dade County, Florida, will have a Hispanic majority and that a culture clash will have to be faced.[2] Europeans may have conquered the Indian population of the Western Hemisphere, and subsequently the North Americans may have broken off from the Europeans; but as the Hispanic influence presses northward, a settling of old accounts is foreseen. Stated in a happier-sounding mode, this migration and potential miscegenation may hasten the day when all residents of the Western Hemisphere will be able to call themselves Americans. But would that be a livable world?

The decision to undertake this study stems from the authors' shared conviction that unless a truly hemispheric community comes into being, and with it true participatory instruments and arenas for hemispheric governance, we may well find the area unfit to live in by the end of the twentieth century. That may very well be the case in other parts of the world as well. We face overburdening problems from uncontrolled population increase, including exhaustion of the world's food stores and threats to our oxygen supply. Also there are threats to peace that emerge from the desperate efforts of regimes to control scarce resources. Unloading one's excess population on a neighboring state can lead, and has led, to war, as we will document. Certain governments today commit genocide against unwanted populations. Benign neglect, the policy of looking the other way as poverty and overpopulation are "solved" through clandestine migration, may be no more than postponement of imminent disaster.

We also became interested in the illegal alien phenomenon because of the contrasting political and economic meanings it has taken on in the United States during recent years. Politically it is often North American labor leaders and police chiefs who scream about the "silent invasion" of Mexicans and others from the South. Economic interests (from agricultural to industrial), in contrast, welcome the coming of cheap and usually docile labor. Congress is divided among spokesmen for the opposing groups, and as a result reform of immigration law does not occur; no effective barriers are mounted, although they could be, nor is a guest-worker program instituted that could legalize and regularize the illegal migration for the benefit of all. Instead, nothing is done in the United States except formalistic talk; and the migration continues unchecked. That is benign neglect in the absence of policy. States and localities are asked to deal with the problem on an ad hoc basis, at least in the United States. Canada, as will be seen, has taken more concrete steps both to regularize clandestine migration and to curtail illegal alienage generally.

Our Latin neighbors present varied responses to illegal migration ranging from absolute silence to diplomatic protest to outright invitations for the illegals to come. Great public fanfare was raised by Paraguay when allegedly illegal aliens from Argentina came in to assassinate Anastasio Somoza, the former dictator of Nicaragua who was living there, in September 1980.[3]. Economically it is the building trades and commercial interests of the Argentine middle classes that absorb the millions of illegal aliens who seek work after having abandoned their own countries. In Latin America, when illegal aliens are treated in the political sense, they are often seen as an evil force. When the question is economic, their migration may be seen as beneficial. Examples of this attitudinal dichotomy will emerge from around the hemisphere in this study. The spectrum runs all the way from ready acceptance of illegal aliens to outright genocide and war against them.

It is difficult to study illegal populations with precision, since one can hardly take a census of them. For that reason our effort will appear quite frequently to be on weak substantive grounds, something we hope to overcome in a future edition after we have benefited from colleagues' criticism plus our own ongoing quest for more precise methods with which to study clandestine populations. We ask the reader to note carefully our broad focus in this volume: let us specify as best we can the principal actors, elements, and influences in the illegal migration, plus the norms that motivate and guide them. We do this so that the socioeconomic malaise that generates clandestine migration can be understood, intervened, and managed on a hemispheric community basis. We are pointing to a critical problem affecting the future existence of the hemisphere and we are saying, "Here are some of the ideas and tools you will need for dealing with it." If we are guilty of conceptual ambiguities, we are also victims of a vacuum in substance, this owing to the inherent difficulties of studying a clandestine phenomenon. For that reason we invite the suggestions of scholars and policy makers as to how we might elaborate an analytic paradigm or schema that could be made operational for hemispheric betterment, toward the goals of creating many Americas and Americans and of sharing the good life equitably with all.

"Ideas and tools" are not employed here as social science jargon. Ideas would be, for example, the notion of livability strategies, long-range plans for achieving a good life whose characteristics are well-specified at any given time by given participants who have agreed voluntarily on a set of acceptable procedural rules. Tools could be the use of deportation statistics as one indicator of the intensity of potentially illegal alienage as experienced in any given nation (to be precise, the case of Canada; see Chapter 3). We assume that many livability strategies are compatible within one hemispheric umbrella strategy, but that some must be excluded. We do not, for instance, see the international dumping of excess population as an acceptable technique for furthering national goals. Nor would we find slavery or genocide acceptable within any concept of hemispheric good. We might, however, be able to make a sound case for a new guest-worker program as part of a larger socioeconomic cooperative plan between the United States and Mexico. We might also make a case for creating international reserves for aboriginal peoples whose cultures might otherwise be lost through forced clandestine migration.

The reader will find certain conceptual overlaps that appear to us unavoidable, at least for now. There are certain nuances of meaning that distinguish clandestine from illegal migration, yet in many cases the two may be one and the same (for example, many, if not most, deportable aliens in Canada entered legally but later became unacceptable, and their continued presence then became illegal). Not all undocumented migration is illegal if the receiving nation (for example, Argentina) chooses in practice to ignore the legal formality of documentation, thereby abrogating it on a de facto basis. Not all illegal Mexican aliens in the United States should be called undocumented: many of them have Mexican documents showing them to be illegal aliens — yet many of them did not enter clandestinely, but submitted to routine entry procedures and later overstayed their visas and/or permits. Other terms that we use interchangeably from time to time are extralegal, surreptitious, fraudulent, unsanctioned, and informal. The complexity of the phenomenon is such as to deny us, at least as of this writing, a comprehensive analytic term or concept.

We also have a human rights goal in this study. We believe in the natural right of all human beings to enjoy the physical and emotional inviolability of one's self. This includes the right to try to find a better life in another country; and it is instinctive for each person to violate that country's immigration laws, if necessary, in the quest for a better life. Obviously the target nation has a countervailing juridical right to try to enforce its laws. The conflict of right against right in this process can, and should, be managed by the hemispheric community so that the human rights of all can be preserved. These include the right to decent space in which to live, enough food to eat, clean air to breathe, and a reasonable expectation that one's offspring can also find a life that is free of want, suffering, and oppression. It also means the natural right of human beings to have an opportunity to fulfill their talents and aspirations, not to be perpetually restrained by artificial political borders.

Finally, we assume that magistrates who satisfy greedy interests by deliberately visiting want and oppression upon others are corrupt. We believe that corruption is a concept that may at times be culture-relative (like the line between a bribe and a tip), but we assert that profiting from the enslavement and torture of others is generically corrupt. Thus we are prepared to argue, for example, that a migrant or refugee resettlement project in one country may be corrupt while (comparatively speaking) in another it may be acceptable, albeit poorly managed, depending on the motives and consequences of what is done. We will cite evidence that during 1979 and 1980 a refugee program in Argentina was managed in a morally corrupt way, while at the same time Canada absorbed many more refugees in an exemplary way. We do express normative judgments in this book, and accept responsibility for them.

Nor should ethnic sensitivities be affected by the assertion that governmental corruption — in Mexico, for instance — contributes to illegal emigration out of that country. To say that a regime (Mexico) is corrupt and can be improved upon is not to argue ipso facto for its revolutionary overthrow; much less does it imply disparagement of persons who share that nation's cultural heritage. Criticism of a government does not imply ethnic prejudice or racism.

If there is a bias in this book, it is that well-managed multiethnicity (different people celebrating each other's differences and living peacefully together)[4] is a desirable goal. We doubt that secession of regions or provinces from any given hemispheric state will, in and of itself, further the good life through ethnic geopolitics. Recognition of the separate ethnic character and integrity of a certain region may, however, be effectively pursued via hemispheric government. Thus, in a hopeful way, we might speculate that creation of a "Chicano Quebec" could be accomplished without destruction of the United States and that French Canadians can preserve their distinct ethnicity without destroying the Dominion of Canada. And we would hope that El Salvador and Honduras might even be merged politically for the socio-economic betterment of both nations and that this could, in the future, be accomplished without war. Following so risky a vision as that, we might even think in terms of hemispheric cooperation to share food, mediate conflict to avoid war, and plan resource and environmental conservation. Starting at the hemispheric level may be less utopian than continuing to expect world government somehow to emerge from the United Nations. But we need something definitely stronger and more independent than the existing Organization of American States (of which Canada is today only an observer, not a member).

In preparing this study we have benefited from the wisdom and goodwill of a goodly number of persons. Kenneth F. Johnson gives sincere thanks to George Jeffs and his colleagues at the Canada Employment and Immigration Commission of Toronto, including Al Naylor, Milt Best, and Ken Lawrence. Other distinguished Canadians who deserve thanks are Sylva Gelber, Peter Duschinsky, Joe Constant, Garnet Quigley, Bill Neville, Jim Versteegh, Jessie Falconer and Brian Dougall. He also extends warmest gratitude to Harry Mellman, Ray Neudecker, and Dorothy Walker of St. Louis for their wise counsel and special understanding. Major debts of gratitude are owed to

W. J. van Staalduinen of the Canadian diplomatic service for his wisdom and encouragement and to the Faculty Enrichment Programme of the Canadian Embassy in Washington, D.C. Professor Johnson also acknowledges special debts of gratitude to two distinguished Latin Americans, Oscar Monroy Rivera of Mexico and Oscar Francisco Risso of Argentina, for their contributions to this study.

A similar number of distinguished persons collaborated in the research of Miles W. Williams and merit his thanks here. These include Pedro Rubiano Sáenz, bishop of Cúcuta in Colombia, and Sister Ana Lucía María B. of the Deportation Reception Center in Cúcuta for their assistance in gathering information about the Colombia-Venezuela border, and Gabriel Murillo of Universidad de los Andes in Bogotá; also to be thanked are Professor Oscar Martínez and the fine staff at the Oral History Institute at the University of Texas-El Paso. Professor Williams is most particularly grateful to Mauro Romero Lara, a wise counsel, trusted friend, and distinguished chronicler of the Mexico-U.S. borderlands culture. Mr. Lara's vision extends from the revolutionary period at the turn of this century and has significantly enriched this study.

Both authors give warm appreciation to Betsy Brown of Praeger Special Studies for her criticism and skillful management of this project and to Steve Mumme for evaluating the manuscript and for his epilogue.

NOTES

1. From *World Press Review*, November 1980, p. 45.
2. Ibid.
3. *Diario las Américas* (Miami), October 8, 1980.
4. "Celebrating our differences" is the motto of a multilingual radio and television operation in Toronto that broadcasts daily in over 30 languages (not counting English and French).

1

POPULATION EXCHANGE IN THE WESTERN HEMISPHERE

MIGRATION AND THE QUALITY OF LIFE

It was hunger for land and the quest for freedom that sent Europeans to colonize and populate the Western Hemisphere. Many settlers came to escape religious and political persecution, to look for land in which to establish a new cultural setting for life. Often this involved the pillage of an established society. The relics of the ancient Aztecs, Mayas, and Incas throughout Latin America are reminders of some of the traumata that colonial immigration brought with it. Indians, Eskimos, and scattered aboriginal subcultures remind Canadians and Americans of similar historical legacies in the northern part of the hemisphere. Between the seventeenth and nineteenth centuries there were wars of conquest and invasion by waves of immigrants from Europe, with lesser migrations coming from Africa and Asia. Settlers tried to expand their numbers — and hence their defenses — vis-à-vis the Indians of the New World, who were, for the most part, displaced and liquidated if they could not be assimilated. To the extent that indigenous subcultures remain today, there is at least symbolic hostility to the reach of "modernity" from without. There also is scientific evidence to challenge the view that the advent of modernity really has brought about the good life when compared with the aboriginal lifestyle of some of the remnant cultures.[1] It may be that the hunting and gathering societies of premodern times had a great deal of "good life" to offer, especially when one considers the contemporary fight for survival within the competitive ethic.[2]

The nineteenth century was a period of consolidation and independence for the once-colonial holdings in much of the Western world. By the time World War II broke out, most of the Western Hemisphere's frontier area had been claimed, although some pioneering opportunity existed later in the twentieth century in such areas as the U.S. deserts and the Canadian territories. By the 1980s a new form of pioneering, the urban variety, had emerged as one-time refugees from central city areas returned to displace the poor from their ghettos, partly as the result of high transportation costs created by the petroleum crises of the 1970s and thereafter. At this point many people began to accept what experts had warned for over a decade, that the crush of people into the urban areas would produce one of the great social catastrophes of our time. Cities became unlivable. They were infested with slums (in the late 1970s it was estimated that half of Mexico City's 10 million inhabitants were slum dwellers). Air was polluted in nearly every major city. A few metropolitan areas like Toronto, with its sophisticated planning and mass transportation, may have been exceptions to this otherwise sorry rule.

From the urban standpoint no new immigrants from anywhere were needed. But they came. Major urban complexes like Caracas and Buenos Aires were circled with rings of depressed, marginal communities. New York was often termed an economic and cultural atrocity. Migration, scarcity of resources, and human deprivation were central elements in this scenario.

Much of the immigration contributed to the growth of identifiable ethnic communities, ranging from the depressed Latin sectors of East Los Angeles, New York, and Chicago to the relatively affluent Chinese sectors of Toronto and San Francisco. Much of the migration into these ethnic sectors was clandestine. Estimating the extent of such clandestine migration is a highly complicated task that will be deferred for the moment. Such migration from other countries was increasingly seen during the 1970s as a causal factor in the displacement of Canadian and U.S. workers. The impact of illegal immigrants on public health and safety, schools, and political representation became a topic for political action and debate. American farmers protested potatoes from Canada and tomatoes from Mexico, but they welcomed illegal migrant agricultural workers from just about anywhere if they kept the price of labor down while production and transportation costs were rising. Even the U.S. census of 1980 was challenged in court, on the ground that the counting of illegal aliens would adversely affect the political and financial fortunes of the less-populated states and their urban areas.[3]

Between Mexico and the United States one sees a spectrum of issues and problems involving both legal and clandestine migration in the Western Hemisphere. Estimates that some 7 million Mexicans lived and worked illegally in the United States during the early 1980s — roughly 10 percent of Mexico's total population — contributed to public concern over what appeared to be an increasing volume of extralegal population transfer into the United States. But at the other end of Mexico, in the South, economic refugees and the war-ravaged from Guatemala and El Salvador poured northward into Mexico. The Mexican government reported that between 800 and 1,000 illegal Central American immigrants were deported each week.[4] Interviews with Mexican government officials produced estimates that for every illegal immigrant caught coming over their southern border, some 30 others got away. At the same time U.S. officials complained that for every illegal Mexican alien eluding the Border Patrol, probably three or four others "got home free." Clearly, during the 1970s and 1980s desperation to abandon one's homeland affected millions of people in the Western Hemisphere.

But along with this migration there was a population explosion by natural means. The Population Reference Bureau of Washington, D.C., cited the mythical continent-island of Populandia that emerged in the Pacific Ocean during 1977, began at once overpopulating itself, and adopted Spanish as its official tongue.[5] Why Spanish? Why not? In the Western Hemisphere that might make sense. But to many in the Western Hemisphere, alarm at over-population and extralegal population transfer also makes sense. At the beginning of the 1980s the issue had become tantamount to survival.

How to survive on the planet Earth is the fundamental socioeconomic and political issue of our times. The 1970s will be remembered for the awakening of a constructive alarm over the possibility that some of us may be living in a life-boat that is unable to hold those clinging desperately to its sides for survival. This school of thought contends that the developed nations of the world are, indeed, lifeboats whose culture and well-being cannot survive except at the expense of others. The "lifeboat ethic" holds that the humanitarian doctrine of "one meal for each mouth" can only result in a totally miserable world for everyone. It will be necessary, therefore, to let starvation purge the Third World as nature's way of castigating those who do not regulate their breeding habits and who fail to develop, conserve, and rejuvenate their natural and human resources in a responsible way. Civil libertarians find this doctrine morally repugnant, but in the face of growing population pressure on the planet, the "lifeboat ethic" is unlikely to go away.

Calculations from the Population Reference Bureau hold that the planet's total population in 1980 is about 4.4 billion, and predict that by 2000 the figure will have climbed to over 6 billion, given current birth and death rates.[6] Some estimates have it that by the end of the twenty-first century the earth's population will have grown to 50 billion, leading to an everlasting war of all against all, the exhaustion of the oxygen supply, and destruction of the entire human cultural legacy.

Many concerned scholars believe such a dire prediction is unwarranted, providing their preferred ethic, the "quality of life ethic," is allowed to function. In the "quality of life" scenario there would be an unleashing of forces that are either latent or incipient in most humans and that would, as in Sweden, achieve an equitable wealth distribution, thereby giving everyone a recognizable and perceived stake in not overpopulating the world. Persons allowed to share meaningfully in their national (or world) wealth would see the benefit in regulating their family size. In Sweden it is said that a birth rate of 33 per 1,000 living persons existed in 1800, but by 1950 it had dropped to 14 per 1,000. As Sweden's wealth distribution became more equitably spread along a normal curve, its birth rate went down to livable proportions.

The "quality of life ethic" also urges structural reforms within socioeconomic and political systems to permit innate human regulating forces to control population growth naturally. This would involve the more developed nations of the world sharing their technology with the crowded and less developed states (such as India) so as to control population and immediately generate more food.

But the structural reforms on which the "quality of life ethic" rests are not always accompanied by corresponding changes in values. During the 1970s India's population control programs failed. Its food production programs came nowhere near meeting the country's desperate needs; and, when given sophisticated technology, India's leadership decided to join the quest for world "prestige" by exploding a nuclear device. That is ironic, because the dropping of atomic bombs on the excess population of the Third World is one of the proposals set forth by a well-known proponent of the "lifeboat ethic" who had countries like India specifically in mind.[7]

Although this book is about the Western Hemisphere and its population transfer problems, the crisis of scarcity and deprivation is worldwide. And there is growing evidence that what happens to scarce resources at one extreme of the map can threaten human well-being at other, noncontiguous locations. Take, for instance, the matter of trees and vegetation. Increasing population means more consumption of trees and plant products. Especially critical is the condition of indigenous and aboriginal populations that depend primarily on the bountiful earth for their subsistence. We could, of course, exterminate such populations in the interest of helping the more "advanced" cultures survive. But that would mean loss of one more piece of the human heritage, and it has been argued forcefully in the case of the Aché Indians of Paraguay and Brazil that both peoples and their cultures have natural survival rights.[8] Thus, both genocide and ethnocide are unacceptable policies. But those victimized indigenous peoples must compete with the growing modern society for the scarce resources of the forest, the field, and the stream. The survival techniques of primitive societies, like slash-and-burn farming, may be incompatible with the conservation goals of the modern world. And we stress that slash-and-burn "living" involves both trees and ground vegetation whose destruction may have deleterious effects on the immediate region and its atmosphere. This, in turn, is tied to the population crisis in a vicious circle, inasmuch as subsistence living is most common among the rural poor who depend heavily on trees and ground vegetation for their sustenance. These basic facts of life should be emphasized. Keeping the Third World alive, not to mention the Fourth World refugees, may impinge on the lifestyle of the rest of us. But what difference, you may ask, does it make to us if the people of Africa and Latin America exhaust their trees?

It is estimated that some nine-tenths of the world's poor people depend on wood from trees for a fuel for cooking and heating. It is also believed that wood users constitute over one-third of the world's total population.[9] As petroleum prices rise and annual world population growth continues unrestrained, the pressure on wood reserves also grows. Massive reafforestation programs, along with population control, will be needed if drastic fuelwood shortages are to be avoided even within the 1980s.[10] Most Indian villages in the Western Hemisphere have no reafforestation program whatsoever. Migration of Bolivian Indians out of the Andean area and eastward into neighboring countries is related to their living on already overworked and overslashed forest and grazing areas. The vegetation scarcity explains the migration in part, but there is an even broader and potentially graver issue.

What are the possible consequences to both the modern world and the Third World of massive deforestations? Climatologists believe that increasing the atmospheric albedo,[11] hence raising the heat and carbon dioxide concentrations, may be a result of major deforestations. Decreasing the amount of standing forest on the Earth's surface, accompanied by over-grazing and exhaustion of ground vegetation, may lead to dire consequences including melting of polar ice caps, a worldwide rise in sea levels and flooding of inhabited areas, and changes in present locations of desert and rain belts.[12] Or, to put it in hard, plain terms, if Brazil's Amazon region were to be turned into the world's largest parking lot (financed, of course, by "development" loans and grants from the United States), it could seriously threaten the Earth's oxygen supply, create unhealthy levels of carbon dioxide, turn the grain-producing plains of North America into deserts, and create famine throughout the world.

This might be acceptable to the "lifeboat ethic" proponents, providing the only people who perished were in India, Tanzania, Bolivia, and other parts of the Third World. Unfortunately, the research of climatologists indicates that drought and famine will not respect political and geographic boundaries. To this one must add the population pressure. If Third World peoples continue to proliferate and to cover vegetated areas with their slums, if they continue to slash and burn forests in quest of firewood and food, and if cities continue to mushroom out and to eliminate vegetation and forest, then a massive worldwide deforestation may be occurring anyway. At that point a "fortress America" concept will be useless. Perhaps what is needed is a "lifeboat Earth" ethic under a world government if civilization and culture are to survive.

The Western Hemisphere is part of that civilization. In this book we will be concerned primarily with hemispheric phenomena and survival, but we do not pretend that they can realistically be separated from the world context in a permanent way. Just like carbon dioxide, heat, famine, and plague, displaced people are drifting across national boundaries. But we do not equate people with plague. We do equate them with the desperate search for a solution to scarcity and a refuge from deprivation. Migration is occurring at a rate that is difficult to estimate because much of it is clandestine. People are trying to escape the overcrowding of their native lands and are searching for perceived opportunity in neighboring countries. In the Western Hemisphere one war, in 1969, was fought between El Salvador and Honduras over the issue of extralegal population transfer and the human rights of the clandestine migrants. Diplomatic and economic relations remained paralyzed for over a decade following that war, which claimed several thousands of lives. And at the moment of this writing El Salvador is still in the throes of violent revolution stemming from the deprivation of its population. Like other natives of the Western Hemisphere Salvadorans look to North America as a place to migrate and escape their ill fate. And therein lies the rub: it is questionable whether North America — Canada and the United States — can continue to absorb these socioeconomic and political refugees. It is from this recognition that the "lifeboat ethic" rhetoric arises, and it should not be dismissed idly.

Earlier in this century the sociologist Maurice Davie wrote of two critical aspects of hemispheric migration toward the United States. First, he feared that the transfer of population from Mexico and Canada into the United States could ultimately result in the loss of U.S. territory to those nations through secessionist movements.[13] Second, he voiced a conviction that the yellow, brown, and black races would be unassimilable and that their exclusion would be indispensable to the welfare of the United States.[14] This dire prophecy has not come true exactly as Davie expressed it. But, ignoring the racist-sounding part of his pronouncement for the moment, we can say that a kind of Mexican irredentism has developed in the American Southwest, where Mexican-American activist groups have proclaimed the territory of Atzlán and have talked of secession, even using the analogy of a "Chicano Quebec." In the twentieth century it is, of course, Mexico — and not Canada — that creates an illegal immigration problem for the United States. Mexico today has great difficulty in absorbing its population explosion (about 3.5 percent annually) because of cultural inhibitions against family regulation, scarce resources, land shortage, uneven economic development, and extensive political corruption. The corruption exacerbates all the other problems. Throughout much of Latin America corruption in government and socioeconomic planning lies behind the emigration and extralegal immigration that have become a hallmark of our times and that may, before this century is over, obliterate the contemporary distinctions between states. (For instance, if all the people of Mexico moved into the United States, and if all Jamaicans moved into Canada, we would have, for all intents and purposes, two fewer nations in the hemisphere, at least potentially.) First let us consider some contemporary trends within the hemisphere itself, on a regional basis.

MIGRATION TRENDS IN NORTH AMERICA

The bulk of North America's immigration around mid-twentieth century was from European nations of the North and West, a trend continuing from the previous century. Table 1.1 shows population migration calculations for 1946-55.

TABLE 1.1
Net Emigration from Europe to North America, 1946-55
(in thousands)

	North America	*Canada*	*United States*
British Isles	512	281	231
Scandinavia	61	19	42
Germany	397	132	265
Netherlands	129	101	28
France	55	26	29
Other	127	70	57
Italy	246	127	119
Portugal	12	3	9
Spain	7	2	5
Greece	41	14	27
Yugoslavia	63	19	44
Bulgaria	2	1	1
Czechoslovakia	47	13	34
Hungary	36	12	24
Poland	271	88	183
Rumania	26	10	16
U.S.S.R.	161	36	125
TOTALS			
Northwest	1,281	629	652
South	369	165	204
East	543	160	383
Europe and U.S.S.R.	2,193	954	1,239

Source: Milbank Memorial Fund, *Selected Studies of Migration Since World War II* (New York: Milbank Memorial Fund, 1958), pp. 18-19.

Immigration into Canada

Agriculture was the mainstay of Canada's economy when the first recorded census took place in 1891. At that time Canada's population was some 3.5 million, with three-fourths of these inhabitants living in Ontario and Quebec. Both federal and provincial governments mounted active recruitment campaigns for immigrants in Europe. Passages by sea were financed for immigrants, and free railway services were available within several eastern provinces. A homesteading policy similar to that of the United States was followed, and railway construction moved toward the western provinces, helping to attract some 50,000 immigrants in 1873. This was also the year when more immigrants declared the intention to remain in Canada than passed on into the United States.[15] During succeeding years, however, the flight of settlers from Canada emerged from time to time as a serious problem. During the early years of the twentieth century, British and other foreign investments in Canada stimulated the production of cereal grains in the hope of feeding British and European proletarian classes. This was accompanied by new drives to increase industrialization and mining. All this spurred new waves of migration. In the decade ending in 1913, over 2.5 million immigrants entered Canada, but many of them became victims of the economic recession of 1914. Opening of the prairie provinces of Manitoba, Saskatchewan, and Alberta drew both immigrants and natives westward, and those areas more than doubled their total population to 326,000 by 1911.

Canada's unemployed were greatly reduced by World War I, which drew thousands into military service and defense-related industries. The war-induced demand for Canadian grains further decreased unemployment, but immigration fell off until after the war, and population loss by emigration continued. An estimate made by R. H. Coats in 1930 set the total Canadian emigration since 1871 at 4.3 million. He ascribed the high figure to the unique relationship between Canada and the United States.[16] Since the two nations had in many respects a common culture, plus an open 3,000-mile border, the economic opportunity and milder climate in the United States constituted a natural population magnet. In the decade ending in 1921, for instance, Canada's immigration was 1,728,921, from which an emigration of 1,297,740 was subtracted. Add to this a natural population increase of 1,150,659 and Canada's rate of population growth lacks only a figure for clandestine population movement to be complete.[17]

During the early years of the twentieth century, Canada shared with Argentina the tendency for settlers to be transient workers or a "floating population." According to Canadian statistician Coats:

> . . . there are numbers who come in from year to year as short-time labor, leaving their families abroad, [which] is of course immediately reflected in the statistics of the money-order business with countries like Italy, Austria, and Sweden, which undoubtedly represents in large measure the remittance of wages to friends. It is also shown by the surplus of males appearing in the immigration from certain countries.[18]

Good numbers of these "floating immigrants" found their way into the United States as part of the population drain mentioned above. Still, there are no hard statistics on Canadian emigration specifically into the United States for the early years of the twentieth century.

Canadian immigration during the nineteenth century was dominated by British and French, and most of those entering Canada via the United States were of continental European origin. Only during the twentieth century did Canada begin to experience a considerable immigration that was both non-British and non-French:

The stocks of continental Europe are of many types, but they may be grouped as two: those of north-western Europe (chiefly Scandinavian and Germanic) and those of central, southern, and eastern Europe (Slavic, Latin, Hebrew). The significant fact is that, while in the opening decades of the century the number in Canada of persons born in northwestern Europe increased by 80 percent, the number born in central, southern, and eastern Europe almost trebled. In 1901 the numbers of the two groups were fairly equal, but in 1921 the foreign-born from central, southern, and eastern Europe were two and one-half times those from northwestern Europe.[19]

Although slightly larger than the continental United States, Canada in the 1930s had a population of over 10 million, about three persons per square mile. Immigration was seen then as part of Canada's agricultural development process; it was also intended to keep Canada predominantly British in character and allegiance.[20] In that decade Canada was the second most important immigrant-receiving country in the hemisphere, having taken some 7 million immigrants, most of whom came from Europe. The United States at that time was the leading immigrant-receiving nation, having absorbed over 35 million immigrants, the bulk of whom came from Scandinavia and Mediterranean Europe. Canadian immigration policy stressed the concept of "assimilable type": French-speaking and English-speaking people supposedly received priority over speakers of other languages. In Table 1.2 the reader can appreciate the broad picture of immigration into Canada during recent years.

In practice the French have been less prone to emigrate than the English, with the result that French-speaking migrants have not taken advantage of their preferred position and other Europeans — Scandinavians and, especially, British and Irish — have taken their place. As of the 1930s Davie noted that settlers from southern and eastern Europe were seen by Canadians as less assimilable than those who spoke English and French. Even more severely restrictive Canadian views prevailed with respect to Orientals.[21] A great deal of Canada's manpower need for English speakers was filled in the British Isles through special programs for relocating juveniles who were wards of British social welfare organizations. Between 1868 and 1930 some 100,000 juveniles were so relocated.

By the 1930s a pattern had been established whereby Canada and the United States served as fertile recruiting grounds for each other. Canada attracted native-born Americans who sought agricultural opportunity. The United States attracted native-born Canadians interested in business, industry, and the professions. Canada's emigration to the United States was roughly equal to its total immigration, so its global problem was that of not losing its balance of people to the United States.

In order to retain its population, Canada's policy during the 1930s was to assist immigrants in securing land, to protect settlers, and to provide special services for females and juveniles. Immigration statutes also prohibited various classes of undesirables from entering the country, and such exclusionary rules were typical of the United States as well. From time to time exclusion was imposed against Hutterites and Mennonites (for their refusal to abide by Canadian educational language statutes) and against Hindu immigrants during times of severe unemployment. Canadian immigration remained generally open to agricultural workers from the Western Hemisphere, Europe, and the British Isles.

Canada's population since World War II has increased more than that of any other industrialized country. By the early 1970s its intake of immigrants reached over 3 million.[22] Western Hemisphere migration is an important aspect of Canadian immigration and its management. American migration into Canada increased steadily after World War II, and the United States replaced Britain as the major source of Canadian immigrants. Americans are now subject to fewer restrictions in migrating to Canada than Canadians face when coming to the United States.

The most recent increase of Canadian immigration has been from the United States, the Caribbean, and Asia.[23] Between 1946 and 1962 immigration into Canada from South America was 0.93 percent of the total. By 1970 it was 3.35 percent of the total. From the United States, Mexico, and Central America combined, immigration increased from 8.72 percent during 1946-62 to 25.59 percent in 1970.[24] From 1946 to 1967 (before new immigration regulations went into effect) immigration into Canada from the United States was 244,280; from Central America, 702; from Mexico, 2,252; and from South America, approximately 32,175.[25]

In 1967, Canada adopted new immigration regulations that were considered nondiscriminatory against any particular country. These laws were based on a system of points for certain personal characteristics and gave increased recognition to family relationships. For example, points were allocated

TABLE 1.2
Canadian Immigration: Top Ten Source Countries, 1966-77

Country	Number	Country	Number	Country	Number
1966		*1967*		*1968*	
Britain	63,291	Britain	62,420	Britain	37,889
Italy	31,625	Italy	30,055	U.S.A.	20,422
U.S.A.	17,514	U.S.A.	19,038	Italy	19,774
Germany	9,263	Germany	11,779	Germany	8,966
Portugal	7,930	Greece	10,650	France	8,184
France	7,872	France	10,122	Austria	8,125
Greece	7,174	Portugal	9,500	Greece	7,739
Netherlands	3,749	Hong Kong	3,749	Portugal	7,738
Hong Kong	3,710	Australia	4,967	Hong Kong	7,594
Australia	3,329	Netherlands	4,401	Yugoslavia	4,660

(continued)

Table 1.2, continued

Country	Number	Country	Number	Country	Number
1969		*1970*		*1971*	
Britain	31,977	Britain	26,497	U.S.A.	24,366
U.S.A.	22,785	U.S.A.	24,424	Britain	15,451
Italy	10,383	Italy	8,533	Portugal	9,157
Hong Kong	7,306	Portugal	7,902	Italy	5,790
Portugal	7,182	Greece	6,327	India	5,313
Greece	6,937	Yugoslavia	5,672	Hong Kong	5,009
Germany	5,880	India	5,670	Greece	4,769
Trinidad/		Trinidad/		Philippines	4,180
Tobago	5,631	Tobago	4,790	Trinidad/	
France	5,549	Jamaica	4,659	Tobago	4,149
India	5,395	Hong Kong	4,509	Jamaica	3,903
1972		*1973*		*1974*	
U.S.A.	22,618	Britain	26,973	Britain	38,456
Britain	18,197	U.S.A.	25,242	U.S.A.	26,541
Portugal	8,737	Hong Kong	14,662	Portugal	16,333
Hong Kong	6,297	Portugal	13,483	India	12,868
India	5,049	Jamaica	9,363	Hong Kong	12,704
Uganda	5,021	India	9,203	Jamaica	11,286
Italy	4,608	Philippines	6,757	Philippines	9,564
Greece	4,016	Greece	5,833	Greece	5,632
Philippines	3,946	Italy	5,468	Italy	5,226
Jamaica	3,092	Trinidad/		Haiti	4,857
		Tobago			5,138
1975		*1976*		*1977*	
Britain	34,978	Britain	21,548	Britain	17,997
U.S.A.	20,155	U.S.A.	17,315	U.S.A.	12,888
Hong Kong	11,132	Hong Kong	10,725	Hong Kong	6,371
India	10,144	Jamaica	7,282	Jamaica	6,291
Portugal	8,390	Lebanon	7,161	Philippines	6,232
Jamaica	8,211	India	6,733	India	5,555
Philippines	7,364	Philippines	5,938	Lebanon	3,847
Italy	5,078	Portugal	5,344	Portugal	3,579
Guyana	4,394	Italy	4,530	Italy	3,411
S. Korea	4,316	Guyana	3,430	France	2,757

Source: Demographic Policy Group (of the Canada Employment and Immigration Commission [CEIC]), "Immigration to Canada: Trends and Policy," in *Immigration to the United States*, Ottawa, published by CEIC, April 1978, p. 397.

for knowledge of French or English, or having a relative who could help establish the applicant in Canada (but not merely be a sponsor). Points (or assessment units) were also awarded on the basis of years of formal education and the demand for specific labor skills in the area of the applicant's intended destination. The regulations also established three categories of immigrants: sponsored dependents, nominated (nondependent) relatives, and independent applicants. Since then, immigration patterns to Canada have changed. In 1967 immigration from Central America and the Caribbean more than doubled over the prior year, and there was an increase of immigration from the United States.[26]

Freda Hawkins suggested that immigration into Canada from the early 1970s on would increasingly be related to social, environmental, and economic factors as well as "manpower" needs. She predicted that the composition would shift toward more immigrants from Asia, Latin America, and the Caribbean. The countries of origin of Canada's immigrants did change substantially, especially after the 1967 regulations. There was an increase in the number admitted from the Caribbean, Hong Kong, India, the Philippines, and Latin America. In 1969 immigrants from the Caribbean and Asia accounted for 23 percent of the total number admitted into Canada, and 18.49 percent in 1971.[27] European migration dropped off during these years, especially because of the European Economic Community and the increased prosperity of many European countries.

Thus, the Western Hemisphere became increasingly important as a source of immigrants into Canada. But herein lay one of Canada's principal immigration dilemmas, one it shared with other First World nations like the United States and Australia. As capsulized in the words of one Canadian scholar:

> . . . it is not easy to profess humanitarianism and racial tolerance and still feel that one must dissuade would-be entrants from coming to Canada because perfect conditions to receive them do not exist, or because their cultural heritge does not make them easily assimilable.[28]

Immigration into the United States

An overview of immigration to the United States might begin as early as 1798, when the first Alien Act (giving the president authority to deport any aliens considered "dangerous") was passed by Congress, but in more realistic terms it may begin with the creation of the Bureau of Immigration within the Treasury Department in 1891. This gave the federal government exclusive jurisdiction over immigration and established extensive categories of inadmissible persons. The early 1880s brought major national demands for restrictions on immigration, a significant change in U.S. public opinion. As in Canada, many Americans were reluctant to see the increased immigration from Greece, Italy, and neighboring countries. This xenophobia was fed by several financial panics during the 1890s that led many to believe that the United States could not feed the large numbers of immigrants who kept coming. Mixed in was religious and racial bigotry. The outstanding example of American xenophobia had been, perhaps, the Chinese Exclusion Act of 1882, the first instance of a given nationality's being singled out for discrimination in United States immigration policy.

In 1903 the Department of Commerce and Labor was created with cabinet status, and all immigration matters, including the Bureau of Immigration, were transferred to it. This seemed to coincide with increased American hostility toward immigrants. One publication carried an extreme view categorizing Italians, Russians, Jews, and several other nationalities as being of "a low order of knowledge, if not intelligence, as well as of physical development," and described immigrants from Germany, Scandinavia, and Great Britain as "better developed physically, and mentally superior to the former class."[29]

After World War I began, immigration decreased. In 1914 there had been 1,218,480 aliens admitted, but the following year the figure was 75 percent lower. Immigration into the United States reached a low of 28,867 admitted to Ellis Island, New York City, in 1918. Recorded immigration to that point in American history had centered on Europeans and Asians. Davie noted that immigration from Latin America during the early years of the twentieth century was too negligible to merit analysis. Also, in 1917, Congress passed a literacy test for new immigrants over President Wilson's veto. The literacy test marked a transition period in American immigration policy. On the surface it added educational qualifications to the traditional individual selection, but its other, very real purpose was to exclude unskilled laborers from southeastern Europe.

The same ban, had it been enforced, could have excluded Mexican and other Western Hemisphere immigrants as well. But when serious labor shortages developed in the sugarbeet fields in 1918, and later in cotton- and fruit-producing areas, the secretary of labor amended the immigration rules to suspend literacy tests and head taxes, and gave temporary work permits to thousands of Mexicans who entered the United States and proved themselves to be superior workers. The temporary work permits were rescinded in 1921, the year of the passage of the first quota system under a new immigration law. Of the 73,000 Mexican workers who were on record as having been admitted between 1918 and 1921, some 21,000 had disappeared and could not be repatriated. This may have been one of the major beginnings of clandestine Mexican worker migration into and within the United States.

As noted below, the Immigration Act of 1921 placed a quota on immigration from European nations but no such restriction on Mexicans. American employers began to accept Mexican laborers, many of them illegal entrants, in numbers previously unknown. Immigration from Mexico in the 1930s was approximately 3,000 per year; depression-hit cities in the United States began to provide transportation back to Mexico for those who could not be absorbed economically and who would likely become public charges. An early trend observed by Davie in the 1930s was for Mexican migrants to come from the states of Jalisco, Guanajuato, and Michoacán, where the greatest number of severely exploited peons were to be found.[30] He listed a population of nearly

1.5 million people of Mexican stock living in the United States, adding that "about one-tenth of all Mexicans now live in the United States. Their leading center is in Los Angeles where they number 97,116 — the second largest Mexican city in the world."[31] Mexicans were well-established during the 1930s not only in the American Southwest but also in the Chicago-Calumet area, where they became an important part of the packing industry's labor supply.

In those years Mexicans were considered highly mobile and were prepared to respond on short notice to varying labor demands throughout the United States. The origin of today's migrant "stream" patterns and "underground railways" for migrant Spanish-speaking laborers can often be traced to this period and earlier. Mexican immigrants then faced the continuing problems of language barrier, poor access to legal remedies, ethnic segregation, discrimination in some public places, and second-class "citizenship" generally. Intermarriage was rare and the Mexicans tended to congregate in ethnic ghettos.

Restricting the entrance of Mexicans into the United States had little support during the 1930s. Some employers, mostly in the Southwest, and especially agricultural-horticultural enterprises, railroads, lumber and mining, and ranches, favored unrestricted Mexican migration. Davie correctly foresaw that quota imposition would make alien smuggling more profitable. Whereas the State Department then opposed extending the quota system to Mexico and Canada, the Labor Department sought to impose quotas in the interest of protecting domestic labor.[32] Illegal alien migration, thus, is not new to the second half of the twentieth century insofar as Canada, Mexico, and the United States are concerned. But its criticality as an issue has been most clearly witnessed since World War II, and especially since the 1970s.

Before 1867 the official statistics for "immigration" into the United States included visitors and tourists, without regard to whether they intended to remain. By 1907 the administrative definition of immigration had come to require that the person in question be an alien, that he or she be officially admitted with formal inspection, that previous residence in a foreign country be established, and that the immigrant declare his or her intention of residing in the United States.[33] Also around 1907 (inception of the administrative practice varied) residents of Canada and Mexico who intended to take up residence in the United States were counted as immigrants. During the nineteenth century, immigrants from those two countries had not been included in official immigration figures. Early notice was taken as well of the extralegal transfer of population across the two U.S. borders, as in the following statement, written during the 1930s:

> No record could be made, of course, of clandestine immigration and there is little evidence upon which to estimate its amount. It was probably large and increased with the growth of legislative restrictions upon immigration, but the evidence in support of a suggestion recently made by the Bureau of Immigration to the effect that the right of

1,400,000 immigrants now in the United States to continue their residence might be challenged does not stand examination and that figure, no doubt, is much too high.[34]

What is reputedly a conservative estimate of the total net immigration (gross immigration less repatriated immigrants) holds that 26.2 million permanent immigrants came to the United States between 1820 and 1930. But the exact number of repatriates is not known. Moreover, as already mentioned, before about 1908 immigrants from Mexico and Canada were not recorded as immigrants, thus making the true migration picture difficult to determine.[35] It was estimated, however, that between 1840 and 1920 some 3 million Canadians and some 468,000 Mexicans migrated permanently into the United States. It should also be noted that until January 1906, an alien who entered and left the United States was counted each time. Before January 1903 an alien traveling in first or second class on a steamship was not counted as an immigrant, but an alien merely passing through the United States enroute to another country was counted as an immigrant. The three foregoing rules were abandoned on the dates indicated, thereby laying a more realistic basis for calculating immigration into the United States.

Between 1918 and 1930 some half-million U.S. citizens emigrated to other countries. One-third of these went to Europe and two-fifths went to Canada. In an estimate given by the Department of State in 1929, there were 273,340 American citizens living in Canada, 77,063 living in Europe, 24, 119 living in Asia, and 12,136 in South America.[36] Writing about population currents generally in the Western Hemisphere ("western world"), Walter Wilcox observed two main currents, one drawn by agricultural opportunity and the other by industrial opportunity. Both currents attracted immigrants to the United States, but industry became the dominant drawing influence in the first half of the twentieth century.[37] This was reflected in the higher percentage of foreign-born concentrating in the large cities and the establishment of ethnic subcultures in the larger urban areas. But this did not mean that all the foreign-born ended up as urbanites. In 1920, 4.4 million – one-third of the foreign-born – were living in rural areas or in communities of less than 10,000 population. Considering that 98 percent of all immigrants into the United States entered through big cities, it can be seen that the attraction of agricultural pursuits was considerable.[38]

The growing national pressure for immigration limitation led to passage of the Immigration Act of 1921, also known as the Quota Act. Under this act alien migration to the United States was limited to 3 percent of the number of foreign-born of each nationality living in the United States as of 1910. The Quota Act of 1921 was a major point of departure in American immigration policy and placed a ceiling of some 358,000 immigrants annually. This formula favored western and northern European nations and tended to give second place to southeastern Europeans, but left Western Hemisphere migration untouched. Migrants were subject to a range of admissibility tests within the quota ceiling

limits. As a result of American xenophobia, the "Red scare" psychology following World War I, and pressures from business and labor groups, another quota
act, the National Origins Act, was passed in 1924 and went into effect in 1929.
This reduced the annual immigration ceiling to some 160,000 by imposing a new
quota formula: 2 percent of the foreign-born population residing in the United
States in 1890. Under this system some 85 percent of the quota preference went
to nations of northwestern Europe.

While both acts restricted immigration, certain classes of aliens remained
exempt. Principal among these were aliens who had resided in a country of the
Western Hemisphere for 12 consecutive months preceding their entry into the
United States. This residence requirements was raised to five years in 1922.
After 1924 an additional exemption was granted to close relatives of American
citizens, to certain professors and clergymen and their families, and to persons
born in independent countries of the Western Hemisphere. This meant that after
1924 a vast amount of immigration could come in over both U.S. borders as
well as through the ports. Also in that year the U.S. Border Patrol was created
to protect American land frontiers. Soon the nonquota immigration began to
exceed the quota immigration, and the roots of hemispheric migration into the
United States were firmly set. It also should be noted that a significant portion
of the quotas that went into effect in 1929 went to southeastern European
countries that could not use the quota because of the more rigid admissibility
requirements. This meant that quotas often went unused while nonquota migration from within the Western Hemisphere increased.

During World War II a series of emergency acts and regulations placed strict
controls on the entry and actions of aliens inside the United States. The Alien
Registration Act of 1940 was the principal enabling legislation during this
period. At the end of the war these controls were relaxed, and special laws like
the Displaced Persons Act of 1948 facilitated the relocation of war victims who
wished to enter the United States. Under this legislation some 200,000 war
refugees were welcomed into the United States in the two years following
its passage.

During the first half of the 1950s, the U.S. Congress made an attempt at
comprehensive immigration legislation, the first such effort since the quota acts
of the 1920s. The Immigration and Nationality Act of 1952 (also known as the
McCarran-Walter Act), as amended, is the basic governing law today for immigration into the United States. A part of the debate over this legislation featured
"national origins" forces against the "melting pot" forces, the former seeking to
maintain the ethnic character of America as predominantly northwestern
European and the latter favoring greater entry and even miscegenation of minorities. President Harry Truman vetoed the bill, but it was passed by a strong
congressional override.[39] The era was that of McCarthyism and the "Red
menace" psychology. From the standpoint of Western Hemisphere migration,
the 1952 act left the independent nations without numerical restrictions. The
growth of industries based on Mexican *bracero* contract labor could proceed

unhampered. The McCarran-Walter Act abolished the national origins quotas as such, but assigned small area quotas within which the various nations could compete. Race and sex were excluded as criteria for citizenship through naturalization. Under the act the attorney general had a broad power to grant exceptions and to facilitate the entry into the United States of many persons who otherwise might not qualify. This benefited the Cuban refugees who began coming to the United States in large numbers during the early 1960s.

Amendments to the McCarran-Walter Act passed in 1965 and 1976 have created a complicated system of preferences for immigration into the United States that stresses skills and family ties. These amendments also fix numerical limits on immigration: an annual limit of 170,000 for the Eastern Hemisphere and 120,000 for the Western Hemisphere. The key stipulation is that no more than 20,000 immigrant visas may be granted any one country in a given year. This puts a premium on the various routes of nonquota entry, including special paroles and "adjustment of status" to refugees and others determined eligible by the attorney general (acting through the U.S. Immigration and Naturalization Service). It also means that illegal entry is the only remaining option for many would-be immigrants and itinerant workers, especially Mexicans. As this phenomenon grew in the late 1970s, so did the intra-U.S. debate over population pressure and worker displacement through immigration generally and through illegal immigration in particular.

Adding to the debate was the issue of the asylum granted to Southeast Asian refugees and "boat people" during the late 1970s. In the spring of 1980, approximately 100,000 Cubans came to the United States in the "Freedom Flotilla." Their initial status was that of illegal alien, but they were accepted as political refugees, further contributing to the growing public anomosity toward new immigrants. The Cubans demanded rapid processing and integration into U.S. society, and Southeast Asian refugees were also beginning to make demands. In the small California town of Arvin (home of the DiGorgio Farms), for example, the refugees made demands on their church sponsors for better household goods and were even moving into rented housing traditionally reserved for the native Mexican-American population. Throughout the United States, Mexican illegals and Haitians who fled the Duvalier dictatorship were classified as "economic refugees," and therefore were not eligible for exceptions to immigration laws or in a position to make demands. Resentment against all aliens grew, and the survivability of "economic refugees" was threatened. Outbreaks of violence within minority communities, such as the one experienced in Miami in mid-April 1980 (at least partially a result of economic competition between ethnic minorities), promised to be more widespread in the years to come.

Indeed, the 1980s may be the decade of Fourth World immigration insofar as the United States is concerned. It may become a decade of refugees seeking to find their niche in America's affluent society.[40] Herein lies the American quandary of optimum population size. Recent research suggests that the U.S. population of 222 million in 1980, and a projected 263 million in 2000, may be controllable at "zero population growth" providing both fertility and immigration can be controlled. It has been suggested that a 5.2 percent drop in American fertility can accommodate an annual immigration of up to 400,000 and achieve a stable population by the end of the century.[41] But America is faced with more, not less, immigration from Latin America. One particularly bitter irony in this is the exodus of Latin Americans from repressive regimes that have been sustained by U.S. aid. The more such aid is given, the greater the problem of clandestine migration is likely to become. So the question of achieving a stable population must be looked at in the context of U.S. foreign policy, not just in terms of domestic fertility and legal immigration.

Migration Trends Affecting Latin America

Major migrations into Latin American countries have historically been from Italy, Portugal, and Spain, with lesser inputs from elsewhere in Europe, Asia, and Africa. Between 1946 and 1955 three Latin American countries – Argentina, Brazil, and Venezuela – received the bulk of this immigration (shown in thousands).

	Italy	*Portugal*	*Spain*
Latin America total	571	205	294
Argentina	362	9	161
Brazil	76	173	35
Venezuela	109	21	61
Other	24	2	37

Source: Milbank Memorial Fund, *Selected Studies of Migration Since World War II* (New York: Milbank Memorial Fund, 1958), pp. 18-19.

During the twentieth century, European migration into Latin America tended to be directed to areas having well-established European populations. During the first 60 years of the twentieth century, three-fourths of all European migration to Latin America is believed to have gone to southern Brazil, Uruguay, and northern Argentina.

Latin America has over 300 million people in the 1980s, and will probably have beyond 500 million by 2000.[42] By contrast, its estimated total population in the 1930s was roughly 100 million.[43] The population density in the 1930s was approximately ten per square mile, one-fourth that of the United States. By the end of the 1970s it was estimated that Latin America's population would double in 26 years, given birth and death rates at the present levels. In the early twentieth century the most favorable employment conditions were offered in Brazil and Argentina; but nowhere in the hemisphere at that time were political conditions favorable to large migrations. Davie observed that "democracy is not a system of government in most of the Latin American countries; it is a legal fiction."[44] In the 1930s it did not appear that Latin America would experience major European and North American migrations. Davie estimated the total immigration into Latin America at the time of his study as not more than 11-12 million, and most of that had gone to Argentina and Brazil. Barriers to European and North American migration were the large-estate pattern of land tenure (latifundia), competition with neofeudal peons and serfs, and political instability. Most of Latin America in the 1930s lacked the middle-class tradition that would be necessary for immigration from more advanced nations to occur.

Argentina

An exception to this rule was Argentina, which aided immigration through policies that gave the foreign-born all the advantages of the native-born but exempted them from such obligations as military service. Between 1857 and 1930 over 6 million immigrants came to Argentina, mostly from Europe, and only about 3 million emigrants departed. It is noteworthy that whereas residence registration was compulsory for native Argentines, it was left voluntary for aliens. Thus many north Europeans and Mediterranean peoples started foreign cultural enclaves within Argentina and saw themselves as working toward their eventual return to "the old country," a phenomenon that had significance later in the twentieth century, when populist movements sought to unite the Argentine proletariat in a new political consciousness or "national accord." The Argentine government also advanced passage money to European immigrants until 1890, when political crises forced an end to that program.

During the first half of the twentieth century, Argentina continued to receive a steady stream of European immigrants; many of these were "birds of passage" who came to Argentina for agricultural work beginning in October and returned to their homelands in May and June. Between 1904 and 1913, Argentina's population grew from about 5 million to 7.5 million. The census of 1914 showed that of nearly 8 million inhabitants, nearly 30 percent were foreign-born (a proportion twice that of the United States). It is believed that since 1857 about half of Argentina's immigrants have been Italians, with the majority of them coming from northern Italy and concentrating in and around greater Buenos Aires. This metropolitan complex has grown into one of the greatest demographic magnets of the twentieth century, and draws both legal and clandestine migrant laborers from Uruguay, Paraguay, Bolivia, and Chile.

Immigration into Argentina from bordering countries came in three waves. From 1914 to 1947 such immigrants tended to settle especially in the provinces of Jujuy and Salta, bordering on Bolivia, and of Formosa, Entre Rios, and Misiones, bordering on Paraguay and Uruguay. Between 1947 and 1960 more of them went to Buenos Aires, and by 1960-70 it was the Buenos Aires metropolitan area that attracted the bulk of the migration from surrounding countries. Bolivians, for example, concentrated only 3.85 percent of their numbers in

Buenos Aires in 1914 and settled 92.65 percent of their numbers in the border provinces of Jujuy and Salta. But by 1970, 36.59 percent of the Bolivians went to Buenos Aires while 46.16 settled in Jujuy and Salta.[45] This drastic change in population flow was strongly influenced by the flourishing construction industry in Buenos Aires, but it also created a large corpus of laborers who lived mainly in the *villa misera* slums of the capital city and Buenos Aires province.

Once migratory labor patterns were established in the first half of the twentieth century, it was not unexpected that they would continue even though steady migration, much of it clandestine, tended to depress wages in the marginal sectors of the Argentine economy. Following the collapse of the first Perón era in 1955, Argentina was beset with waves of inflation and monetary devaluations. Employers found that their profits could be protected either by demanding more work for the same wages or by paying less. This would have been difficult had the powerful General Workers Confederation (CGT) of the Peronist political sector been able to control the entire labor market. But clandestine migrant workers, especially from Bolivia and Paraguay, were willing to work for less. These illegal aliens tended to work in "stagnant" industries like food, textiles, construction, and domestic services, where the employment of illegals kept wages down. This was especially true of the Buenos Aires construction industry: "The presence of immigrants appears more directly linked to employers' strategies of profit maximization than to a global expansion of production and employment."[46] By 1970 nearly 50 percent of the immigrants from bordering nations were concentrated in greater Buenos Aires, not only creating depressed social conditions but also contributing to the stagnation of much of the labor market since there were always new illegal immigrants (*cabecitas negras*) who were willing to work for subsistence wages.

In the years since 1970, then, labor immigration into Argentina has been a function of reaction to economic crisis, rather than a consequence of economic growth (as in Canada) that would have drawn immigrant workers to fill a void (as seems also to have been the case in Venezuela during roughly the same period). As of 1970, in Argentina there was a clear tendency for employers to prefer hiring immigrants, legal or clandestine, as a way of defending profit margins. This corresponded with stagnation in commerce and services that offered underemployment to immigrants who no longer found good employment prospects in the industrial and goods-producing sectors of the economy.[47] It was not surprising, then, to hear government-sponsored television and radio announcements in Buenos Aires during the late 1970s that urged the illegal alien workers to "regularize" their status so that the work force could be more accurately estimated and "channeled."

As noted above, there is a tendency for the majority of immigrant workers (especially Bolivians and Paraguayans) to be absorbed by the construction and domestic services industries. Personal observations and published analyses reveal two factors in this process. First is the concentration in Buenos Aires of wealthy sectors (wealth drawn from provincial agriculture, manufacturing, import-export commerce, or "politics") that create steady demands for high-rise housing, offices, and stores. The second is the practice of subcontracting and using temporary labor: "Subcontracting tends to reduce total labor costs by permitting firms to avoid the payment of social benefits, and it helps to reduce fixed costs and spread investment risks . . . the presence of surplus labor also helps to explain the survival of older, inefficient, low-productive, building techniques."[48]

The use of labor-intensive techniques and the conscious maintenance of a "floating reserve" of transient labor, people who are expected to live in wretched, marginal circumstances and sell their health and labor cheaply so that the wealthy will have a cushion against inflation and devaluation, are part of a scenario that is all too prevalent in the Western Hemisphere. Much "successful capitalism" is based on such exploitation; the migrants are expected to be a malleable and movable labor force who are docile and don't demand social benefits. Indeed, one impressionistic study based on interviews in the slums of Buenos Aires produced testimony that in a given neighborhood, some 80 percent of the residents were Bolivian immigrants and that at least half of them were undocumented.[49] In the two years subsequent to that study, it was learned that the Argentine government had forced the residents out of their precarious community and relocated them on the far periphery of the capital city without regard for their need to travel to their jobs.

Although this picture is drawn from Argentina, it represents the way migrant populations are typically treated in Latin America. The Venezuelan government in the late 1960s bulldozed slums on the rim of the valley overlooking Caracas so that they would not present an "eyesore" for a new American-owned hotel that was being built. Many of those abruptly moved were extralegal migrants from Colombia and other countries. Such treatment of migrants, whether they are documented or not, raises serious policy and human rights questions.

Brazil

It is important in this survey to consider Latin America's largest nation, Brazil, whose 1980 estimated population is 120 million. This figure is expected nearly to double by the end of the century. Today Brazil has over three times the population of either Argentina or Canada, and has a greater land mass than the United States.

Twentieth-century immigration into Brazil has had similarities with that into Argentina. During the first half of the twentieth century, about 85 percent of all Brazilian immigration went into the state of São Paulo or into the port city of Rio de Janeiro, where the expansion of coffee production and exportation attracted foreign laborers. Over 1.5 million workers migrated to the state of São Paulo alone, and some 600,000 of these had their steamship passage refunded by the São Paulo government.[50] The Brazilian federal government also had a program of subsidized passage and operated a land distribution program not unlike the homesteading practice in Canada and the United States.

In Brazil the states had powers of immigrant recruitment apart from those of the federal government, and could admit foreigners as immigrants on their own terms. The 1920 census showed the state of São Paulo with over 800,000 foreign-born inhabitants, more than any other Brazilian state.

Immigration statistics for Brazil prior to 1850 are of doubtful accuracy. Between 1820 and 1926 it is estimated that over 4 million immigrants were landed in Brazil, with 1,462,000 coming from Italy, 1,219,000 from Portugal, and 565,000 from Spain. The low levels of literacy among these immigrants contributed to the 75 percent illiteracy that was reported for Brazil in 1920.[51] Germans constituted another major immigration group, with 190,000 during 1820-1926. Whereas the immigrants from Latin countries tended to blend into the proletarian classes, the Germans tended to buy small farms and to settle the southern parts of Brazil, which were cooler and better suited to the German way of life. German cultural influences grow stronger as one progresses south into Uruguay and Argentina, and the Germans generally did well after immigrating. The Italians and Portuguese were less favored, despite their superior numbers. They fell into the exploited position of many sharecroppers in the United States; they labored for low wages and a small plot of land, and became indebted to a company store. Bad as the situation was, however, the Italians kept coming. In 1902 the Italian government even restricted emigration to Brazil in an effort to maintain its own work force.

It is not known how many immigrants entered Brazil extralegally during these years, but there is evidence that Brazilian authorities were aware of such immigration. From the west and north, clandestine immigration from Colombia and Venezuela was, and still is, difficult owing to jungles and mountains. The bulk of early clandestine migration into Brazil came from Paraguay, Uruguay, Bolivia, and Argentina, to the south and west, where the natural barriers to population movement were fewer and government inspection was less rigorous (often nonexistent). But there were also numerous Italians and Portuguese — estimated at some 167,000 out of the total registered immigration — who came in extralegally, and a substantial number (not estimated) of Brazilian nationals who were foreign-born and who entered Brazil more than once, thereby inflating the total of 4,167,000 immigrants between 1820 and 1926. Given the size of Brazil and its vast frontiers and unguarded boundaries, it is to be expected that the opportunities for clandestine immigration are legion and that estimating it will always be risky.

Venezuela

The attraction of Venezuelan oil has been a mixed blessing as far as migration into that country is concerned. In the mid-twentieth century a good number of migrants from Europe and elsewhere came to Venezuela, but relatively few stayed. It was reported that only one out of three immigrants remained permanently in that country in 1956, and that "Venezuela's more than

100,000 immigrants were supposed to help augment agricultural production, but they have tended to drift from land projects into the cities."[52] Between 1952 and 1957 some 492,517 immigrants entered Venezuela, placing that nation's total immigration for those years above that of any other in Latin America.[53] One pattern of migration stands out for Venezuela: the lure of petroleum wealth and the myth of a better life in the capital city. Caracas is a powerful population magnet. So many Venezuelans have abandoned the countryside for the cities that campaigns have been launched by agricultural interests to recruit illegal migrants from neighboring Colombia. In recent years the abuses suffered by Colombian peasants who went to work (many who went under homestead promises) in Venezuela have caused open friction between those two nations.

According to recent research, Venezuela had fairly open immigration laws until 1958. In that year immigration was restricted "partly in recognition of both its failure to fulfill the expected functions and also the preponderance of foreigners in jobs that could have been performed by consequently unemployed Venezuelans."[54] Since 1973 immigration policy has been linked directly to specific production needs and ultimately related to petroleum, whose revenues constitute over 70 percent of state revenues.[55] Since the 1960s there has been a major flow of undocumented workers into Venezuela's rural areas from other Latin American countries, thus changing the predominant pattern of the 1950s and before, which featured European nations (principally Spain, Portugal, and Italy) as sending countries. As with the clandestine migratory patterns elsewhere in the hemisphere, it is very difficult to estimate the size of these extralegal population transfers into Venezuela. Nevertheless, perhaps more published results are available on this case than on any other hemispheric migratory pattern save that between Mexico and the United States.

It has been quite openly admitted that Venezuelan agriculturalists have recruited illegal labor in neighboring Colombia. Because of the closing of the borders while the two governments disputed this and related issues, the recruitment of Colombians had to be extralegal. One estimate is that between 1960 and the early 1970s some 1.5 million Colombian workers entered Venezuela illegally.[56] In part this demand can be explained by pressures imposed by the oil economy on the agricultural sector for increased production, and by the prevalance of labor-intensive agricultural techniques and low levels of mechanization. It is doubtful whether mechanization can proceed rapidly enough during the 1980s to reduce the need for transient labor, especially that supplied by Colombia.

Since 1974, Venezuela's immigration policy has been more selective and many undocumented workers have received legal status. Since 1976 it has been difficult for residents of other Latin American nations to come to Venezuela as tourists without providing a bond or other guarantee that they will depart as required by law. A freeze also has been imposed on changes of status for persons who enter Venezuela as tourists or temporary workers and later seek to become landed immigrants. Venezuela now has a National Council of Human Resources that controls the allocation of work permits and entry visas. Employers are required to submit their requests for foreign labor to the Ministry of Planning (CORDIPLAN), which publishes these requests and consults with labor leaders about the availability of resident Venezuelan labor. Indications are, however, that illegal recruitment of Colombian workers continues and that the bulk of Venezuela's immigration today is clandestine. The seriousness of this conflict, in both human and nation-state terms, is seen in reports like the following, which have been frequent since 1970:

> The Colombian Parliament met in secret session to hear testimony concerning the massacre of undocumented Colombian workers in Venezuela. The Chancellor, Diego Uribe Vargas, declared that the Venezuelan government had promised formally to investigate the murders which allegedly took place on the border area of the two countries.[57]

Add to this an analysis of Colombian census data showing that between 1963 and 1973 some 600,000 emigrated from Colombia, the majority to Venezuela, and that of this number 148,000 were legal migrants and 452,000 were illegal. Although the study does not give exact figures for migrants destined for Venezuela, it found that 70 percent were men and that 60 percent of these were 20-34 years old, the most probable laboring class.[58] The Venezuelan/Colombian migratory nexus reflects the apparent tendency for regional wealth centers to develop throughout Latin America and to act as population magnets affecting the work force in many countries.

TOWARD A SCHEMA OF ANALYSIS FOR
EXTRALEGAL POPULATION TRANSFER

Hunting and gathering societies of early times still exist in the forests of the Western Hemisphere. In this type of society the members of the group enjoy equal access to the group's resources and contribute to the common stores as their abilities allow. Status and prestige are derived from generosity and from give-away rituals, not from intragroup competition. Generosity is a prerequisite for continuing influence and power in the hands of any given person or persons. These are face-to-face participatory societies that localize responsibility, credit, or blame, and reduce the need for penal sanctions. Tribes dispute and fight for territory, but the concept of private property is generally unknown.

At some threshold point hunting and gathering societies and tribes have had to split up because of the sheer crush of numbers; it was divide or find a new technology for making life livable. Migrant alien societies, one of the subcultures of today, may be remnants of such tribes. If populations grow to exceed the pressure limits in today's Third World countries, as they did in the early societies, some nations can be expected to split apart. Thus, serious questions of viability as a nation are raised for states like Mexico, Colombia, India, and the Philippines, which will have doubled their populations within this century and whose technological capability has not controlled their population increase. Societies threatened with breakup may find a temporary solution in clandestine emigration.

The predicament in which the clandestine migrants find themselves may, however, be one of continual conflict and competition in which few or none of their security needs are met by the host nation. Indeed, the clandestine migrants are usually without a formal host, save the employer. Their status is unprotected. To the degree that clandestine migrants can blend in with the local population, or even be welcomed, as in Argentina and Venezuela, their condition of life may be somewhat more tolerable. But illegal population subcultures tend to compete with each other, and the ethic of generosity that may prevail within families and small groups is usually replaced by cutthroat competition when one group's survival is pitted against another's in the cloudy world of illegal work and living.

Robert C. North's "tooth and claw" model may be useful here.[59] In this scenario there is a definite struggle for survival that exhibits Social Darwinian norms of behavior. It is not, however, a question of genetic determinism. Subcultures, transplanted by clandestine migration into a dissimilar cultural milieu, compete to survive — at each other's expense. To an extent one could say that zero-sum game conditions prevail, although this would be a dangerous generalization if applied to all subcultures under study here. There is a certain sounding of William Graham Sumner's dictum on the menace of the "unfittest" in the struggle among the subcultures. One set of migrants may gain legality in a receiving country and subsequently feel threatened by the continued migration of their compatriots. Strong evidence of such intraethnic rivalries emerges from the interviews conducted by the present authors among Bolivians, Colombians, and Mexicans who have emigrated. The same phenomenon was found by one of the authors in Canada. At a Spanish-speaking cultural center in Toronto, it was clear that there is little reality in the claim for the existence of "Latin Americans abroad" with a common cultural bond cemented by language. In that setting Chileans kept to themselves, and competed with Argentines and Colombians for survival. Mexicans sought to "Canadianize" themselves away from identity with other Mexicans. The goal was to learn English as soon as possible, so as not to seem "different" from the remainder of the community — a somewhat strange logic, given Canada's strong multiethnic tradition and highly visible ethnic subcultures.

Our analysis of the impact and meaning of extralegal transfer of population in the Western Hemisphere can benefit from an assessment of the degree to which the clandestine migration comes to be seen by the receiving country as an "alien invasion." Valuable work in this regard has been done by Ellwyn R. Stoddard.[60] In considering the illegal migration in the United States-Mexico borderlands, he raised a series of questions, from which the following have been adapted for our purposes:

1. Does a given nation have an identifiable but flexible immigration policy that allows immigration crises to be handled administratively and without public discord (as with the granting of amnesty to illegal aliens in Argentina and Canada)?

2. Do national borders serve not only as barriers that preserve political and territorial integrity, but also as a "permeable membrane through which symbiotic exchanges of persons" can be accomplished?

3. Is illegal immigration the result of both an imposed disposition to leave the sending country and an unofficial and/or informal, but nonetheless real, invitation to come to the receiving country?

4. Can we generalize cross-nationally within the Western Hemisphere about "borderlands" experiences and behaviors in a way that would lead to theoretic propositions that would be testable in various intrahemispheric settings?

5. To what degree have existing nation-states become artificial political contrivances that continue to exist for the convenience of political elites despite the transfer and mixture of populations to a degree that would suggest merging them into a more viable socioeconomic union (for example, Honduras and El Salvador since 1969)?

In addition, one of the most critical hemispheric and world problems is that of balancing food supply with people. Can Argentina, Canada, and the United States keep the Western Hemisphere stocked with grain and meat? And, as one concerned critic puts it, "What would happen if the populations in these fortunate nations were allowed to grow until their food-exporting capacity were overtaken by domestic food needs? Whose interest would such a turn of events serve?"[61] There is a strong humanitarian component in this research undertaking. We are concerned with the consequences, in concrete human terms, of the interaction between immigration, population growth, and food supply. We are also interested in the consequences for existing nations of rivalry between the ethnic subgroups formed by clandestine migration.

A critical and broad question seems to be how much rivalry between ethnic subgroups a given society can stand before competing "mafias" pitch the society toward atrophy. In concrete terms, how much rivalry between the West Indian or *antillano* blacks and the mulattos and mestizos can Panama absorb before the social order is damaged? How much resentment can Argentine society tolerate between groups of Bolivians and Paraguayans before ethnic strife starts? Colombians in Canada have already created violent confrontations with the state, as have Jamaicans and Haitians. Violence in the United States by Cuban and Puerto Rican subculture groups is well documented. Clashes between American Chicanos and Mexican *bracero* workers have been more frequent than the former might like to admit. An additional question was posed at the outset of this chapter, that of the viability of existing nation-states in the Western Hemisphere, should clandestine migration move the bulk of a nation's inhabitants into another country. We will keep in mind throughout this book the possibility that "disincorporation" of states and their merger into broader regional communities (as in metropolitan cooperation among municipalities) may be the road to creating a genuine hemispheric community of nations in which the human needs and rights of all can effectively be pursued and even guaranteed.

Tables 1.3 through 1.8 reproduced below are intended to give the reader a statistical overview of key dimensions of legal population input into the United States. They are presented as self-explanatory.

TABLE 1.3
Western Hemisphere Immigrants to the United States, by Country of Last Permanent Residence, 1820-1977
(in thousands)

Country	1820-1977, Total	1951-1960, Total	1961-1970, Total	1971-1977, Total	1973	1974	1975	1976	1977	Percent 1820-1977	Percent 1961-1970	Percent 1971-1977
Total	8,784	996.9	1,716.4	1,314.7	179.6	178.8	174.7	169.2	223.2	18.2	51.7	45.3
Argentina	90	19.5	49.7	20.0	2.9	2.9	2.8	2.7	3.1	.2	1.5	.7
Brazil	55	13.8	29.3	12.4	1.8	1.6	1.4	1.4	1.9	.1	.9	.4
Canada	4,081	378.0	413.3	112.5	14.8	12.3	11.2	11.4	18.0	8.5	12.4	3.9
Colombia	134	18.0	72.0	44.6	5.3	5.9	6.4	5.7	8.2	.3	2.2	1.5
Cuba	497	78.9	208.5	208.2	22.5	17.4	25.6	28.4	66.1	1.0	6.3	7.2
Dom. Rep.	197	9.9	93.3	93.8	14.0	15.7	14.1	12.4	11.6	.4	2.8	3.2
Ecuador	81	9.8	36.8	33.9	4.2	4.8	4.7	4.5	5.2	.2	1.1	1.2
El Salvador	39	5.9	15.0	18.0	2.0	2.3	2.4	2.4	4.4	.1	.4	.6
Guatemala	37	4.7	15.9	15.5	1.8	1.6	1.9	2.0	3.7	.1	.5	.5
Haiti	77	4.4	34.5	37.6	4.6	3.8	5.0	5.3	5.2	.1	1.0	1.3
Honduras	31	6.0	15.7	9.6	1.4	1.4	1.4	1.3	1.6	.1	.5	.3
Mexico	2,031	299.8	453.9	438.5	70.4	71.9	62.6	58.4	44.6	4.2	13.7	15.1
Panama	44	11.7	19.4	13.0	1.7	1.7	1.7	1.8	2.5	.1	.6	.4
Peru	43	7.4	19.1	16.0	1.8	2.0	2.3	2.6	3.9	.1	.6	.6
W. Indies	689	29.8	133.9	169.3	21.6	24.4	22.3	19.6	27.1	1.4	4.0	5.8
Other	660	99.2	106.2	71.9	8.8	9.1	8.9	9.3	16.1	1.3	3.2	2.5

Source: U.S. Bureau of the Census, Statistical Abstract of the United States: 1979 (100th edition.), Washington, D.C., 1979, p. 89. The regional totals are not consistent with the totals for the countries in those regions. This is a result of the Bureau of the Census figures, not an error in our calculations.

TABLE 1.4
Aliens Naturalized in the United States
by Country of Former Residence, 1970-77

Country of Former Residence	1970	1975	1977
Canada	6,340	3,548	3,759
Central America	2,480	2,773	3,094
Colombia	970	1,699	2,029
Mexico	6,195	5,781	6,301
Cuba	20,888	15,546	20,506
Dominican Republic	538	1,518	1,904
Haiti	433	1,966	1,870
Jamaica	479	2,152	3,849
Other West Indies	337	1,510	1,802

Source: U.S. Bureau of the Census, *Statistical Abstract of the United States: 1979*, p. 96.

TABLE 1.5
Immigrants to the United States, by Country of Birth, 1951-77
(in thousands)

Country of Birth	1951-1960, Total	1961-1970, Total	1971-1977, Total	1970	1973	1974	1975	1976	1977	Percent 1961-1970	Percent 1971-1977
North America	769.1	1,351.1	1,101.8	129.1	152.8	151.4	146.7	142.3	187.3	40.7	38.0
Canada	274.9	286.7	70.5	13.8	9.0	7.7	7.3	7.6	12.7	8.6	2.4
Mexico	319.3	443.3	436.1	44.5	70.1	71.6	62.2	57.9	44.1	13.3	15.0
West Indies	122.8	519.5	521.0	61.4	64.8	63.0	67.4	66.8	114.0	15.6	18.0
Barbados	1.6	9.4	12.8	1.8	1.4	1.5	1.6	1.7	2.8	.3	.4
Cuba	78.3	256.8	216.4	16.3	24.1	18.9	26.0	29.2	69.8	7.7	7.5
Dom. Rep.	9.8	94.1	93.8	10.8	13.9	15.7	14.0	12.5	11.7	2.8	3.2
Haiti	4.0	37.5	39.1	6.9	4.8	3.9	5.1	5.4	5.4	1.1	1.3
Jamaica	8.7	71.0	84.1	15.0	10.0	12.4	11.1	9.0	11.5	2.1	2.9
Trinidad and Tobago	1.6	24.6	45.3	7.4	7.0	6.5	6.0	4.8	6.1	.7	1.6
Central America	44.6	97.7	73.7	9.3	8.8	9.2	9.7	9.9	16.5	2.9	2.5
El Salvador	4.8	15.0	18.0	1.7	2.0	2.3	2.4	2.4	4.4	.5	.6
Guatemala	4.1	15.4	15.3	2.1	1.8	1.6	1.9	2.0	3.6	.5	.5
Panama	9.7	18.4	12.6	1.6	1.6	1.7	1.7	1.7	2.4	.6	.4
South America	72.2	228.3	167.6	22.0	20.3	22.3	23.0	22.7	33.0	6.9	5.8
Argentina	14.3	42.1	15.7	3.4	2.0	2.1	2.2	2.3	2.8	1.3	.5
Brazil	8.9	20.5	8.7	1.9	1.2	1.1	1.1	1.0	1.5	.6	.3
Colombia	17.6	70.3	44.6	6.8	5.2	5.8	6.4	5.7	8.3	2.1	1.5

	1960	1965	1970	1972	1973	1974	1975	1976	1977	1978
Ecuador	9.5	37.0	33.9	4.4	4.1	4.8	4.7	4.5	5.3	1.1	1.2
Guyana	1.0	7.1	24.5	1.8	3.0	3.2	3.2	3.3	5.7	.2	.8
Peru	5.7	18.6	15.6	.9	1.7	1.9	2.3	2.6	3.9	.6	.5

Source: U.S. Bureau of the Census, *Statistical Abstract of the United States: 1979*, p. 90. The regional totals are not consistent with the totals for the countries in those regions. This is a result of the Bureau of the Census figures, not an error in our calculations.

TABLE 1.6
Foreign Laborers Admitted to the United States, by Country of Last Permanent Residence, 1960-78

	1960	1965	1970	1972	1973	1974	1975	1976	1977	1978
Agricultural laborers										
Mexico	427,240	103,563	—	—	—	—	—	—	—	—
Canada	7,804	8,149	3,156	1,895	1,458	1,250	970	572	399	312
West Indies	10,874	15,397	15,895	12,171	11,712	11,625	11,245	11,568	11,661	10,955
Japan	969	31	—	—	—	—	—	—	—	—
Spain (Basque sheepherders)	213	453	463	321	381	322	211	185	206	274
Others										
Canada (woodsmen)	NA	13,281	8,238	7,373	8,310	5,685	3,671	2,696	2,303	2,059
U.S. V.I. workers	NA	13,514	15,459	11,580	10,582	9,901	7,286	5,967	4,304	3,077

NA = not available.

Source: U.S. Bureau of the Census, *Statistical Abstract of the United States: 1979*, p. 92.

TABLE 1.7
Border Patrol Immigration Activities, 1965-78

(in thousands)

	1965	1970	1972	1973	1974	1975	1976	1977	1978
Persons apprehended*	53.3	233.9	373.9	503.9	640.9	602.2	701.6	820.4	870.6
Deportable aliens located	52.4	231.1	369.5	498.1	634.8	596.8	696.0	812.5	862.2
Mexican	44.2	219.3	355.1	480.6	616.6	579.4	678.4	792.6	841.5
Canadian	5.8	7.8	8.2	8.7	7.4	7.3	5.9	5.8	6.5
Other	2.5	4.1	6.2	8.9	10.8	10.1	11.7	14.1	14.2

*Covers deportable aliens located and U.S. citizens engaged in smuggling or other immigration law violations.

Source: U.S. Bureau of the Census, *Statistical Abstract of the United States: 1979*, p. 93. The total number of deportable aliens located listed in this table does not correspond exactly with the nationalities of those aliens. The inconsistency was found to exist in the census figures reported in this source.

TABLE 1.8
Western Hemisphere Nonimmigrants Admitted to the United States, by Country of Birth, 1966-78
(in thousands)

Country	1966-70 (avg.)	1971-75 (avg.)	1975	1977	1978
Total*	1,501	2,831	3,477	3,750	4,213
Argentina	41	62	96	90	116
Bahamas	62	83	71	87	108
Brazil	36	71	93	68	86
Canada	133	193	223	275	262
Colombia	45	86	91	121	152
Dom. Rep.	87	121	149	155	167
Ecuador	21	32	38	59	78
Guatemala	25	31	33	50	58
Haiti	16	33	43	52	62
Jamaica	60	106	124	128	143
Mexico	633	1,537	1,997	1,990	2,150
Panama	15	28	29	36	41
Peru	30	40	47	47	45
Trinidad and Tobago	25	42	43	52	62
Venezuela	50	71	87	176	247

*Includes countries not shown separately.

Source: U.S. Bureau of the Census, Statistical Abstract of the United States: 1979, p. 94.

NOTES

1. As treated in Robert C. North, *The World That Could Be* (New York: Norton, 1976), passim.

2. Ibid., p. 39.

3. The suit by Federation of Americans for Immigration Reform (FAIR) was turned down by the Supreme Court in March 1980. FAIR contended "that illegal immigration . . . had grown to such an extent that counting illegal residents of the United States would distort the apportionment of Congress and would seriously dilute the voting power of those who don't reside near large concentrations of illegal immigrants," and asked that the U.S. census of April 1980 exclude illegal alien residents. See FAIR, *Immigration Report 1*, no. 7 (April 1980) and other issues in that series.

4. As reported in *La voz del norte* (Nogales), April 6, 1980.

5. From *St. Louis Post-Dispatch*, October 29, 1978.

6. Population Reference Bureau, *1979 World Population Data Sheet* (Washington, D.C.: Population Reference Bureau, 1979).

7. See Garrett Hardin, "The Immorality of Being Softhearted," *Stanford Alumni Almanac*, January 1969. Also see Barry Commoner, *The Poverty of Power* (New York: Knopf, 1976).

8. See Richard Arens, *Genocide in Paraguay* (Philadelphia: Temple University Press, 1976).

9. Patrick C. Fleuret and Anne K. Fleuret, "Fuelwood Use in a Peasant Community: A Tanzanian Case Study," *Journal of Developing Areas* 12 (April 1978): 315-22.

10. One example is the Tanzanian village of Kwemzitu, which is typical of many primitive subcultures in the Third World as far as wood fuel is concerned. Through the use of trees directly for fuel or for making charcoal, some 476 cubic meters of wood are consumed by that village each year. "To keep pace with their consumption, Kwemzitu people would have to plant 1,360 trees every year." On all the evidence they are not even coming close to doing that. Ibid., p. 321.

11. The albedo is the ratio of the sun's light that is reflected by a planet or satellite to that which it absorbs. Raising the albedo means raising the amount of light Earth reflects back into the atmosphere, hence more heat and more chance of drought and famine. Deforestation raises the albedo of the planet. See Stephen H. Schneider, *The Genesis Society* (New York: Plenum Press, 1976), p. 165 and passim.

12. Ibid.

13. Maurice Davie, *World Immigration (With Special Reference to the United States)* (New York: Macmillan, 1939), p. 209.

14. Ibid., p. 368.

15. Walter F. Wilcox, *International Migrations*, vol. II, *Interpretations* (New York: National Bureau of Economic Research, 1931), p. 125. (Authorized copy by University Microfilms, Ann Arbor, Mich.)

16. Ibid., cited on p. 129.

17. Ibid., p. 130.

18. Ibid., p. 132.

19. Ibid., p. 136.

20. Davie, *World Immigration*, p. 417.

21. Ibid., p. 419.

22. Freda Hawkins, *Canada and Immigration* (Montreal: McGill-Queen's University Press, 1972), pp. 35-36.

23. Ibid., p. 12.

24. Ibid., p. 57.

25. Ibid., p. 55.

26. Ibid., p. 57.

27. Ibid., p. 362.

28. Daniel Kubat, *The Politics of Migration Policies* (New York: Center for Migration Studies, 1979), p. xxi.

29. From *Leslie's Weekly*, August 7, 1902, p. 126.

30. Davie, *World Immigration*, p. 214.

31. Ibid., p. 215.

32. Ibid., pp. 218-19.

33. Wilcox, *International Migrations*, vol. II, p. 86.

34. Ibid., pp. 86-87.

35. Ibid., pp. 90-91.

36. Ibid., p. 106.

37. Ibid., p. 108.

38. Ibid., p. 111.

39. President Truman's reasons, outlined in his veto message, were essentially that the legislation still contained many racist and discriminatory provisions, and that it set forth a morass of legalisms that would prove unworkable administratively. See Benjamin Ziegler, ed., *Immigration: An American Dilemma* (Lexington, Mass.: D.C. Heath, 1953), pp. 97-103.

40. Paul R. Ehrlich et al., *The Golden Door* (New York: Ballantine Books, 1979), pp. 50-91 passim.

41. Kubat, *The Politics of Migration Policies*, p. 64.

42. Population Reference Bureau, *1979 World Population Data Sheet*.

43. Davie, *World Immigration*, p. 444.

44. Ibid.

45. Juan M. Carrón, "Shifting Patterns in Migration from Bordering Countries to Argentina: 1914-1970," *International Migration Review* 13, no. 3 (Fall 1979): 475-76.

46. Ibid., p. 483.

47. Ibid., p. 486.

48. Adriana Marshall, "Immigrant Workers in the Buenos Aires Labor Market," *International Migration Review* 13, Special Issue No. 3 (Fall 1979): 499.

49. Ibid. Also see Kenneth F. Johnson, "Life and Death of Carlos Mujica," *Latin American Digest* 2 (Fall 1976): 8-12, passim.

50. Wilcox, *International Migrations*, vol. II, p. 162.

51. Ibid.

52. Anthony T. Bouscaren, *International Migrations Since 1945* (New York: Praeger, 1963), p. 149.

53. Ibid., p. 151.

54. Saskia Sassen-Koob, "Economic Growth and Immigration in Venezuela," *International Migration Review* 13, no. 3 (Fall 1979): 456.

55. Ibid.

56. Ibid., p. 458.

57. From *Diario las Américas* (Miami), March 24, 1979.

58. Alberto Bayone Núñez, *Cobertura del censo de población 1973* (Bogotá: Pontificia Universidad Javeriana, 1977), pp. 41-42.

59. North, *The World That Could Be*, pp. 60-65.

60. Ellwyn R. Stoddard, "A Conceptual Analysis of the 'Alien Invasion': Institutionalized Support of Illegal Mexican Aliens in the U.S.," *International Migration Review* 10 (Summer 1976): 157-89, passim.

61. John Tanton, *Rethinking Immigration Policy* (Washington, D.C.: FAIR, 1979), p. 25.

2

STRATEGIES FOR HANDLING ILLEGAL ALIENS IN THE WESTERN HEMISPHERE AND ELSEWHERE

LABOR MOBILITY AND INFORMAL ACCOMMODATION

We have dealt with some of the roots of illegal migration, including poverty, political violence, and the attraction of a better life in a nearby state. Labor mobility across national borders, both legal and clandestine, is an economic fact of life throughout the world and is not unique to the Western Hemisphere.

In the Middle East, Yemen, for instance, exports over 500,000 workers to Saudi Arabia yearly. The Yemeni workers are desired because they are prepared to work long and hard under adverse circumstances. In this respect they are similar to many of the extralegal migrants in the Western Hemisphere. But the Yemenis have a cultural compatibility with their neighboring states that does not always prevail in the Western world. Most Yemenis do not intend to settle in Saudi Arabia. They accumulate funds there to return to Yemen and establish businesses and build homes. The coming and going from Saudi Arabia is easy because no work passes are required. Hence this informal migration may not always be strictly illegal.

Also, in most cases Saudi Arabia prevents Yemeni workers from taking their families, thereby creating some guarantee that the workers will eventually return to their native land. Nor does Saudi Arabia permit foreign workers to buy homes, start businesses, or receive social security benefits. This is in contrast with the treatment the same Yemenis may have encountered when migrating to the United States. In fact, "the American Consulate in Sana, Yemen, sends out social security checks monthly to Yemenis who have retired and come home."[1] There is, thus, a considerable flow of expatriate savings into Yemen. It was estimated at $1.5 billion for 1980. The result is that there is virtually no male unemployment in Yemen and the country has an annual economic growth rate of about 8 percent. The Yemenis work abroad so as to live well at home. Their prime minister boasts that there is not even a "brain drain."[2]

Such is not the experience of most nations in the Western Hemisphere, certainly not insofar as the impact of extralegal worker migration is concerned. There are great variations in the benefits and ownership privileges that illegal aliens in the Western Hemisphere may expect to receive from their host countries. From the United States, generally speaking, they can send money home and repatriate savings. Aliens can own property and receive social security benefits in the United States regardless of their alienage. The Social Security Administration says it tries to prevent the granting of account numbers to illegal aliens, but we have found that it is very easy to circumvent this in practice.

In Canada it is more difficult to secure social security benefits or enroll in the system if one is an illegal alien. The Canadian system of SIN (social insurance number) requires that any applicant other than a Canadian citizen or resident be given an SIN starting with 9, and that any such SIN card, when presented, must be accompanied by a special work permit. There is a stiff fine for employers who violate this requirement, thereby making illegal work in Canada risky for both the employer and employee.

In other Western Hemisphere nations it is quite easy to work illegally, but very difficult to secure any social security benefits. Most social security benefits in Mexico, Argentina, and Venezuela are contingent upon one's belonging to a specified trade union or an officially sanctioned association. Competition for these benefits is fierce, and the illegal migrant worker is likely to try to conceal that status rather than to apply for benefits, an act that might jeopardize employment.

The United States is probably the principal target of illegal worker migration within the Western Hemisphere, and perhaps this is true worldwide. A typical media report early in 1980 stated flatly that "hundreds of thousands of foreigners from Asia, Latin America, and the West Indies are bribing, forging or sneaking their way into the country."[3] Some of these aliens, fleeing the political violence of their home country, became the victims of unscrupulous smugglers or "coyotes" who abandoned them in treacherous terrain once they had crossed the United States/Mexico border. One such group of refugees from El Salvador was so abandoned in the Arizona desert during July 1980, and more than a dozen of their number perished in the severe heat.[4]

The U.S. Immigration and Naturalization Service (INS) became the focal point for congressional investigation as evidence of corruption emerged. American immigration policy was frequently described as "benign neglect" and, if compared with that of Canada, the criticism was justified. For instance, it remained legal to hire illegal aliens. No one except the organization known as FAIR (Federation for American Immigration Reform) seemed willing to make a campaign issue out of immigration reform in 1980. Political forces in the U.S. Congress — agricultural and commercial-industrial groups — fought immigration policy reform to a standstill against the American labor groups that sought to protect U.S. citizens from the competition of immigrants. President Carter promised in 1980 that he would name a "blue ribbon commission" that would, once again, look into the matter of immigration reform. In the meantime, the United States remained one of the world's principal magnet nations insofar as illegal migration was concerned.

AMNESTY AS A MEANS OF FORMAL ACCOMMODATION

If a country feels itself being inundated with illegal aliens and has little enforcement capability to deport them, then the granting of amnesty is a temporary solution. It has been tried during recent years, at least in the Western Hemisphere. For this solution to work, even on a short-term basis, it is important that the aliens in question be generally perceived as welcome additions to the host country. Such was the case in Argentina during the 1970s.

Throughout much of the twentieth century, Buenos Aires acted as a magnet for human migration from the Argentine provinces and from neighboring countries. Construction of the Argentine railroad system in the nineteenth century by British interests helped to direct migration into Buenos Aires because all commerce destined for Europe passed through its port. The railroad system converged there to make Buenos Aires the natural locus for human growth. Perhaps because of the city's middle-class European tradition, the people of Buenos Aires frequently disdained manual labor, and the practice of employing Paraguayans, Uruguayans, and Bolivians to do this work became well established.

By 1974 it was estimated that Argentina, a country of 25 million people, almost half of whom lived in or around the capital city, had some 2 million illegal aliens, most of whom were living and working in the principal urban areas. Most of these immigrants were from countries bordering on Argentina (Uruguay, Paraguay, Brazil, Bolivia, Chile), and had either crossed the border without documents or had overstayed a visa and work permit. Argentina's governmental system, it should be noted, had been so often at the mercy of political chaos that it is easy to understand how millions of foreign migrant workers might enter illegally, with virtually nothing to stop them from crossing the long, unguarded borders. The migrants usually were motivated by poverty and the lure of relatively better salaries in Buenos Aires. Most of them shared a common language, so it was not too hard to blend into the local population.

In January 1974 the Argentine government began promoting a new amnesty decree in the public media. Radio and television were employed to encourage undocumented workers to appear at the national immigration headquarters, located inside a naval base at the port of Buenos Aires. Long lines formed, and continued through the night for weeks and months. The staff was too small to handle the demand of Bolivians, Paraguayans, and others who sought to regularize their status. Thousands of people formed serpentine lines, cooked over charcoal fires, and moved the fires and ashes along as the lines surged forward at the pace of a tortoise. Not surprisingly, many of the illegals decided that clandestine living was preferable to spending days in a line just to secure the promise of social benefits through legal status. Others stayed away because of the fear that they would be deported should the amnesty offer turn out to be a trick.[5]

The second Perón government, a short-lived constitutional dictatorship of sorts, sought to enlarge its proletarian ranks of supporters via the amnesty. But the formal reasons given were those of humanitarianism and Argentina's need for a permanent work force, especially in the construction industry. The Perón government was ended by a military coup in March 1976.

Argentine officials stated in 1980 that it was much more satisfactory for them to allow the presence of millions of illegal alien workers than to confront the bureaucratic dilemma of documenting them.[6] But Argentina is one of the hemisphere's "underpopulated" nations, something one would not gather by visiting Buenos Aires, where nearly half of the country's some 26 million inhabitants lived in 1980. The remaining provinces, however, do appear to be underpopulated, and the Argentine government tries to attract immigrants into those areas. Especially difficult to settle is the southern region, Patagonia, with its long, frigid winters that frustrate the quest for a vast subsoil wealth.

In short, the limited availability of social security benefits and welfare, plus the need for seasonal manual labor and the desire to keep wages low, make it convenient for Argentina to encourage illegal worker migration simply by looking the other way. The immigrants, of course, are the victims because Argentina's legal system does not protect them.

A different situation obtains in Canada. There many benefits of the welfare state are available to illegal aliens, at least until the moment of their deportation. The Canadian legal system is subject to long appeals and delays in the disposition of many deportation cases. There is a motive for becoming an illegal alien in Canada, at least on a short-term basis. It is to be kept in mind that Canada, unlike most nations of the Western Hemisphere, does not receive most of its illegal aliens across its borders or on its beaches. The vast bulk of illegal aliens in Canada entered legally, usually through one of three or four airports, and then remained past their 90-day authorized stay. Canada has not required that all tourists secure a visa or even a tourist card in their home countries. Most visitors to Canada arrive at a major international airport and try to convince the PIL (primary inspection line) officer that they are bona fide tourists who will not become public charges. Most are granted 90-day visas. It is unclear how many of this number overstay and thereby become illegal aliens. During the 1970s Canada began increasing the number of countries whose nationals must obtain visas in their home countries. Naturally, in many cases this was seen as a punitive act (which it usually was). The requirement that visas be obtained in home countries is thought to have stemmed the flow of persons from some countries, whose nationals traditionally tended to become illegal aliens in Canada. It is doubtful, however, whether it has alleviated Canada's illegal alien problem in global terms.

Amnesty was tried in Canada. The Canadian version was much more sophisticated than that in Argentina, and vastly more complex. The results were uncertain. A 1967 immigration regulation made it possible for people already inside Canada as visitors to apply for permanent (landed) immigrant status without returning to their country of origin. If an applicant was refused, there were rights of appeal. It was discovered that the appellate procedure was lengthy, thereby allowing the visitor to remain in Canada even though the authorized stay had expired. The longer one stayed in Canada, the greater one's cause for claiming the right to stay. During 1970 some 45,000 visitors overstayed their visas while applying for permanent immigrant status. The numbers grew alarmingly until November 3, 1972, when the Canadian government revoked that part of the statute allowing visitors to make in-Canada applications for immigrant status. The November 3 announcement was intended to end the immigration abuses associated with the loophole in the 1967 law, but it hurt a number of bona fide visitors who might have wanted to stay for nonopportunistic reasons. To avoid inequities, the Canadian government declared a sort of reprieve for 60 days between August 15 and October 15, 1973, during which time all "visitor" aliens could apply for regularization of status. It is estimated that along with the bona fide visitors, some 50,000 illegal aliens were able to acquire permanent (landed) immigrant status during that period. The Canadian government's official position was that this was not a formal amnesty, even though that is what it amounted to.[7] Canadian officials believe that the reprieve, amnesty, or status adjustment program (as it can be called) encouraged other attempts by illegal aliens to regularize their status, efforts that generally met with frustration.

The illegal alien subculture of the United States, estimated at between 6 and 10 million in 1980 by the INS, poses special dilemmas for the application of amnesty. This is seen in President Carter's amnesty proposal of 1977. At the first meeting of his future Cabinet, well before inauguration day, he requested proposals to meet the problem of illegal immigration. He asked the attorney general to head a task force representing the departments of Labor, State, Justice, and Health, Education and Welfare for that purpose.

The task force reported to the president in April 1977, with a comprehensive set of options. In this and several subsequent meetings the president requested and heard the range of views and analyses of the issues. The options were sharpened and additional ideas were researched at his direction. At the same time, meetings and discussions were held with interest groups and affected parties within and outside government. The results were reported to him and used to recast the proposals in several important respects.

The policy that emerged drew upon many assumptions and views; principally, however, it is believed to be a statement of the choices and ideas of the president himself. Formally announced on August 4, 1977, in a message to Congress, it includes both administrative directives and legislative proposals. The legislation has been under consideration by the Congress (Judiciary Committees), and is called the Alien Adjustment and Employment Act of 1977 (S. 2252 and H.R. 9531).

The program is based on two primary assumptions:

— There is no single solution to the problem of illegal immigration. Rather, we must undertake a combination of related actions both within the United States and in other countries.

— The problem is an outgrowth of stubborn social and economic forces, and therefore cannot be eliminated overnight. However, we must take steps now to establish control and prevent the growth of more serious problems in the future.

In brief, the major features of the program are the following:

— Make unlawful the hiring of undocumented aliens, with enforcement by the Justice Department against those employers who engage in a "pattern of practice" of such hiring. Penalties would be civil — injunctions and fines of $1,000 per undocumented alien hired. Criminal penalties could be imposed by the courts against employers violating injunctions. Moreover, employers and others receiving compensation for knowingly assisting an undocumented alien to obtain or retain a job would also be subject to criminal penalties.

— Increase significantly the enforcement of the Fair Labor Standards Act and the Federal Farm Labor Contractor Registration Act, targeted to areas where heavy undocumented alien hirings occur.

— Adjust the immigration status of undocumented aliens who have resided in the United States continuously from before January 1, 1970, to the present and who apply to the INS for permanent resident alien status; create a new immigration category of temporary resident alien for undocumented aliens who have resided in the United States continuously from prior to January 1, 1977; make no status change and enforce the immigration law against those undocumented aliens entering the United States after January 1, 1977.

— Substantially increase resources available to control the southern border, and other entry points, in order to prevent further illegal immigration and control alien smuggling rings.

— Promote continued cooperation with the governments that are major sources of undocumented aliens, in an effort to improve their economies and their employment opportunities.[8]

The proposed amnesty for illegal aliens was never enacted by Congress. But even the public revelation that such a proposal existed generated false hopes among many aliens, especially Mexicans, and spread the belief that merely crossing the U.S. border would be tantamount to gaining "amnesty" and even citizenship. The proposal created a lively black market in "old rent receipts" and other spurious documents that would-be migrants bought in the hope that they could get into the United States and remain. These false hopes further choked the border areas with Mexican migrants hoping to get part-time work in one of the industries with plants on both sides of the border, or *maquiladoras*. This depressed wages and living conditions for all concerned.

Other serious defects of the amnesty proposal were its creation of classes of aliens within the illegal alien subculture. It would have given preference to those illegals who had been in the country for the longest period. And those were also the most likely to be under the protection of crime syndicates. In this respect, then, the Carter proposal sounded like a reward for the Mafia and a penalty against the law-abiding Mexican who waited legally in Mexico for his or her name to come up under the immigration quota as administered by the American consulate there. And for those aliens who might, under the proposal, demonstrate that they had resided continuously in the United States since before January 1, 1970, there was a collateral question: Had they filed income tax returns for all of those years? And, if not, would they be given a tax amnesty also?

Amnesty poses thorny issues throughout the hemispheric community. Costa Rica has for years allowed travel agencies and airlines to issue tourist cards for 30-day visits and longer stays. But Costa Rica has no administrative mechanism for enforcing the departure of these tourists. Many of them remain in Costa Rica indefinitely. Costa Rica opened its borders to the Nicaraguan refugees in 1979, and during prior years had allowed its territory to be used as a staging area for the revolution against the Somoza dictatorship. Costa Rica, in effect, gave amnesty to both political and economic refugees who entered that nation illegally; knowledge that one group of political exiles had de facto amnesty attracted others. Members of guerrilla organizations like the Tupamaros of Uruguay and the Montoneros of Argentina have found a comfortable haven in Costa Rica, thanks to the de facto amnesty that prevails.

As a solution to the illegal alien problem, amnesty seems to be a stopgap measure. It depends upon the willingness of the illegals to step forward and be counted. This, in turn, depends upon the aliens' perceiving the amnesty offer by the host government as bona fide. If the host government has a reputation for being repressive (as in Argentina), the amnesty will have less success than in a country like Canada, where the political system is generally viewed as benevolent and accountable. One of the greatest dilemmas posed by amnesty is the magnetic effect it may have on potential migrant populations outside the borders of the host country. If amnesty is misunderstood or misrepresented, and attracts an even greater flow of illegal aliens (as seems to have been the case in the United States), then its population effects are likely to be adverse.

Amnesty is not a long-range strategy for accommodation of illegal aliens. It tends to exacerbate the inherent force in extralegal population transfer: that as the peoples of the Western Hemisphere blend themselves informally, there is a blunting of national identities. This may challenge the viability of the continued, perhaps artificial, separation of the Western Hemisphere peoples into "distinct" politico-geographic units. Such an alternative future, as we have already set forth, is one of the central concerns of this book.

ACCOMMODATION BY CREATING FOREIGN COLONIES

Granting legal status to foreign immigrants who create distinct colonies within a given state is a more permanent approach to the absorption of illegal aliens or potentially illegal migrants. Canada has allowed the establishment and growth of large, easily identified Chinese communities in Toronto, Vancouver, and elsewhere. In the Canadian prairie provinces there are identifiable communities of Ukrainians and Lithuanians. The fact that there are "two" Canadas, one French and one predominantly English in culture, may have made it easier for Canada to accept ethnic pluralism on a regional and even local basis. There is, for instance, a television channel in Toronto devoted almost exclusively to non-French and non-English broadcasting. It is possible to hear the evening news broadcast first in Portuguese, then in Italian, and finally in Greek.

However, it has not been Canadian policy to encourage ethnic and linguistic fragmentation to the degree that could be termed colonization. Canadian citizens are required to send their children to either French- or English-speaking schools, even if they also send those same children to schools using other languages. This requirement has led some Canadian subgroups to migrate to countries where they are permitted to form ethnic colonies apart from the national population. Canadian Mennonites from Manitoba and elsewhere have set up colonies in Mexico and South America under promises from host governments that they may use German as their exclusive educational language. Some of those Mennonites, now under pressure from Mexico's growing dispossessed population, are reconsidering the wisdom of their colonial status.[9]

One of the Western Hemisphere countries that is best-known for its policy of encouraging the selective migration of foreigners on a neocolonial basis is Bolivia. Obviously, if Bolivia encourages foreigners to come, they are not illegal aliens. But some of them were in fact illegal aliens before the legalizing invitations were offered. In 1953, Bolivia decided to legalize the extralegal transfer pattern of German-speaking Mennonites who had been entering Bolivia from neighboring Paraguay and other nations as distant as Canada. The recruitment of Mennonite families, mostly farmers, into Bolivia continued into the 1960s and gave these people freedom from military service, religious and linguistic freedom, and some limited government support. By settling groups selectively, on an ethnic and geographic basis, Bolivia legalized an existing migratory pattern and used that newly created subpopulation to guard against other, continuing (illegal) migrations into a given area. The vast Santa Cruz farming region of eastern Bolivia has been the location for most of the Mennonite colonies. It is generally believed that Bolivia's food production capacity has been significantly enhanced by this legalized migration.[10]

Bolivia also welcomed colonies of Japanese and Okinawan migrants during the 1950s and 1960s. In the case of the Okinawans there was no major issue of illegal migration, the agreement having been negotiated between the governments of Okinawa, the United States (which had held Okinawa as a trust territory after World War II), and Bolivia as part of that country's policy of selective immigration. Word of the selective colonization did, however, motivate other Latin Americans to seek the same preferential status. The Bolivian government's thinking seems to have been motivated partly by the desire to attract more industrious people into the nation's agriculture and partly by the ambitions of some government officials who might enrich themselves through the colonizing process.

The Japanese colonies and the Okinawan settlements in Bolivia experimented with communal ownership of the land. The Mennonites opted for individual ownership with communal service obligations imposed on all members. In their colonies in Bolivia, Mexico, and elsewhere, Mennonites usually insist that only German be spoken in the homes and schools, but they are willing to speak the national language for commercial and marketing purposes. In fact, the aggressive mercantilism of the Mennonites has enabled them to overshadow native agriculturalists in many cases. Some local resentment has been the result. In Bolivia the aggressive land acquisition practices of the Mennonites, Japanese, and Okinawans have further depleted the supply of available land. This has created more incentive for creation of new agricultural land by slash-and-burn methods. Further, it has meant that displaced Bolivian peasants have been obliged to migrate illegally into Brazil and Argentina in search of economic opportunity. Moreover, those who abandon Bolivia's *altiplano* highlands fare poorly in their search for land in the rich Santa Cruz lowlands.

Therefore, "many of eastern Bolivia's potential colonists are lost to the sugar mills of Argentina that pay their laborers' fares; many thousands have taken up permanent residence in that country, moving on to the cities after the six-month cane harvest."[11] It is known also that the foreign colonists enjoy, on the average, "four times as many acres per settler in rice and corn"[12] than their Bolivian counterparts. Thus, the Bolivian government has legalized both real and potential illegal migration and has given aliens preferential treatment over its own nationals. The latter are forced to migrate illegally into Argentina, where their presence helps depress wages for native Argentines and contributes to the economic parasitism on which Buenos Aires traditionally thrives. The displaced Bolivians are twice the victims of their own illegal migration: as part of a regional socioeconomic phenomenon and as the result of a deliberate immigration policy that is foisted upon them.

Creating foreign colonies to handle both actual and potential illegal migration gives the receiving country an opportunity to select those migrants who are most likely to benefit it (and its officials) in areas where there is a shortage of labor and entrepreneurial skills. Its long-range benefits may overcome the short-term disadvantage of causing political alienation among the local population, resentment among natives who are outraged to see special credit and land tenure advantages being given to foreigners. But, as in the case of the Canadian Mennonites in Mexico, it may also be that in the long run the receiving country will become inhospitable and the original sending country will face the issue of repatriating its former nationals. The Bolivians displaced into Argentina may have long-range political effects on several nations should the alienation of the migrant subgroups be channeled into subversive political movements.

Overall, however, the creation of foreign colonies appears more viable as a strategy than does amnesty. The *antillanos negros* (West Indian blacks) of Panama are, perhaps, a case of the successful creation of a foreign colony. There is resentment over these immigrants, to be sure, but not such as to threaten the stability of Panamanian society. The West Indian blacks and their descendants are required to become Panamanian citizens, even though many claim to hold dual nationalities. They fulfill valid economic roles in the society without displacing major population segments. A similar observation could be made concerning the Lebanese in Colombia; they have been so thoroughly integrated into that nation that one of their number became the nation's president in 1978. The integration of Europeans into Venezuelan, Chilean, and Costa Rican societies provides still more evidence that foreign "colonization" can be a successful long-range alternative to illegal migration and a better strategy than such stopgap measures as amnesty. The same may be said for the colony of Cubans in Miami. It is true that in the past certain South American nations have had constitutional restrictions barring the immigration of Orientals. But the creation of colonial subgroups within a greater but tolerant society promises to continue to be a viable partial accommodation to some of the demands of international demographic change.

REFUGEES: SPECIAL PROBLEMS OF ACCOMMODATION

During May and June 1980, over 100,000 Cuban refugees arrived in the United States as the result of an offer by Fidel Castro, the Cuban head of state. It was Castro's idea to show the world that Cuba did not want to continue maintaining political prisoners or to see families remain separated. The offer was that if the existing Cuban exile colony in Miami (numbering in excess of 500,000) wanted to send boats to the Cuban port of Mariel, they could pick up their relatives who were political prisoners, along with other Cubans who were not prisoners but wished to leave the island. Very soon it was clear that Castro had much more in mind than freeing political prisoners. Most of the boats arriving at Mariel had to accept Cuban "deportees" on a first-come basis, and transport them to the United States in the order in which the Cuban authorities specified. This included persons who were criminals, the elderly, and the insane. Estimates that 8,000-10,000 felons had been deported began to circulate. It was reported that Castro used all his diplomatic influence to keep the refugees from getting to other Latin American countries, where their presence might damage the revolutionary image of Cuba. The tactic was to force the Miami exiles, desperate for reunification with their families, to pay the price of bringing back additional and undesirable human baggage. Many of these refugees died at sea.

The U.S. government vacillated, first trying to enforce the law against illegal entry, then appropriating special emergency funds to help the Cubans who arrived, then impounding the boats being used to bring more refugees. Members of the Cuban exile community in Miami made it clear that they would defy the federal ban on bringing the refugees, and would continue to do so until all those wishing to be free of the island had left it. Cuban relocation centers were set up in Arkansas and Florida as the federal government sought to decide what to do with the Cubans and to separate those considered undesirable.

The Cuban refugee crisis was not an isolated event. Globally, some 16 million refugees were estimated by FAIR as constituting a Fourth World during 1980. All of these people would like to enjoy the welfare benefits of the United States. The United States, with some 8 percent unemployment in 1980, a severe economic recession in which tens of thousands of workers were being laid off, and an estimated 17 million undernourished children, had to question its policy of continued refugee absorption. Several hundred thousand refugees from southeast Asia had been admitted the year before, and with the revolutions in Nicaragua and El Salvador there were tens of thousands more seeking to enter the United States and Canada.

One congressional response to this population pressure was a bill introduced by Senator Walter Huddleston that would set a fixed limit of 650,000 immigrants of all kinds (including refugees) to be admitted into the United States during 1980.[13] The problem was that the American government seemed to have no policy on refugees at all, except the vague proposition that economic refugees would not be considered outside existing quota limits, whereas political refugees would be. The hundreds of Haitians landing illegally in Miami each week were every bit as politically motivated as those from Cuba, yet the INS took the position that the Haitians were economic refugees and therefore illegal aliens, since they had entered without inspection and visas. Civil rights groups challenged this before the courts, contending the Haitians were being discriminated against because they were black. During May and June 1980 there were uprisings in Miami over alleged police brutality against blacks. Black community leaders cited the treatment of the Haitian refugees as proof of the American establishment's racism – the Cuban refugees being admitted under irregular circumstances were predominantly nonblack.

The refugee problem in the Western Hemisphere grew complex. Refugees from the military dictatorships of Argentina, Chile, and Uruguay were found throughout the hemisphere, with a great number going to North America. Brazil's military regime had declared an amnesty during 1979 that allowed most political exiles to return, but it is uncertain how many accepted the offer. More exiles began to appear from Central America, especially from Nicaragua and El Salvador. Some 10,000 Nicaraguans who had been given temporary refuge in the United States when the Somoza dictatorship fell during 1979 requested and received a 90-day extension of their temporary residence visas on July 1, 1980. This was to give them the opportunity to request political asylum in the United States or another country. These exiles were predominently nonblack and of the upper middle class, another source of resentment among the Haitians and their black American sympathizers.

It should be noted that supporters of the fallen Somoza dictatorship had backed one of the world's most brutal tyrannies; scores of thousands of lives were lost in the struggle by the Sandinista Liberation Front to free Nicaragua. The new revolutionary government sought extradition of those who had taken refuge in the United States and elsewhere. Some of the Nicaraguan exiles created a united front called FOND that held marches and conducted demonstrations in the United States demanding permanent resident status[14] (the exercise of such tactics under the Somoza dictatorship would have brought almost certain repression and incarceration). Nor should it be forgotten that the United States supported the Somoza regime financially and diplomatically; hence it was U.S. foreign policy that had helped cause the refugee problem to which it must now attend.

In Canada the policy of accepting refugees from within the hemisphere created visible strains. New visa requirements that were put into effect in December 1979 threatened the access of would-be Chilean refugees who sought asylum in Canada. The changed rule made it necessary for Chileans to apply for refugee status at the Canadian Embassy in Santiago. Previously they could make their way to Canada by any means available and then apply for political asylum once safely across the Canadian border. A spokesman for Chileans resident in Canada who wished to aid their friends and relatives in escaping (military repression is well documented in Chile) told of the risks to anyone going to the Canadian Embassy in Santiago to make such an application: "They may disappear the next day."[15] During the first 11 months of 1979, over 5,000 Chileans came to Canada as visitors; 257 of them claimed and were granted refugee status.[16] It was possible in Canada (as with the Nicaraguans in the United States) for the Chileans to stage a demonstration against the changed immigration policy, without reprisal for their action and with reasonable certainty that the Canadian government would at least consider their complaints.

Refugees often concentrate in relatively identifiable areas of a country, such as the Cubans in Miami and the Nicaraguans in New Orleans and San Francisco. Chileans, Uruguayans, and Argentines seem to have spread out from New York to Toronto, with sizable clusters in other cities. Looking only at Toronto, and the Spanish-language subculture press that is readily available there, one finds moving expressions of the human dimension of the refugee. From the monthly journal *LATINO:*[17]

> Since 1974 we have resided permanently in Venezuela. Moreover, 16 other countries including Canada have received us in a fraternal spirit. We are a theatrical company of Latin Americans and during the past 20 years we have been the vehicle for the popular expression of oral theatrical history in various countries. We are agents of hope who bring the message of a Chile that should be free and happy. One day it will be. But now we live in Venezuela for reasons that are well known.

> Two Argentinian exiles describe a routine of violence that differs little from the classical mode: prisoners with their limbs spread apart, electric currents, torture of children in the presence of their parents, sexual violations, total humiliation. The fundamental difference, when we compare the procedures used for repression in Argentina with those of other Latin American dictatorships, is the final outcome of the prisoners. Whereas in other countries there may be at least the appearance of some legal trial by law, in the majority of cases in Argentina the execution of the prisoners takes place swiftly within the same immediate military jurisdiction in which they were first detained. Transference . . . is a euphemism for execution in Argentina and in these days it most frequently means that while people are being "transferred" they are dropped from airplanes into the sea. This will explain the nearly daily appearance of cadavers, almost all with signs of torture, that have appeared washed up on the beaches of cities in Argentina and Uruguay.

> In Latin America, where 90% of the women are illiterate and have little other opportunity than watching the misery of their children, there is at least one country which enjoys three other records of notoriety. Uruguay is the country with the most political prisoners in Latin America, Uruguay has the 'principal' torture chamber of all the Americas, and it is the country with the most emigration. It is estimated that out of a total of 2½ million Uruguayan citizens, over half a million of them have fled their country for exile. These thousands of exiles have organized with the goal of destroying all dictatorships. LATINO spoke today with one of these exiles: she is Diosma Fonceca, an Uruguayan 48 years of age, who has been a political refugee in Canada for a year and a half. Today we pay homage to the women of Latin America on this INTERNATIONAL WOMEN'S DAY. Diosma is divorced and has two children; one, a 26-year-old daughter, Maria, lives with her in Canada. She says, "In Uruguay I worked in a jewelry store, I am a jeweler by trade, and I belonged to a union. I was also active in workers' political organizations. Following the military coup of 1973, until 1976, I went underground and later my daughter and I went into hiding for two more years in Buenos Aires. Because we had no papers we were expelled from Argentina, but thanks to the

mediation of the United Nations we finally arrived in Canada. I got a job in a factory in Canada that made furniture and I had to stand on my feet 9 hours at a time until I developed a spinal ailment and the doctor ordered me to stop doing this work. We lived in bad conditions. There were no other Latin Americans there but I came to know a Portuguese lady and we talked as best we could. The solitude was hard to bear. Now I am receiving welfare and my daughter is working whenever she can." LATINO asks Diosma if she thinks the women of Latin America have the same problems as the immigrant women and whether she thinks it is possible for women to organize worldwide. Diosma replies in the affirmative because all the women everywhere are discriminated against and receive the same bad treatment. "For example, I know of a factory where many people work that is called 'The Death Trap' where the work is hard, unhealthy, and the people who work there must breathe poisonous gases. When somebody suggested that they should organize to fight this, many women urged their husbands to stay out of such politics so as to save their jobs; but if they do, the same situation will befall their children."

[Editorial note: it is not clear from the text of the article to which province Diosma refers in her story of the bad working conditions, but it is clear that refugees from Latin America can encounter severe difficulties in Canada just as they can in the United States. It should also be noted that the governments of both Canada and the United States make available to Latin American immigrants, migrants, and refugees instructions printed in Spanish as to how to avail oneself of social welfare benefits.]

Finally a brief note is in order concerning the resettlement of hundreds of thousands of southeast Asia refugees, or "boat people," in the Western Hemisphere. Most of the public attention to this process was directed toward the United States, which absorbed the bulk of that displaced population. Two of the less publicized stories run the gamut from unsavory to excellent. In the first case our interviews[18] during 1980 indicated a great amount of dissatisfaction with the resettlement program in Argentina. It was stated that some 300 Laotian families were taken by Argentina, with much publicity, and then dumped in provincial areas without adequate financial support, without even adequate language training to help them make the cultural transition.[19] Protests by the Laotians in Argentina caused the Interior Ministry to issue a statement claiming that only 47 out of 293 families had experienced difficulties.[20] Argentina suspended admission of Laotians, many of whom were reported trying to migrate illegally into Paraguay after violent conflicts with the Argentinian population.[21]

A brighter picture emerges from the Canadian program of accepting the southeast Asian refugees. Canada set 50,000 as a target figure for southeast Asians to be absorbed during 1979-80. Canada pledged $15 million to aid the refugees, who were given extensive medical examinations and treatments at

Canadian staging areas and, thereafter, appropriate language instruction. One language specialist pointed out that teaching English to the southeast Asians was no different from teaching it to anyone else, with the exception that Spanish-speaking immigrants might find the language conversion slightly easier due to phonetic similarities. "The job of the teachers, however, goes far beyond language teaching. They find themselves acting in a number of roles to help immigrants adapt to Canadian life. The instructor often becomes the trusted contact between the student and landlords, employers and institutions."[22]

Many of Canada's ethnic subgroups – the Czechs, for example – joined in the relocation effort, remembering their own situation in times past. High American officials lauded Canada's refugee program, saying that in per capita terms Canada had done more than any other nation to help the refugees.[23] It should be noted, however, that Canada has a strong tradition of ethnic pluralism, which no doubt helped its refugee acculturation effort. Also, in all fairness, it should be noted that Spanish-speaking countries probably would not be chosen by most southeast Asians as places of exile if they could go to either English-speaking or French-speaking societies.

WAR AS A CONSEQUENCE OF ILLEGAL MIGRATION

In recent years undoubtedly the worst example of a breakdown in hemispheric strategies of accommodation and response to the challenge of illegal migration emerged from the "Football War" between El Salvador and Honduras in 1969. That war is not officially over, the Central American Common Market has been virtually wrecked, the Pan American Highway was still closed well into 1980, and both El Salvador and Honduras are facing determined forces of social revolution from within.

One scholar has referred to the people of El Salvador as "the Japanese of Central America," meaning that they are willing to work long and hard, under adverse conditions, for their economic security;[24] and they are willing to cross almost any Central American border in order to find work. Moreover, at least between El Salvador and Honduras, it was traditionally very easy to cross the border with nothing more than one's national identification card. Technically, if those people who crossed the border did so without a special work permit, they were illegal aliens. But traditionally no distinction was made, and the Salvadorans entered the territory of Honduras by the thousands seeking work.

Thus, in order to understand the "Football War" it is important to contemplate a basic reality of Central America, one that relates to a central theme of this book: In socioeconomic terms the five countries of the isthmus could effectively be one.[25] But their geographic isolation from one another and their separate political developments have made this impossible. Still, the dream of Central American unity has persisted in the minds and actions of each country's leading political figures.[26] In 1951 the Organization of Central American States was created in an effort to restore something of the nineteenth-century Central American union that collapsed in 1842. In 1961 economic integration was attempted by the creation of the Central American Common Market. But the heralded and much-publicized success of these efforts was seriously weakened by the Football War, and many believe the Common Market experiment has been permanently damaged.

During the early 1930s thousands of Salvadoran peasants fled their nation because of political turmoil and violence. In later years this migratory trend continued because of the predominantly rural composition of the country's population (about 62 percent) and the scarcity of land because of latifundia. Although the peasant migrants from El Salvador went in all directions, the northeastern region of Honduras was the most inviting because of its relative underpopulation. The foreign banana companies along Honduras' northern coast contributed to the migration by recruiting Salvadoran peasants to work on their plantations.[27] High levels of rural unemployment in El Salvador (estimated roughly at 33 percent but easily twice that), aggravated by latifundia problems and the country's high population density, continued to favor this migrational pattern until more than 250,000 Salvadorans, called *guanacos*, were believed to be living illegally on Honduran soil.

On the other hand, Honduras did not have a latifundia problem until after 1958,[28] and overall there was much more land and many fewer people. When the war broke out in 1969, Honduras had an approximate population (not counting the illegal aliens) of 2.5 million (3.5 million in El Salvador), with only 56 persons to the square mile (compared with 421 persons per square mile in El Salvador). This coupled with a higher population growth rate than that of El Salvador (2.5 to 3.4), made Honduras a most likely, and natural, migratory site.[29]

It is understandable that Salvadoran migrants were unwelcome visitors. Honduras had at least a limited latifundia problem but, worse, its public treasury was low, in part because of minifundia. There were at that time some 64,000 Hondurans, called *catrachos*, who were subsistence peasants without land; and there were more than twice that number who were barely existing on small plots. None of these small-scale endeavors was earning any foreign exchange for the country's depleted coffers. In addition, large parcels of land were held idle, many of them by U.S. banana companies. This injected an international element into the bases for mutual resentment between the two countries. The Salvadoran migrants generally believed that they were denied access to idle lands because the Honduran government was in league with the United Fruit Company against the entire peasantry. The threat to private landholdings became so great that the principal U.S. fruit companies hired "rangers" and "special employees" to repel or punish trespassers.[30] In April 1969 the Honduran government began displacing *guanaco* squatters by force and turning their lands over to *catracho* peasants. It was an open secret that many of the expropriated lands went to some of the Honduran militarists who did the "expropriating."

A treaty on migration signed by the two countries in 1965 should have avoided the population conflicts that were mounting. But, as is the case in most of Latin America, the signing of a treaty is a formalism; treaties are like constitutions, mere "scraps of paper" to be invoked only when it is convenient to do so. This treaty expired in January 1969 and Honduras refused to renew it, insisting that El Salvador must put a stop to the illegal migration of its citizenry. The Honduran refusal is said to have motivated El Salvador to begin moving weapons to its borders early in 1969.[31] Honduras was also suffering a trade deficit because the Central American Common Market seemed to be working to the advantage of the more industrially competitive El Salvador. The Salvadorans appeared to be a favored party whose economy was expanding and whose excess human baggage was being dumped in the neighbor's yard. The Honduran government and its citizenry shared the belief that El Salvador was solving its excess population problem by doing nothing about the illegal migration. Honduras argued that El Salvador was best equipped to control the extralegal population transfer, although in terms of normal international practice the task should have been shared by Honduras.

The Honduran military government of Colonel Oswaldo López Arrellano (which seized power in 1963) had used force and duplicity to break up a nationwide labor strike in September 1968, and was now under pressure by local industrialists to stop the influx of cheap merchandise from El Salvador. Ironically, however, many of the same Honduran industrialists were perfectly content to import cheaper Salvadoran labor. El Salvador also had internal problems that contributed to the international tension. Its military president (through an ostensibly "honest" election in which major out-groups participated but were not given full access to the nation's mass media during the campaign) was General Fidel Sánchez Hernández, who in 1968 had announced plans to modernize his nation's military establishment. Honduras could subsequently point to this arms buildup as evidence that the *guanacos* were planning war.[32] Given these well-established antagonisms between the two nations, which were real and in no way figments of the political imagination, it is not surprising that a major public insult to the national pride of either nation should occasion extreme reactions leading to reciprocal violence. In other words, only an "incident" was needed to spark conflict.

Here, before the story can continue, we must explain as best we can a feature of the Latin American personality, the passions of football (soccer). Can the North American reader accept the notion that football may take on political significance? The survivors of several thousand victims of the 1969 war take it quite seriously. In Latin America, generally speaking, soccer is a sport attended only by males. Women usually do not attend because it is an arena for the men to release their passions and frustrations, and to say whatever they would like to be able to say directly to the socioeconomic elites who dominate their lives. This, of course, they cannot do except at a soccer game or through extralegal means. The soccer game provides an emotional catharsis, much as do the bullfights (in the nations where they are allowed), whereby emotions may be discharged and/or sublimated. It is at once an exercise in machismo (whereby the male combatant exhibits his manliness and virility) and a flirtation with death (for the violence is often greater in the stands than on the soccer field). When the catharsis is limited to intranational competition, the personal experience is likely to take on no more than regional significance in terms of individual spectators' loyalties. But when nations are in competition, especially nations whose governments offer the people little or nothing to inspire national pride, then the success of a national champion soccer team becomes a profound experience.[33] All of this may appear incredible to the North American who has not been exposed to the Latin American culture, but it is nonetheless a reality.

Let us consider, then, the national teams of El Salvador and Honduras in 1969, both countries seething with political and socioeconomic hostilities. The winner of their encounter could go into the world finals, to be held in Mexico City, by defeating the Caribbean area representative, Haiti. Therefore, the timing of the soccer playoff series between Honduras and El Salvador could not have been worse in terms of its potential for touching off a war. When the two soccer teams met first at Tegucigalpa, Honduras, on June 8, 1969 (for the first match in the best-of-three series), the population of each country united behind its team. It was as if each citizen were on the field to fight a much-despised opponent.

In a very tragic sense this constituted a psychological simulation of political participation, inasmuch as the political systems of the two countries offered little with which the citizen of either could identify proudly or could be involved in effectively. This is a psychological key. Let us put it this way: "If I cannot be proud to be a *guanaco* or a *catracho* because of the socioeconomic realities of my country, and the political freedom it affords me, then perhaps an athletic success that commands world headlines (the Jules Rimet World Cup) may serve as a temporary substitute." This, we believe, was the subconscious (or perhaps the conscious) thinking of many, if not most, Salvadorans and Hondurans as the soccer games got under way.

It is not idle speculation that the climatic conditions surrounding the playing of these games contributed to the atmosphere in which violence could explode. The games were held during the rainy season, when human emotions are often frayed and food is less plentiful. But the background for conflict had been generated earlier in socioeconomic terms: Honduras believed that El Salvador was indifferent to the economic problem that its unchecked flow of illegal migrants was causing; El Salvador believed that Honduras was evicting Salvadoran nationals from their farmlands in Honduras. These claims, although substantially true, had elements of the apocryphal; but they were believed and acted upon nonetheless, and this is the most critical element from a social science point of view. To a surprising extent the two-country soccer contest became the "new rage" around which each country's nationals planned their activities and structured their near-future expectations.

One American scholar writing from El Salvador described the soccer matches that helped to ignite the war as follows:

> The first game was held in Honduras and, naturally, Honduras won. The second game was played in El Salvador June 15. The Salvadorean crowd took no chances. For two nights they serenaded the visiting team in the Gran Hotel with fireworks and sirens to make sure they were properly rested for the game. The visiting Honduran fans got hopping mad. In the two days of rioting before the game three people were gunned down. El Salvador won the rather anti-climactic game, 3-0.[34]

The aftermath of these games was the spark that ignited the "Football War" even though the essential issue was illegal migration and the treatment of illegal aliens.

Tensions were released immediately after El Salvador's soccer victory. Honduras claimed that Salvadorans had attacked its banner carrier, that the Honduran flag had been desecrated, that Honduran soccer players had been assaulted, and that Honduran women had been raped in broad daylight outside the soccer stadium. The Salvadoran side of the ledger was similarly lined with charges of indiscretions committed by Hondurans: "the destruction, burning, plundering, and looting of large and small business establishments owned by many Salvadoreans in Honduran territory"; "the beatings, mutilations of all kinds, infliction of wounds, and even murders perpetrated in Honduras against Salvadorean men, women and children"; "persecuting and mistreating physically [the] Salvadorean consul in Juticapa and Danlí"; and "the massive expulsion" of Salvadorans from Honduras.[35]

The "beatings" of Salvadorans residing in Honduras were allegedly done by irate Honduran citizens as reprisals for the abuses they had suffered in El Salvador. But within a day or two "bands of thugs and vagabonds" perpetrated a second, more vicious and systematic, round of attacks in Honduras, "looting the business establishments of Salvadoreans and of Hondurans selling Salvadorean products."[36] News broadcasts openly fanned the already unquenchable fires of anti-Salvadoran sentiment, and a handbill calling on Hondurans to boycott Salvadoran products was widely circulated.[37] In this climate of provoked hatred and runaway passions, deliberately stimulated and prolonged by partisan propaganda and the laxity of the Honduran government in protecting its foreign residents, thousands of people, guilty only of their nationality, became victims of a collective reprisal. By July 9, two refugee centers, established at the border points of El Poy and El Amatillo, had registered and cared for some 13,820 persons of Salvadoran nationality, allegedly evicted from Honduras. The International Red Cross in El Salvador estimated that it had processed more than 21,000 refugees between June 15 and August 8, 1969.[38] Obviously, most of these refugees — as seen by their physical circumstances (at least 80 percent needing immediate medical attention, according to Red Cross informants, and having no possessions with them) – had left Honduras in great haste and against their will.

Even a cursory study of this period reveals singular simplicity on the part of Salvadoran officials who believed that the inter-American system would be immediately sympathetic to their petition and would then be capable of intervening in Honduras on behalf of persecuted Salvadorans still residing there. (The OAS's past performances reveal no such sympathy nor capability.) The procedure, after calling upon the Commission of Human Rights of the Organization of American States (June 24, 1969) to verify Honduras' violation of the rights of Salvadorans living in Honduras, was to compile "lists of thousands of notable acts" and "many documents" to prove "the genocide perpetrated on hundreds of Salvadoreans located in Honduran territory." El Salvador's "many documents" consisted of "tape recordings, films, publications, and innumerable photographs," which on July 4 were shown to unimpassioned representatives of the OAS Subcommission on Human Rights in San Salvador. To the dismay of an entire nation caught up in the compelling tragedy of the thousands of uprooted and tormented compatriots returning from Honduras, the OAS took 16 days to arrive in El Salvador and exhibited "only the mildest interest in trying to control the happenings in Honduras."[39]

On July 14, El Salvador launched its national army and air force against Honduras, an act presumably undertaken after a warplane, disguised as a commercial airliner and bearing the initials SAHSA, strafed Salvadoran troops along their border positions.[40] July 14 was, essentially, the beginning of the "Football" or "Hundred Hour" War.

There had already been an estimated 2,000 casualties when the OAS achieved a cease-fire at 5 P.M. on July 17. But the cease-fire was not immediately communicated to Salvadoran troops operating in the far-flung reaches of Honduras, so that the two-country war entered a fifth and last day. Through August 1969 not even lavish military celebrations could overshadow the continuous flow of terror-stricken Salvadorans back into crowded El Salvador. Fear existed for the fate of the 10,843 incarcerated Salvadorans in Honduras. For the majority of Hondurans there were the realities of intensified poverty and social disorder, magnified in the aftermath of a devastating war. As the inflow of Salvadoran refugees reached a cumulative total of approximately 36,700 on October 8, 1969, El Salvador vigorously renewed its pre-withdrawal conditions, and more OAS meetings were held in October 1969. Although the seven-part OAS document, "Resolutions of the OAS in Its Second Session in Washington, October 1969," issued on October 27, reaffirmed a position of "respect for human rights" and of "rights to life, personal safety, liberty, property, and family," El Salvador felt that the document could not have real meaning until a similar attitude and disposition should exist on the part of Honduras. Again, however, the OAS was stressing the general view of hemispheric unity and solidarity. Its diplomacy was directed more to obtaining an end to the hostilities and restoring diplomatic relations between the contending countries than to determining the interests of each country or resolving particular problems.

Both countries appeared to be disturbed by the apparent detachment and ineffectiveness of the OAS in its mediation of the conflict. Therefore, attempts were made to work through the United Nations. But top-level discussions between UN officials and the foreign ministers of both countries (Tiburcio Carías Castillo of Honduras and Francisco José Guerrero of El Salvador) at the annual UN General Assembly meeting in New York (September 1979) were no more fruitful in reaching mutually satisfactory solutions. There seem to have been no imminent or certain solutions through diplomacy, regardless of scope (regional, hemispheric, or worldwide).

Amid the charges of genocide, desire for territorial conquest, torture, involvements of U.S. business interests, allegations of the presence of the CIA and/or Fidel Castro, and myriad confusing charges that remain unclear, it is difficult to render a final judgment on the "Hundred Hours War." Several things are certain, however, even if it is too soon to judge their ultimate ramifications. It is clear that El Salvador's illegal migration problem had become a plague to all neighboring states, especially to Honduras. It is also clear that many of these Salvadoran migrants were gainfully employed in Honduras, thus depriving Hondurans of jobs; and it is certain that Hondurans took reprisals against these unwelcome illegal aliens. It is believed on good authority that some 2,400 military fatalities occurred and that there were at least 2,000 civilian deaths.[41] This, in and of itself, makes the conflict a major war. There are still uncertainties about the fate of some of the Salvadoran migrants who may still be trying to subsist, illegally, in Honduras. Also uncertain is the exactness of the boundary between the two states, a matter not settled as of mid-1980. As a result of the boundary dilemma, there continues to be an obvious ambiguity as to the citizenship of thousands who reside near the frontier.

Certain bizarre aspects of the war's conduct tended to inspire derision of each of the national combatants and to obscure the more profound ramifications of what happened: events humorously related by the U.S. press, such as Honduran bombs that fell but did not explode and the Salvadoran Army's using oil-company road maps to find its way into Honduran territory. Some Central Americans believe that the Salvadoran president, General Sánchez Hernández, took advantage of perhaps the only chance in his entire career to issue combat orders, and seized upon the occasion to solve his country's overpopulation problem through conquest of the lands that his compatriots had already occupied. His desire for territorial expansion was easily fed by a Salvadoran campaign, supposedly not sponsored by that government, which consisted of the distribution of maps showing El Salvador as it was and as it would be after the planned take-over of most of Honduras' Caribbean seaboard. These maps were seen throughout the area.[42] In addition, there was fear in El Salvador of a Honduran paramilitary organization known as the Mancha Brava. This was told to Kenneth F. Johnson by Guatemalan congressmen who had become privy to confidential information concerning the war. The Mancha Brava was said to be poised to make retaliatory incursions into El Salvador.

Honduras argued after the conflict, in testimony elicited in field interviews by Paul R. Hoopes, that if the Salvadoran government were truly interested in the welfare of its nationals, it would never have risked the invasion. In addition, Hoopes found considerable grounds for economically based resentment in Honduras. Bitter conflict had characterized the economic relations between Honduras and El Salvador (in which Honduran industrialists had lost more than 50 percent of their national market to Salvadorans) before the war of July 14-18, 1969. Even before the operation of the Central American Common Market, the two countries had had precarious trade relations. Once the Common Market had begun to operate, Honduras found itself unable to compete with El Salvador.

Not to be forgotten are the human and material losses that were suffered as a direct result of the conflict. The figures on human casualties have already been cited (some 2,000 unofficial combat casualties for Honduras and 89 officially recognized casualties for El Salvador; an additional 2,000 civilian casualties in Honduras). In addition, some 36,700 Salvadorans were expelled from Honduras up to October 8, 1969; and 10,843 Salvadorans were believed to be incarcerated in 32 concentration camps in Honduras. Of the some 100,000 Hondurans living in the war zone, at last 40 percent were directly affected by the conflict. Also, an estimated 20,000 civilians fled into the interior before the advancing Salvadoran troops in July 1969. These figures do not reflect the total human impact of the conflict, since the invasion and resistance to it were national efforts that mobilized, united, and engaged much of each country's population. Such extensive participation implies extensive influence; nearly every national inhabitant had to have been affected in some way.

This analysis could speculate about the material losses suffered in the conflict without adding significantly to anyone's knowledge. It is sufficient to refer to intra-Central American trade in 1968 to visualize the subsequent economic impact of the war upon each country's economy in 1969. El Salvador lost its principal Central American market, valued at $22.9 million in 1968, $18.6 million (81.4 percent) of which consisted of manufactured products; Honduras lost a $14.8 million market, $10.3 million (69.7 percent) of which was in raw materials and foodstuffs.

No two nations of Latin America have more reason for collaboration, and ultimately integration, than do Honduras and El Salvador. Their separation is due to political factors and historical accidents, and has produced an unwholesome and unnatural socioeconomic situation in which national passions can be triggered into a full-scale war by a soccer game. Thousands of lives could have been spared. Millions of dollars spent on armaments could have gone to socioeconomic development.

One of the best analyses (and one of the most complex) of the "Hundred-Hour War" was done by Paul R. Hoopes.[43] Within a "strategical sociological" context of analysis, he looked at questions such as "Did the war have to occur?" and "Was the war strictly between El Salvador and Honduras?" and "Were the war's consequences necessarily bad?" Although there is a risk that Dr. Hoopes might not approve of our extracting a piece of "conventional wisdom" from his work, it appears that many analysts of the war would agree that the conflict occurred because (1) misbehavior by nationals of both countries at a series of soccer matches was the pretext for going to war over another series of long-standing and highly complex international differences; (2) this involved a recent history of border disputes and clashes, illegal migration, and the specter of one country being a receptacle for the unwanted excess population of another; (3) elite politics and exaggerated ego sensitivity among ruling groups created a war psychology leading to a certain naive geopolitical imperialism on the part of El Salvador; (4) there was a wanton disregard for the tradition of diplomatic immunity by Honduras; (5) illegal aliens and latifundia problems plagued both nations.

Perhaps no other case in the Western Hemisphere so clearly demonstrates the blunting of national political identities as does the socioeconomic artificiality of the boundary between El Salvador and Honduras. These peoples could, and should, be one nation. The selfish quest for separate political domain, however, makes that impossible for the time being. But the opportunity is there. And natural socioeconomic migratory and collaborative patterns point the way. What remains is for enlightened leaders to emerge and to learn the art of compromise, and for them to be able to take pride in this for themselves, thereby generating satisfactions for their people. Once again the competitive ethic and the "tooth-and-claw" model of behavior are called into question. The "Football War" was one of the worst recent evidences in the Western Hemisphere of these excesses run wild. Late in 1980 El Salvador and Honduras signed a peace treaty that promised to restore the Central American Common Market, which was largely wrecked by the 1969 war. No genuine solution to the illegal migrant problem was contained in the treaty, but it was a step toward such a solution.

LIVABILITY STRATEGIES AND ILLEGAL ALIENAGE

Humans who migrate as illegal aliens find this to be a natural but hazardous livability strategy. If the relations between two states are as amicable as those between Yemen and Saudi Arabia (to give a distinct cultural comparison), there is no problem; instead of calling the phenomenon "illegal migration," we talk of "international labor mobility," regardless of legal technicalities. This is approximately the situation now existing between Argentina and its neighbors in the Rio de la Plata region. The "Football War" of course represents the complete opposite; yet with a more rational set of political norms and structures, a situation approaching "labor mobility" could be achieved throughout most of Central America. The Nicaraguan revolution could, of course, come to mean that that nation's labor force would be exempted from any such scenario. The migratory problem between Colombia and Venezuela (touched on in Chapter 1 and dealt with more fully in Chapter 4) falls in between the extremes.

Political alienation, its sublimation, and its avoidance are essential to any livability strategy for handling illegal alienage. Aside from the problems between Venezuela and Colombia over homesteading and border migrations, it is possible to look at the former (receiver) nation and draw quite a pleasant picture. During the presidential campaign of 1978, the Acción Democrática candidate, Luis Piñerúa Ordaz, told the Venezuelan Congress of Naturalized Citizens that he would give the cold shoulder to hemispheric dictatorships if he were elected.[44] Some 4,000 delegates representing 250,000 immigrants who would vote that coming December were composed of immigrants from Argentina, Chile, Cuba, and Colombia. But the largest groups represented were from Spain, Portugal, and Italy. These people were probably once a mixture of legal and illegal aliens, but they had achieved citizenship and apparently supported the incumbent regime. It is rare in Latin America to find a national association of immigrants that is seen as worthy of a presidential candidate's attention in such a formal way.

On the other hand, the alienated immigrant, legal or illegal, will differ sharply from the integrated immigrant in more than numerical minority status. Immigrant alienation appears to be more acute in Venezuela than, for instance, in Canada. Less than 4 percent of immigrant householders in Toronto were found to be alienated, according to one Canadian study.[45] The ratio, we should add, would most likely be higher in many of the major cities of Latin America, but in the absence of empirical studies one can only speculate on the basis of limited observation. The Canadian study found that the alienated immigrant had less than ten years of education, had lived in the host country for less than five years, and had been sponsored by a relative or had entered "as a visitor who stayed on without obtaining landed-immigrant status"[46] — that is, illegally. Further, the alienated immigrant in Toronto is likely to be deficient in English, is poorly acculturated, has a family in "the old country," and may be socially isolated and at the mercy of the unskilled labor market. In short, he or she feels worse off than most other Canadians.

The great success of Canadian multiculturalism is that it has been able to keep such alienation (albeit oversimplified here) at a minimum level. Even when the unity of the Canadian federation was challenged by Quebec separatists, the issue was not settled by warfare, as in Central America, but temporarily by a provincial election in May 1980. Canada was surely not being torn apart in a fight over alienated illegal immigrants. Nor do we wish to hold Canada up to the world as a standard of excellence; but it is a multicultural nation that has been able to absorb a great deal of legal and illegal immigration without internal atrophy. Multiculturalism, for Canada, is a livability strategy.

But multiculturalism is not likely to work where migrants are deliberately allowed to come in by governments that employ *la vista gorda*, looking the other way. This is likely to be the case in countries that have some abundance of liquid capital but whose economic interests do not want to deplete that capital by long-range commitments to a given labor supply. The handy thing about illegal aliens in a labor pool is that they can be ignored (as in Argentina) or be sent back when they are no longer needed (as in Venezuela). Canada, it should be stressed, has *bracero* or contract-labor programs with several countries in the hemisphere. Mexicans, for instance, are flown at Canadian expense to specific agricultural locations for a harvest; once it is over, they are flown back to Mexico (except those who illegally enter the United States, despite Canadian governmental efforts to prevent this). This is not the same as allowing Colombians to homestead in Venezuela and then expelling them once their efforts have become worth confiscating, a practice that was also intimately involved in the complaints in Central America leading to the "Football War." Worker aliens who are illegally in a country, without legal and social welfare benefits, do contribute a flexibility to production decisions and do enhance profit levels. The aliens, thus, are expendable.[47]

It is true, of course, that exploitation through opportunism is not adequate to explain why countries become receivers of clandestine movements of workers. In the twentieth century, movements of workers to the sugar plantations of Cuba or to the refineries of Curacao occurred because of labor demand generated by the expansion of a specific economic sector. Upon completion of these projects, many migrants returned home and others moved on to other countries. Both the United States and Canada have set up, from time to time, official recruitment programs for the orderly bringing of Caribbean migrant workers north for fixed periods. But this has probably inspired much illegal migration, since there is already severe population pressure in many Caribbean nations and the lure of permanent residence to the north will be greater than temporary employment.[48]

A specific case in point is that of Barbados, whose biggest social problems stem from chronic unemployment. The Barbados government has tried in recent years to persuade other governments to accept its citizens, and tries to provide skills to its people in the hope of making them more able to work abroad. Such a governmental policy must provide a migration mentality that could easily induce extralegal migration. Because, historically, migrants from British or French West Indian countries encountered poor health and living conditions in the Hispanic Caribbean countries, there was a natural tendency to direct migrational streams toward North America or non-Hispanic Caribbean possessions. The United States, for instance, campaigned to expel illegal aliens from the Virgin Islands during the early 1970s; this produced charges of brutality against the American government. Immigration of all sorts from the Caribbean to North America increased during the 1960s and 1970s as the result of less restrictive policies adopted by the United States and Canada. There is reason to believe that following the more restrictive immigration policies of the past would have led to even greater illegal migration from the Caribbean northward.[49]

Any consideration of livability strategies vis-à-vis illegal aliens must consider a range of human rights issues, a sampling of which are reflected in the following questions: Do receiving governments protect prospective entrants from unscrupulous "counselors" and "lawyers" who make a profit by encouraging clandestine immigration? Do governments campaign actively against smugglers of aliens? Are apprehended illegal aliens only jailed before deportation, or are they also given medical help and immigration counseling? Is the option of political asylum available to aliens who might otherwise become illegals? Is the granting of political asylum administered selectively? In short, does the state really do anything to keep aliens from becoming illegal, and does it protect the basic human rights of illegal subgroups once they are de facto part of the work force?

Few nations are totally free of illegal migration. Even the Federal Republic of Germany has a subgroup of illegal alien Turks and Moroccans estimated at over 250,000, some of whom were smuggled in.[50] The German guest-worker program of the 1960s gave impetus to migratory patterns that later grew to include smuggling of aliens.

The human rights policy of a receiving nation is determined largely by the decision to treat the illegal alien either as an economic refugee or as a criminal. In this regard two of the Western Hemisphere's most democratic nations may have a poor human rights record vis-à-vis the illegal alien. The first case is the United States, whose policy of benign neglect and haphazard immigration enforcement amounts to no policy at all. Early in the 1970s one scholar was led to comment:

> . . . there can be no doubt that the Immigration and Naturalization Service should compile more precise statistics citing the number of persons who have been admitted to the United States and those that departed. It is curious that if the government believes that "illegal aliens" pose a significant problem . . . they have virtually no statistics.[51]

Yet the U.S. government maintained detention centers for the Haitian economic refugees (treated as criminals) and relocation and job services for the Cubans (treated as political refugees). In the face of this policy inconsistency, black citizens of Miami during 1980 could understandably feel that the U.S. government preferred foreigners to them. After all, "the Cubans are organized, articulate, they have 4 radio stations and one television channel. The only Black radio station is owned by a white person."[52] Illegal alienage was making itself felt unmistakably in the human rights politics of Florida as a consequence of the lack of a clear and consistent immigration policy.

The second case is Venezuela. The press report below is typical of commentaries on the Venezuelan policy toward illegal aliens.

> Venezuela, a supposedly democratic country, is violating human rights through its brutal treatment of "undocumented" persons. Incapable of stemming the flow of illegal immigrants from economically disadvantaged countries, the Government has made them scapegoats for the ineffectiveness of its public services.[53]

The report states that hundreds of persons are returned to Colombia or deported to other countries after having been beaten by the Venezuelan police. The new Venezuelan government of COPEI, the Social Christian party, is said to have sought to distract the public from its ineptness by launching a national crusade against illegal aliens. Some Venezuelan officials have been exposed as sellers of visas. Arresting an "illegal alien," even though all that distinguishes the person from most others is his or her accent, has become a way for the Venezuelan police to rob someone behind a facade of law enforcement. Peruvians, Argentines, Uruguayans, and some North Americans have been similarly mistreated in Venezuela under the claim that they were illegal aliens.[54]

Thus, whereas in one scenario Venezuela looks like the land of happy legal aliens-become-citizens, in another scenario it appears as the violator of human rights. The United States, with its public officials campaigning for human rights, has a vacillating admission and enforcement policy that subsidizes one group of aliens, declares another group in nearly identical circumstances to be illegal, and practices benign neglect on still other groups of clandestine migrants. What is needed is a hemispheric approach to immigration, one that would accept the possibility that archaic political boundaries need to be redrawn and/or erased, and one that might ask that some political empires be sacrificed in the cause of preserving mankind. Multiculturalism, hemispheric population planning, and hemispheric international government should be considered as alternative livability strategies to what we now have: illegal migration, repression and deportation, amnesty, foreign colonies, regional wars, and the continued population explosion and clandestine migration that threaten to engulf us all.

NOTES

1. As reported by Christopher Wren in *New York Times,* May 10, 1980.
2. Ibid.
3. *U.S. News and World Report,* April 21, 1980, p. 70.
4. *St. Louis Post-Dispatch,* July 7, 1980.
5. As observed by Kenneth F. Johnson during November 1976.
6. Field interviews by Kenneth F. Johnson in Buenos Aires during June 1980.
7. From Desmond Storer, Freda Hawkins, and S. M. Tomasi, *Amnesty for Undocumented Migrants: The Experience of Australia, Canada, and Argentina* (Staten Island, N.Y.: Center for Migration Studies, 1977), pp. 11-17.
8. Based on a U.S. Department of Justice information bulletin dated April 28, 1978, and issued by Doris M. Meissner, deputy associate attorney general.
9. Field interviews by Kenneth F. Johnson in Manitoba during October 1979.
10. See Raymond E. Crist and Charles M. Nissly, *East from the Andes* (Gainesville: University of Florida Press, 1973), pp. 125-54.
11. Ibid., p. 151.
12. Ibid.
13. FAIR, *Immigration Report* 1, no. 9 (June 1980): 1. FAIR's position was "While we do not need to forsake the tradition of this country as being a haven for refugees from throughout the world, we do need to recognize that there are some limits, particularly at

this time when our people are straining under the inflationary spiral that we suffer from in this country, when our economic resources are being sorely tested, when our energy supplies are in short supply. The resolution sets a limit of 65,000 legal immigrants for 1980 and requires an annual limit on all immigration, including refugees, to be set each year by the president."

14. From *Diario las Américas* (Miami), July 2, and July 6, 1980.

15. From *Globe and Mail* (Toronto), January 26, 1980.

16. Ibid.

17. *LATINO* (Toronto), March 17, 1979, passim.

18. Interviews by Kenneth F. Johnson with foreign diplomats in Buenos Aires during June 1980.

19. Ibid.

20. *Diario las Américas* (Miami), July 1, 1980.

21. Ibid.

22. Employment and Immigration Canada, *NEWSLETTER: Indochinese Refugees* (Ottawa) 11, no. 1 (January 24, 1980): 12.

23. Ibid., p. 17. Canada's official policy on refugees from Latin America is seen in events between 1973 and 1979, when Canada accepted over 7,000 Chilean refugees, more than any other country. However, the number of resettlement requests from Chilean and Argentine refugees has decreased markedly, reflecting the view of the UN high commissioner for refugees that, with individual exceptions, the major resettlement needs from this area have been met, at least, for the present. However, Canada maintains interest in helping individuals in South America who are victims of persecution, and therefore will continue to respond to requests from those Latin Americans who are Convention refugees as well as those falling within the parameters of the Latin American designated class: Chileans, Argentines, and Uruguayans within their own countries who have a well-founded fear of persecution. This class includes 100 Argentine political detainees and their families for whom a program was initiated in 1978.

While other countries in Latin America have been experiencing refugee-creating situations owing to political or social instability, this has not resulted in a significant demand for resettlement in third countries, since most people are generally able to return home upon normalization of the situation or to be accommodated in neighboring areas.

24. Thomas P. Anderson, "El Salvador Against Honduras: The Great Fútbol War," *Commonweal*, August 8, 1969, p. 480.

25. Much of this section is based on unpublished work done by Paul R. Hoopes and Kenneth F. Johnson.

26. See Placido García Reynoso, *Integración económica latinoamericana* (Mexico City: CELA, 1965).

27. As early as 1928 the United Fruit Company alone had more than 87,000 hectares of Honduran land under cultivation, and expansion continued well into the 1950s.

28. Idle lands accounted for some 85 percent of the total national territory of Honduras as of 1958.

29. Religious conservatism has generally been held responsible for the unusually high birthrate in El Salvador.

30. Marco Virgilio Carías, *Análisis sobre el conflicto entre Honduras y El Salvador* (Tegucigalpa: Universidad Nacional Autónoma de Honduras, Facultad de Ciencias Económicas, 1969), p. 24.

31. Ibid., p. 52.

32. Colonel Fidel Sánchez Hernández, *Informe presidencial: Primer año de gobierno* (San Salvador: Imprenta Nacional, 1968), p. 11.

33. See Thomas G. Sanders, "The Social Functions of Fútbol," *American University Field Staff Reports* 14, no. 2 (1970): passim.

34. Anderson, "El Salvador Against Honduras."

35. Paul R. Hoopes and Kenneth Johnson, research files.

36. Carías, *Análisis sobre el conflicto* . . . .

37. Hoopes and Johnson, research files.

38. Ibid.

39. Statement issued by Residents of the United States of America in El Salvador, "The Truth About the Conflict Between El Salvador and Honduras" (San Salvador, 1969). (Mimeographed.)

40. Hoopes and Johnson, research files.

41. Ibid.

42. Ibid.

43. Paul R. Hoopes, "Strategical Sociology and the Study of International Conflicts: Central America's Hundred-Hour War Revisited," paper presented at the annual meeting of the Southwestern Political Science Association, San Antonio, Texas, March 26-29, 1975.

44. *Diario las Américas* (Miami), October 3, 1978.

45. Anthony H. Richmond, *Aspects of the Absorption and Adaptation of Immigrants* (Ottawa: Information Canada, 1974), p. 43.

46. Ibid.

47. See Dawn Marshall, "The International Politics of Caribbean Migration," in Richard Millett and W. Marvin Will, eds., *The Restless Caribbean* (New York: Praeger, 1979), pp. 42-50, passim.

48. Ibid.

49. Ibid.

50. Kurt Glaser and Stefan Possony, *Victims of Politics: The State of Human Rights* (New York: Columbia University Press, 1979), p. 338.

51. Austin T. Fragomen, *The Illegal Alien: Criminal or Economic Refugee* (Staten Island, N.Y.: Center for Migration Studies, 1973), p. 7.

52. *Diario las Américas* (Miami), June 7, 1980.

53. *Atlas World Press Review*, May 1980, p. 58.

54. Ibid. There is, to be certain, a potential for xenophobia that is active and disturbingly real within the United States. An organization in point would be the Christian-Patriots Defense League. This group's racism is directed against almost anyone not Christian and white. They write off the entire eastern seaboard as hopelessly contaminated by blacks and Latins who must be "shipped back"; the Southwest gets the same treatment because of Mexicans; Chinatowns in the big cities will have to go. The only "pure" zone is the Middle West, ranging from western Nebraska to Pittsburgh, down to Atlanta, and west to Lubbock, Texas. After the Christian-Patriots Defense League carries out its revolution, the "Negroes will voluntarily return to Africa . . . and . . . white Europeans will migrate to this country . . .," leaving Europe to fend for itself against Orientals. This is not to argue that such sentiments are typical of North Americans generally, but we do point out the potential for alienated reaction to continued uncontrolled migration, both legal and clandestine, which could generate severe reactions among the migrants themselves (based on a story in the *St. Louis Post-Dispatch*, July 20, 1980).

3

ILLEGAL MEXICAN AND
OTHER ALIENS IN NORTH AMERICA

The controversy among scholars and activists as to whether illegal immigration from Mexico is a "problem" for the United States is certain to become one of the burning issues of the 1980s. Here are some basic facts about the factors that compel Mexicans to migrate north clandestinely. In 1980, Mexico had approximately 68 million inhabitants; at the population growth rate of 3.5 percent, that figure would double by the end of the century. About 65 percent of Mexico's population is under age 21. By U.S. standards Mexico has chronic unemployment of at least 50 percent. In the capital city over half of the metropolitan population of 12 million are underemployed and undernourished. The Mexican government's family planning and vocational relocation programs, satellite industrialization experiments, and other efforts to alleviate the national distress have not worked. This failure is due largely to governmental corruption, not to a lack of good social and economic planners.

To put it in less abrasive terms, one writer has talked about two general beneficiaries of the illegal alien traffic northward: "Mexican political and economic institutions perpetuating the country's maldistribution of income between the very few rich and the multitudes of the very poor; and the multinationals not only operating within Mexico, but trading with her and other nations as well."[1] Poverty, overpopulation, Mexico's low extractive and distributive capabilities, and governmental corruption are the root causes of the moving north of millions of economic refugees. These are the bulk of the illegal aliens in North America.

There is an emotional debate forming in North America (both Canada and the United States) as to the nature and importance of illegal aliens. There are those like FAIR (Federation for American Immigration Reform) that are concerned to fix numerical limits on immigration into the United States and that

THE WESTERN HEMISPHERE

would ultimately reduce the number of permanent immigrants to near zero. There are others, amply represented among liberal scholars and journalists, who would virtually "let the aliens in" without limit, as one article has suggested.[2] Some within the liberal-permissive school strenuously object to the terms "illegal" and "alien" on the ground that both are unacceptably pejorative. They stress, quite rightly, the danger of doing injustice to Americans of Mexican origin by associating "illegal alien" with brown skin and Spanish-sounding surnames. It is further asserted that estimates of America's illegal immigrant population constitute a hazardous game that can whip up hysteria and xenophobia to no good purpose. It is interesting to note that one writer who disparages such estimates by likening them to the Vietnam War "body counts" goes on, on the same page, to employ other estimates about the fluidity of the American underground labor market.[3] The same writer deplores the term "illegal aliens" but uses it freely nonetheless, and points out three mistakes in the U.S. government's computations. These are worth citing.

The first is that deportations are assumed to be indicators of the actual presence of illegal aliens. The second is that there is no way of knowing how many illegal immigrants leave the country clandestinely, often within a year of their entry (here the author embraces "estimates" that 70-90 percent of the clandestine migrants leave the United States). Third, it is argued that since enforcement is concentrated along the Mexican border, a distorted profile may appear, showing Mexicans to constitute a greater percentage of the illegal entrants than is really the case.[4] This, of course, is just as speculative as any of the other "estimates" and "games" to which the author refers, as is the subsequent allegation that strict enforcement along the Canadian border might generate a more accurate illegal alien profile. The problems of speculation notwithstanding, this argument has merit and will be considered.

During 1980 the U.S. Congress commissioned an effort to survey what is reliably known about illegal aliens within the United States. This was done by the Select Commission on Immigration and Refugee Policy. Its *Semiannual Report to Congress*[5] contains the following generalizations, which seem to reflect a spirit of moderation in coming to grips with the illegal alien phenomenon. The *Report* states that there are some 6 million illegal aliens in the United States at any one time, and probably fewer most of the time; that only half of these are Mexicans; that there is no basis on which to generalize about the overall impact of the illegal migrants; and that if the U.S. annual rate of population increase of 1.8 percent continues along with a net immigration of 750,000 annually, the country will reach a stable population by the year 2030.[6] It is noteworthy that this last prediction excludes illegal migration as an unknown variable and makes no effort to generalize about the expected livability conditions for immigration in the year 2030.

The *Report* acknowledges a deeply felt dispute over whether illegal aliens have an adverse effect on the nation's economy, and states:

There is widespread belief that the presence of a substantial number of illegal aliens in the United States is bad for society apart from its controversial effect on the economy. The reasons given: they are vulnerable to economic exploitation; they are easily preyed upon by criminals; they do not report health problems; many of their children are not in school; and their presence corrodes confidence in a government which presumes to apply laws consistently and equitably.[7]

The *Report* concludes by stressing the need for a more professionalized Immigration and Naturalization Service (INS) and for reforms in immigration law and enforcement policy.

It is obvious that the United States could put up a militarily enforced "cactus curtain" to the south, and a "prairie curtain" to the north, and by stepping up patrols of the beaches and airports could virtually end illegal migration. This could seriously damage our friendly social and economic relations with Canada, and it would surely help to provoke governmental collapse and social revolution in Mexico. The United States also could abandon immigration enforcement and try to absorb everyone. Neither of these drastic measures is likely to occur within the 1980s, although the "curtain" option is clearly more likely than that of "absorption." The question is, then, what can Mexico and Canada do to alleviate the flow of illegal aliens across their borders into the United States?

Mexico presents the greater problem, since about half of that nation's labor force is unemployed and the drought conditions of 1980 intensified the push factor moving Mexican peasants north. A conservative estimate of Mexico's unemployed is 9 million, almost equal to the population of Mexico City.[8] The Mexican birth control program initiated in the early 1970s could be made more effective if it were accompanied by education for the target population and if corruption were removed from its administration. It seems that the traditional proletarian Mexican sectors are the ones that contribute most to the excess population, and the capital-intensive modern sectors seeking to benefit from import substitution are unable to absorb Mexico's excess working population. Thus, even though Mexico may show aggregate economic growth rates of 7 percent and more – high by Third World standards – the capital-intensive basis for this growth absorbs few people into the work force. The poor remain poor, and their numbers proliferate. Northward migration becomes imperative for them. The part of Mexican agriculture (accounting for approximately half the population) that benefits from capital-intensive modern methods of fertilization and irrigation does not embrace the millions of *minifundistas* whose subsistence plots can take no further burdens.[9]

The northward thrust toward the United States, and eventually Canada, may be "only the leading edge of a new world-wide response to economic disparities"[10] that may become a massive and uncontrollable force. Management and investor elites in Mexico are not eager to volunteer profit-sharing with their employees as a way of keeping people from emigrating. Government-decreed cuts in managements' profits would cause a decrease in investor confidence, undermine the Mexican currency through flight of capital, and probably lead to a political crisis through withdrawal of elite support for the established single-party "democracy."

Will Mexico's newly found oil riches spew out over the population, representing a cornucopia for all? They might, if they were effectively and honestly administered and were used to bolster genuinely progressive policies of social and economic change. Barring some drastic change in the Mexican governmental mentality (such as the norm of corrupt self-enrichment giving precedence to community goals), the oil wealth of Mexico is not likely to alleviate poverty any more than it did in Iran. Also, oil is not a labor-intensive industry. It will generate some skilled manual jobs and quite a few white-collar jobs, but they will not help the bulk of the unemployed Mexican labor force. Mexico might develop internal (away from the border areas) consumer goods manufacturing enterprises, as Japan, Taiwan, and Hong Kong have done. There has been a proposal that Mexican expertise might be marshaled through cottage industries that would provide repair and other service functions for North American machinery and appliances.[11]

Ultimately, some reform of the governing norms of Mexico is requisite if the clandestine emigration problem is to be handled from that side of the border. That will not come peacefully. Mexico is governed by a kind of plural dictatorship (that is, by a dominant class).[12] Despite its defects the Mexican regime is not so odious as was the Somoza dictatorship in Nicaragua. It is easier to focus outrage on a single tyrant and his family. In Mexico it is much more difficult to isolate the most appropriate, and most vulnerable, targets for revolutionary ardor. The government may keep life poor, so that most have to emigrate, but it is hard to focus revolutionary sentiment in any one place. Social change, when it comes in Mexico, will be a bloody, cataclysmic affair that could drag the hemisphere into it. About all the United States can do is to prepare for the Nicaraguan socialist revolutionary scenario, multiplied a hundredfold, to emerge on its southern border.

In the short term there is at least one adaptive measure that the United States can try. That involves restoration of the *bracero*, or guest-worker, program that existed from the 1940s until 1964. But there were numerous and gross abuses of human rights during that program, especially in the treatment of the illegals who came along with the contract *braceros*. A guest-worker program will work only when the basic rights of the workers are guaranteed and when traffic in illegals is ended. A change of values north of the border will then be imperative. American employers who prefer hiring illegals to keep wages down must be severely punished. There are simply too many people chasing too few resources in the hemisphere, and some redistribution of wealth is bound to come — via revolution, if that is the only way.

IMPACT IN CANADA

Because the impact of illegal Mexican aliens in Canada is minimal, at least when compared with the United States, we will treat the Canadian scenario first and only briefly. The differences between Canadian and American immigration laws are such that a bona fide Mexican visitor-tourist in Canada may have crossed the United States illegally to get there. Such is often the case with Mexican migrant workers who are able to persuade the Canadia PIL (primary inspection line) officer at the border that they are tourists with sufficient funds for a 90-day sojourn and the means to return to their country of origin. The fact that these persons may have crossed the U.S. illegally does not necessarily prevent them from entering Canada. Canada's liberal visa requirements (no visa at all for most nationals, with only a handful of exceptions) attract many visitors who then cross the vast, unguarded border into the United States. Canadian officials believe that although Mexican immigration to Canada is minimal (only about 6,000 landed immigrants 1953-79), a good number of Mexican and other Latin American and Caribbean migrants use Canada as a back door to the United States. Probably no three nations anywhere in the world have more mutual reasons to cooperate in the control of illegal migration than do Canada, Mexico, and the United States.

According to one study, Canada's seasonal workers in recent years have come primarily from Portugal, the West Indies, and Mexico. Many have, of course, come illegally, and the study cites the 1973 amnesty program that gives the number of illegal immigrants who were given legal status as 15,000.[13] Visitors and migratory workers who want to stay longer than three months must register with Canadian officials outside Canada; those coming to work for shorter periods must obtain an employment permit. The Canadian SIN (social insurance number) card is controlled much more tightly than in the United States. Aliens residing legally in Canada receive a SIN card whose number begins with 9; to be employed legally, they must also have a work permit. This requirement, as noted in Chapter 2, is enforced, and stiff penalties are imposed on employers who hire aliens not qualified to work. That in itself is one reason why Canada has nowhere near the illegal alien problem found in the United States.

Problems faced by illegal migratory workers in Canada – along with the usual immigrant problems – result from their precarious condition. Children seldom go to school. Pay rates are usually low and living conditions are frequently bad. The Ministry of Manpower and Immigration assigned a federal task force in 1973 to investigate conditions of seasonal migrants in Ontario and Quebec. They discovered instances of entire families working but only the head of the family being paid. One case in Quebec revealed a family of ten working for a total income of $60 per week. Housing was frequently substandard, and there were many instances of children working in the fields. Both legal and illegal migrants were included in this study. Canadian labor brokers sometimes recruited farm workers, charging a fee of $500 per person, and the fee was often deducted from the worker's salary. Mexicans often had to pay their transportation costs in and out of Canada, even though the trucks carrying them frequently originated in Canada.[14]

Agreements exist between the governments of Canada and Jamaica, Barbados, and Trinidad and Tobago. They cover the recruitment of agricultural workers, their guaranteed weekly minimum wage, accommodations, and transportation. A Canadian employer notifies a Canada Manpower Centre of his needs. If the position cannot be filled domestically, the governments of the above countries are contacted and asked to recruit workers, and a specific contract between the employer in Canada and the workers is set up. Each country has liaison officers stationed in Canada to handle complaints by the workers or their employers, and to help with transportation arrangements. The Canadian government shares the cost of these liaison officers. In 1973 over 3,000 workers came to Canada under this program.[15] It is known that some overstayed their contract illegally, but exact figures are unavailable.

In June 1974, Canada signed an agreement with the Mexican government that regulates the flow of migratory workers, in an effort to guarantee the improvement of their treatment in Canada. Mexicans aged 18 and over would be recruited by the Mexican government for harvesting jobs in Canada. The agreement includes a standard weekly wage; transportation and living expenses are to be partially paid by the farmers hiring the workers. Though there are obvious advantages for both worker and employer, there are also disadvantages. The workers pay income tax for certain social services but rarely derive benefits from them. Health insurance benefits are unavailable to them, although health protection is provided while working; the Mexicans can make only limited, if any, use of educational facilities, and they are ineligible for unemployment insurance, even though they pay premiums for it.[16]

The study also states that a comparison can be drawn between East Indian immigrants and other migratory workers in Canada.[17] The East Indian community has the advantages of legal residence, relatively large numbers, urban concentration, settled housing, job skills, educational attainment, and developed association. Not all groups have all these advantages, and the difference between East Indians and the other migratory workers has been great. In comparison, many, if not most, migratory workers suffer from ineligibility for permanent residence, small and scattered populations, unsettled living arrangements, little or no formal education, lack of vocal leadership, and fear of detection and deportation. Strict application of the SIN card employment criterion makes illegal employment hazardous for all concerned. This is said to be a factor in drawing illegal migrant workers south into the United States.

Without dwelling further on the oft-stated impossibility of certifying the size of an illegal/clandestine population, let us consider a single indicator of the proportions of illegal aliens in Toronto, one of Canada's most important metropolitan areas, which is conspicuously a multiethnic city. It is unfortunate to be forced to recur to deportation data as a reflection of illegal alienage.

Deportations still do not tell us the size of an underground population. Reducing deportations to numbers, each representing a traumatic experience for someone, will seem cold and inhuman. But there seems no remedy for it. Since the impact of illegal migration on Canada is still minimal when compared with the United States, and since many illegal aliens in Canada may have the United States as a planned final destination, we thought it well to present some new and heretofore unpublished data that yield a glimpse of the illegal alien phenomenon in Canada.

Before doing so, a word of caution is in order. The table below should be taken in a relative context, given the fact that Mexico is not the nation that causes the greatest illegal alien/deportable alien problem for Canada (as it is for the United States). In point of fact, more U.S. citizens have been deported from Canada during most recent years than the nationals of any other country. From April 10, 1978, to December 1, 1978 (to give a brief but illustrative example), 636 U.S. citizens were deported from Canada for a wide range of causes. (This is taken from a special tabulation made available to us by Canadian immigration headquarters in Ottawa. The same source shows that for the same brief period, Guyana had 192 of its citizens deported from Canada, Greece had 110, France had 61, and El Salvador had 35. In that period there were only 29 Mexican deportees from all of Canada.)

Table 3.1 provides a composite picture of the deportable alien in the Toronto district.[18]

TABLE 3.1
Profile of the Deportable Alien in The Toronto Immigration District, July 1-December 31, 1979

	Number	*Percent*
Port of entry		
Toronto Intl. Airport	265	69.2
Montreal Intl. Airport	26	6.8
Vancouver Intl. Airport	3	0.8
Halifax Intl. Airport		
Winnipeg Intl. Airport	1	0.3
Edmonton Intl. Airport	2	0.5
Calgary Intl. Airport		
Gander Intl. Airport		
Ottawa Intl. Airport		
Other airport	1	0.3
Niagara Falls	8	2.1
Ft. Erie	30	7.8
Lansdown	1	0.3
Sarnia		
Windsor	26	6.8

(continued)

TABLE 3.1, continued

	Number	Percent
Cornwall		
Pigeon River		
Blackpool		
Other Que. border	8	2.1
Other Can. border	3	0.8
Not available	9	2.3
Total	383	100
Age		
15 or less	2	0.5
16-19	32	8.4
20-25	130	33.9
26-30	106	27.7
31-35	48	12.5
36-40	29	7.6
41-50	27	7.0
51 +	9	2.3
Total	383	100
Nation of Origin		
Antigua	1	0.3
Argentina	10	2.6
Chile	5	1.3
Colombia	2	0.5
Ecuador	9	2.3
Egypt	1	0.3
El Salvador	2	0.5
England	7	1.8
Fiji	1	0.3
Germany	2	0.5
Ghana	3	0.8
Greece	15	3.9
Grenada	2	0.5
Guyana	69	18.0
Hong Kong	1	0.3
Hungary	1	0.3
India	17	4.4
Ireland	1	0.3
Italy	1	0.3
Jamaica	98	25.6
Mexico	5	1.3
Nigeria	1	0.3
Pakistan	3	0.8

(continued)

TABLE 3.1, continued

	Number	Percent
Peru	2	0.5
Philippines	1	0.3
Portugal	29	7.6
St. Vincent	1	0.3
Trinidad	14	3.7
Turkey	2	0.5
U.S.A. 62	62	16.2
Uruguay	1	0.3
Yugoslavia	2	0.5
Other	12	3.1
Total	383	100
Cause for removal		
Visitor overstay	105	27.4
Student overstay	5	1.3
Worker overstay	20	5.2
Illegal work	133	34.7
Subversive-terrorist	—	—
Criminal conviction in Canada	37	9.7
Elude border inspec.	2	0.5
Bypass port of entry	—	—
Elude inquiry	13	3.4
Elude removal	15	3.9
Escape custody	1	0.3
False documents	5	1.3
False claim	2	0.5
Return deportee*	19	5.0
Departure notice (failed to comply)	—	—
Ship jumper	10	2.6
Inadmissible		
Medical	—	—
Criminal record	15	3.9
Known criminal record	—	—
Public charge	1	0.3
Other	—	—
Total	383	100
Illegal entry		
Assisted	5	1.3
Unassisted	15	3.9
Smuggled	1	0.3
Other	4	1.0
Not applicable (legal entry)	351	91.6
Unknown	7	1.8
Total	383	100

(continued)

TABLE 3.1, continued

	Number	*Percent*
Use of SIN card		
Using own card – regular series	64	16.7
Using own card – 9 series	13	3.4
Using card loaned by other person	46	12.0
Using stolen card	22	5.7
Using counterfeit card	12	3.1
No card – using fictitious number	17	4.4
No card – no number	208	54.3
Unknown	1	0.3
Total	383	100
Occupation in Canada		
Agriculture	13	3.4
Manufacturing, industry	87	22.7
Restaurants, hotels, food service	40	10.4
Commerce, sales, service	31	8.1
Janitorial, maintenance, domestic	67	17.5
Construction worker	14	3.7
Without employment	125	32.6
Entertainer – legal	1	0.3
Entertainer – illegal	5	1.3
Total	383	100
Method of travel to Canada		
Air	301	78.6
Sea	10	2.6
Train	2	0.5
Bus	28	7.3
Auto	40	10.4
Other	–	–
Unknown	2	0.5
Total	383	100
Sex		
Male	202	52.7
Female	180	47.0
Not on form	1	0.3
Total	383	100

(continued)

TABLE 3.1, continued

	Number	Percent
If female, number of children in Canada		
Males coded as "0," and females with		
no children in Canada	356	93.0
One child	17	4.4
Two children	8	2.1
More than 2	2	0.5
Total	383	100
Marital status		
Single	284	74.2
Separated	9	2.3
Widowed	1	0.3
Married	76	19.8
Divorced	8	2.1
Unknown	5	1.3
Total	383	100
Status at entry		
Visitor	334	87.2
Student	9	2.3
Worker	8	2.1
Other	32	8.4
Total	383	100
Time between violation and detection		
Less than 3 months	149	38.9
3-6 months	43	11.2
6 months-1 year	66	17.2
1-2 years	45	11.7
2-3 years	20	5.2
3-4 years	18	4.7
4-5 years	17	4.4
5-7 years	18	4.7
Over 7 years	2	0.5
Not applicable or unknown	5	1.3
Total	383	100
Source of referral		
Private informant	132	34.5
Met. Toronto Police	168	43.9
Ontario Prov. Police	1	0.3
Royal Can. Mounted Police	38	9.9
Other municipal agency	1	0.3
Other provincial agency	1	0.3

(continued)

TABLE 3.1, continued

	Number	*Percent*
Other federal agency	1	0.3
Internal CEIC-Toronto detection	15	3.9
Factory raid	8	2.1
Other (as indicated)	17	4.4
Not indicated	1	0.3
Total	383	100
Degree of cooperation when arrested		
Fully cooperative	188	49.1
Highly evasive (verbally)	165	43.1
Attempted flight	20	5.2
Physically aggressive	8	2.1
Not indicated	2	0.5
Total	383	100
Place arrested		
Residence	121	31.6
Employer	73	19.1
Police station	114	29.8
Other	75	19.6
Total	383	100
Length of stay granted, port of entry		
Less than 1 month	21	5.5
1-3 months	128	33.4
3-6 months	197	51.4
6 mos.-1 year	15	3.9
Not applicable	16	4.2
Unknown	6	1.6
Total	383	100
Number of extensions granted inland		
1	128	33.4
2	197	51.4
3	15	3.9
4	16	4.2
9	6	1.6
Not applicable	21	5.5
Total	383	100

*Returned after one deportation and is deported again (potentially).

Some total percentages have been rounded off.

Source: Kenneth F. Johnson and Nina M. Ogle, "Profile of the Deportable Alien in the Toronto Immigration District," an unpublished research report presented to the Canada Employment and Immigration Commission, March 1980. Pages are unnumbered.

The deportation profile data speak for themselves within the limited time frame they represent, the last six months of 1979. We will attempt no further analysis here, since yearly comparisons seem to be most promising and they must await the passing of time. One can see, however, that Mexico has a tiny impact on Canada in terms of its deportable aliens in Toronto. Jamaica, Guyana, and Argentina have a much greater impact. This, of course, assumes that Toronto is typical of Canada.

Perhaps the most critical factor about Canada in North American immigration is its use as a jumping-off point for illegal migration into the United States. It must be stressed that not all the illegal aliens, not even all the Mexicans, come across the southern U.S. border or onto the Caribbean beaches. A new breed of smuggler seems to have emerged in the 1980s, the north-to-south smuggler who brings illegal aliens into the United States from Canada. According to one detailed account, some of the smugglers operating out of Canada are so confident they give "money-back" guarantees to their clients.[19] Most of this activity occurs along the nearly 800-mile stretch of the border between Canada and Vermont, New Hampshire, and Maine. Most of the aliens are from Caribbean and South American countries. As already noted, it is relatively easy to enter Canada without a visa by convincing the PIL officer at a Canadian airport or entry station that one is a bona fide tourist-visitor, whereupon one may receive a three-month visitor's permit. Thousands are believed now waiting in metropolitan Canada (Toronto to Montreal) for the chance to go south, with or without a smuggler.

Smuggling via Canada has been openly advertised in Haiti.[20] Many people sell their belongings to buy enough "earthly goods" and traveler's checks to look like bona fide tourists to the Canadian authorities. Then, they disappear. Buying a round-trip ticket from Haiti or from Mexico to Montreal is one of the more obvious covers. U.S. Immigration officers report Canadian smugglers using the latest radio equipment and decoy vehicles to facilitate crossing the poorly patrolled northern U.S. border. At least eight eastern points of entry are unwatched during the night, and on the prairie borders there are many more. It is obvious that with alien smuggling rampant, it will be even more difficult to determine the numbers of illegal aliens in either the U.S. or Canada and their cost impact. The governments of Canada and the United States can probably work together much better than has been the case with Mexico. What they need, essentially, is more manpower to enforce the immigration laws of both countries, thereby making unnecessary the setting up of fences (which exist between the United States and Mexico).

IMPACT IN THE UNITED STATES

Over 1 million Mexican aliens were deported from the United States during 1980, a record high since 1954, when about a million were deported during "Operation Wetback,"[21] a concerted paramilitary effort involving the governments of Mexico and the United States in stopping the flow of illegals at the height of the *bracero* program. The impact of the illegal Mexican aliens in the United States in the late 1970s and early 1980s is subject to the eternal problem of estimation, since it is difficult to generalize about an illegal and clandestine population. The illegals seem to prefer urban areas because of higher wage structures, but the majority find work easier in rural areas where only the minimum wage ($3.10 per hour in 1980) or less is paid. This, of course, is a generalization based on the authors' interviews and observations. It seems clear that if the illegals take jobs from Americans, this happens most often in urban industries and less often in agriculture. Most recent scholarship seems to agree that the impact of the illegals on social welfare services in the United States is minimal. In the micro view of the illegals presented below, evidence of tax evasion is cited.

Money sent back to support families in Mexico is an important outcome of the illegal migration. The authors' field interviews confirmed other reports of considerable financial ties between employed illegal aliens and their families in Mexico, who were supported by the dollar earnings that were mailed south. One analyst depicts the dependency relationship as follows:

> If two million Mexican illegals work for some period of time in the U.S. each year, these workers represent more than 13% of the Mexican labor force; and if (as my research indicates) each illegal supports an average of 5.8 dependents, that would mean that some 13.6 million Mexicans − 21.3% of the total population of Mexico at present − depend to some extent upon U.S. earnings in any given year. The dependence of such a large segment of the Mexican population upon cash income earned in the U.S. is clearly undesirable as well as risky to those involved in this dependency relationship.[22]

Such dependency is, of course, better than doing without. And when the workers in question are treated as expendable, as slaves to be used as circumstances and weather permit, then a family's income may be erratic, an anxiety-producing circumstance affecting the emotional and physical well-being of the worker.

It is true that farm and manufacturing machinery has eliminated many jobs that in the past were done by hand. What remains is often the menial task of "feeding the machine," as in lettuce harvesting. In the cutting of spinach it is possible to use machines if there has been no rain recently. In dry periods, as observed in eastern Missouri, the majority of the workers stand by without pay while a few of their number "feed the machine." When the land is wet, all can work and are paid for cutting the spinach by hand. In between, the workers may not get paid, much depending on the weather. The availability of fresh spinach in American markets depends directly on the semi-slavery of those who are willing to wait their "chanza" without pay. This is a direct benefit for the North American consumer. Without the Mexican laborer, willing to accept such income uncertainties and the accompanying living hardships, there would be no fresh spinach in North America – or it would be available at a price only the rich could afford.

There seems to be great variation between areas as to the pay that illegals receive. Existing studies indicate that rural Texas pay scales for the illegals are among the worst in the country, frequently only a fraction of the legal minimum wage. Rural pay in California is generally better. In both rural and urban portions of Missouri and Illinois, we found the legal minimum wage generally paid by employers. In these midwest areas the underpayment of illegal aliens occurs most frequently in foundry and metal salvage operations, where $3.25 is paid (versus a union pay scale of over $7 for the same work). It is generally true that legal Mexican migrants earn more than their illegal counterparts, since the former are not afraid to bargain and to travel openly. Also, in labor-intensive industries that are adversely affected by foreign competition (shoes, clothes, tools), the illegal alien who will work for less enables the American enterprise to maintain its desired profit margin, which would be lessened substantially by paying the "going" wage for U.S. citizens. This is also true in fruit and vegetable operations, where the labor force is needed during only part of the year, an income situation that few Americans are prepared or willing to accept.

The migrants spend a portion of their earnings while they are in the United States, pay taxes, and contribute to the Social Security system, which most of them will never use. It has even been speculated that should the Social Security contributions of all illegal aliens working within the country be suddenly shut off, the system would shortly go bankrupt (again, this is speculative, but the micro view presented below tends to support it). This led researcher Wayne Cornelius to conclude:

> . . . Mexican migrants represent a windfall for the United States, in the sense that they are young, highly productive workers, whose health care, education, and other costs of rearing have been borne by Mexico, and whose maintenance during periods of employment and retirement is also usually provided by their relatives in Mexico. The significance of this windfall becomes apparent when we consider that as of 1977 the cost of preparing a U.S.-born man or woman for integration into the U.S. labor force was about $44,000.[23]

There are, of course, less charitable feelings toward the illegal Mexican aliens. When the Los Angeles County Department of Public Social Services started checking the legal statuses of aliens in 1975, the program reduced the numbers of illegals who gained welfare benefits, but it offended some Chicanos who felt they were being harassed on an ethnic basis. The INS field office in Los Angeles estimated that this procedure saved taxpayers some $5 million in welfare benefits that would otherwise have been paid out to illegal aliens, the vast majority of them Mexicans. Similar figures were reported on medical services. Many hospitals along the border report costs into the hundreds of thousands of dollars stemming from medical services provided to Mexican nationals having no U.S. address of record. In education the Los Angeles Unified School District refuses to identify illegal alien students, and therefore the costs are unknown. It has been determined, however, that in 1976 the district had about 24,000 students who spoke no English.[24] Interviews confirm that a similar situation prevailed in 1980.

The Los Angeles Police Department prepared a briefing paper in 1977 that contended that the illegal alien population of the city had increased some 200 percent since 1971 and that Los Angeles would have a "hidden population" of well over 1 million by 1981.[25] The department argued that its officers were responsible for an official population of 2.8 million residents, but that the real population was some 23 percent higher because of the illegal aliens, most of them Mexican. Thus, instead of the official ratio of 2.63 officers per 1,000 inhabitants, the real ratio was calculated at 2.14 officers per 1,000. The Los Angeles Police Department also questioned the traditional image of the illegal alien as a servile person who avoids trouble. Even if the illegals committed no more than their proportional share of routine violations requiring police service, this could be costly. It was estimated that illegal aliens cost the city of Los Angeles some $37 million annually in crime-related activities.[26] Police departments, like hospitals, may have a vested interest in exaggerating the demand for their services. Yet it seems clear that illegal aliens do create hospital and police costs, especially in the larger cities. Our studies in Missouri and Illinois indicate that the illegal Mexican aliens who are employed in agriculture create vastly fewer such demands than do their urban counterparts employed in industry and commerce.

Tables 3.2 and 3.3 contain statistical dimensions of the legal and illegal Mexican migration to the United States during parts of the twentieth century.

There is probably no purpose served here in quoting extensive figures supplied by governmental agencies as to the cost impact of illegal Mexican aliens in the United States. As already pointed out, the health and police cost figures include all illegal aliens, not just Mexicans, and it is not always certain that all of the "illegals" are properly categorized. If governmental agencies were able to document exactly who is illegal and who is a Mexican illegal, then a more factually based analysis could proceed. Such documentation would be an important contribution, providing civil and human rights were safeguarded and controls were built in to prevent deliberate inflation of "body counts" by agencies bent on augmenting their appropriations.

TABLE 3.2

Mexican Immigration to the United States, 1900-77

Fiscal Year/Years	Immigrants
1900-10	49,600
1910-14	82,600
1915-19	91,100
1920-24	249,200
1925-29	238,500
1930-34	19,200
1935-39	8,700
1940-44	16,500
1945-49	37,700
1950-54	78,700
1955-59	214,700
1960-64	217,800
1965-69	213,800
1970	44,500
1971	50,300
1972	64,200
1973	70,400
1974	71,900
1975	62,200
1976	58,400
1977	44,600

Source: U.S. Immigration and Naturalization Service, *Annual Report* (Washington, D.C.: U.S. Government Printing Office, selected years).

TABLE 3.3
Illegal Mexican Aliens Apprehended in the United States, 1965-78

Fiscal Year	Apprehensions
1965	55,300
1966	89,800
1967	108,300
1968	151,700
1969	201,600
1970	265,500
1971	348,200
1972	430,200
1973	576,800
1974	710,000
1975	680,000
1976	781,000
1977	954,800
1978	963,000
1979	976,667

Source: U.S. Immigration and Naturalization Service, *Annual Report* (Washington, D.C.: U.S. Government Printing Office, selected years).

LOCAL IMPACT: THE CILANTRO EXPERIMENT

Rather than cast more oars into the choppy waters of the national immigration macrocosm, let us look briefly at a micro view, albeit a somewhat superficial one, of the impact of illegal aliens in eastern Missouri and southern Illinois during 1979. This is drawn from a current and continuing longitudinal study in which a researcher became friends with, and works among, groups of illegal Mexican aliens as a paid co-worker. Biographies are developed slowly, and an attitudinal-value measuring instrument is administered as circumstances and discretion allow. Only preliminary findings are reported here as they relate to the local impact of illegal aliens.[27]

The geographic scope of this research is the St. Louis metropolitan area and southeastern Illinois (the Chicago region is not included). A concept developed early in the Cilantro Experiment[28] is that of "stranded" Mexican aliens. In the rural area beyond the suburban fringe of St. Louis, a group of stranded Mexican aliens performs a valuable agricultural service to the consuming public. They help to provide food at affordable prices by doing jobs that most unskilled American citizens will not take. The stranded Mexicans are illegal aliens. A few of their co-workers have secured legal residence papers; they are not necessarily stranded. To be "stranded" near St. Louis means, as it does in similar American locations, that the alien worker dares not leave the immediate area of employment for fear of detection by law enforcement authorities. The alien usually has no car, and cannot negotiate the language barrier for driver's credentials. Others must provide occasional transportation into the city. Since America allowed most of its urban transportation systems to atrophy in the 1950s, we are all in some degree "chained" to the car. Therefore, the illegal alien is stranded in part by this infrastructure defect in American society. In Mexico one can go almost anywhere by bus. The U.S. employer is afraid to provide regular transportation into an urban ghetto because of legal strictures against "transporting" or "abetting" illegal aliens. This means that the alien worker must live near the work location, but not on the employer's property because of an INS ruling in early 1979. Employers who once provided decent housing to alien workers must now leave the illegal aliens to the mercy of slumlords.

In the case under study, this means that one IMA (illegal Mexican alien), a native of Tamaulipas, must now live in a shack behind a rural slumlord's dwelling. There is no running water nor sanitary facilities. The man from Tamaulipas pays $100 per month to live in conditions slightly worse than he left in Mexico. For $100 he could have a comfortable and decent apartment in an older part of St. Louis. But fear of detection prevents his going there. There are only two kinds of housing near where the man from Tamaulipas works, the very expensive and the very miserable (at exorbitant prices). Money must be sent home to support a wife and family he has not seen for years. This IMA works the longest hours possible to increase his earnings. By overwork and precarious living he risks his health, suffers anxiety, and violates his basic human right to emotional and physical inviolability. This, capsulized, is the dilemma of being stranded near St. Louis. Some complex socioeconomic, political, diplomatic, and human rights issues are raised in the process. Among them is the profit motive, as summarized by Alejandro Portes:

> Reasons why these employers want to hire illegal labor are as trans-parent as those that propel illegals to come in the first place. Employers benefit from the lower wages, longer hours, lesser alternative oppor-tunities, and overall greater degree of exploitation which can be imposed on illegal workers. . . . Illegal immigrant labor is allowed to come precisely because it can be made not to. It is this situation which directly guarantees the insertion of the worker in the most disadvantag-eous terms *vis a vis* employers and, hence, aids in maintaining profit-ability in threatened sectors of the economy. . . . The logic of capitalist investment is one which constantly searches for the most vulnerable sources of labor to be put to work under less expensive conditions than those existing previously.[29]

If American agriculture, and horticulture in particular, is a threatened sector of the economy, then many growers in the greater St. Louis area are in a somewhat anomalous position: they may be forced, or feel that they are forced, into exploiting the dilemma of the IMAs in order to stay in business and provide food to the consuming public. The perhaps inevitable tragedy of this is that basic rights of the illegal alien workers may be sacrificed thereby. Must Mexicans forever toil under difficult, indeed unjust, circumstances for Americans to continue eating? And if they refuse to toil, what then?

Human Rights and Psychological Issues

A decision within the enforcement branch of the INS affects the well-being of many illegal aliens now living and working inside the United States. Section 1324 of Title 8 of the U.S. Codes pursuant to the Immigration and Nationality Act (1952) makes it a crime to "harbor" illegal aliens. It was decided by INS that this would be enforced strictly in certain parts of the United States. One grower of vegetables and plants in Kentucky paid a $10,000 fine for having "harbored" IMAs.[30] Although the statute in question has not been amended, an administrative policy decision, motivated by some weighty political considerations, changed the existing interpretation. From February 1979 on, employers providing housing for illegal aliens on their own premises could be subject to prosecution. Corporations as well as individuals would be cited. But it was still not illegal to hire the illegal aliens; it was only illegal to be one or to house one on an employer's property. Another party could rent to aliens with impunity, provided there was no attempt to "conceal" the illegals. Word games? Or politics![31]

Such policy decisions, pursuant to a statutory mandate, have affected the environment of work in the United States for thousands of illegal aliens whose labor contributes significantly to the U.S. economy. This makes it imperative to point out some livability and human rights issues that should be raised in evaluating U.S. immigration policy and enforcement. What the INS and its fellow agencies do to the foreigners who are attracted to this country is of great importance to students of, and activists for, human rights and livability causes. We are interested in both the emotional and the physical well-being of aliens as they may be affected by immigraiton law enforcement policy in the United States.

Let us consider the emotional dimension first. Severe anxiety (such as the constant fear that one may be apprehended by immigration authorities) can turn into an illness or a neurosis.[32] In the case of the illegal Mexican aliens now under study, there is high anxiety resulting from the housing uncertainty recently created by the INS. This is coupled with additional anxiety over what will happen to loved ones at home who are dependent on monthly remittances. A basic concern is that emotional and physical inviolability is among the most fundamental of human rights, and should be protected by the state. Whether people are wetbacks is one issue. But they are not usually hardened criminals;

their illegal entry across the Mexican border is a misdemeanor committed out of desperation for work and food, two increasingly scarce "commodities" in their home country. The illegals are also human beings. It may be quite fair to arrest and deport them, but it is morally wrong to create a continuously terrifying environment in which they must suffer emotionally, and ultimately physically.

Most Mexican wetbacks came north because they were goal-oriented: "to earn money for my own social mobility and to support my family at home." But after living in the environment of fear created by the enforcement policy on immigration laws, they may develop unhealthy levels of anxiety. "The anxious person tends to become threat-oriented rather than goal-oriented, to inflate existing fears and to create new ones."[33] When a Mexican is transformed into a wetback who escapes the Border Patrol and finds employment, the chances are that he or she will soon move from being goal-oriented to being threat-oriented. The anxiety level and the adaptation to it raise some critical human rights and livability questions that grow out of the context in which enforcement policy is made.

Here it is necessary to repeat a semantic caveat in the interest of better communication and improved ethnic relations. We do not use the terms "wetback" and "illegal alien" disparagingly. But we do not see how verbal fantasies like "undocumented persons" do much to aid those who are interested in studying the migrant worker phenomenon. Persons who jump the boundary fence in the Arizona desert and enter the United States without proper inspection are illegal aliens. Many of these people have documentation showing them to be Mexican citizens who have entered the United States illegally. There is, however, a valid area of concern within human rights circles over the possibility that the unrestrained use of the epithet "illegal aliens" might, by informal custom, grow into an unfair stigma on many people of Latin American parentage. In the light of this fact, we would like to use the expression "Spanish-speaking migrant workers" wherever possible, to avoid contributing to an unfortunate ethnic stigma. But, like it or not, foreigners who enter surreptitiously and without inspection are illegal aliens.

Another caveat is also needed. It relates to our use of the term "stranded." This refers to Mexicans who, through a series of circumstances related below, cannot easily return to their native land. Many once illegal Mexican aliens have become U.S. citizens or legal resident aliens (another reason for using the expression "Spanish-speaking migrant workers"), and the fact of their highly prized legal status does not alter their frustration — indeed anxiety — over being impeded from returning to Mexico because of economic circumstances.

Finally, it should be remembered that our micro view cannot be separated from its broad context: the United States-Mexico border is more than just a line nearly 2,000 miles long. It is a symbol of challenge for those pledged to defend it, and it is a barrier to the socioeconomic progress of those who must try to cross it; one might say that the border is a permanent monument to conflict, an undeclared war zone between two opponents, each of whom has a great deal of right on its side. What happens to Spanish-speaking migrant laborers at northern locations like Missouri and Illinois relates closely to the micro war games that are played out daily along the U.S. border with Mexico. Some profound and complex human rights and livability questions are raised in the process.

The Causes and Costs of Being a Stranded Mexican Alien

To the extent that the border is easy or hard to cross, there are likely to be more or fewer stranded illegal Mexican aliens within the United States. The stranded IMAs cannot readily go back to their native land for various reasons, including injuries, ill health, or misfortune; debts and economic dependency; detention by law enforcement authorities; partial acculturation in the United States, accompanied by loss of social and family roots in Mexico; loss of personal prestige. These reasons are not mutually exclusive, and do not exhaust the range of circumstances under which the aliens might be stranded. Each of the above reasons should, however, be explored briefly in the light of broader studies of illegal immigration from Mexico and in relation to both in-depth interview material and limited statistical data from the Cilantro Experiment.

Injuries, Ill Health, or Misfortune

A family of four (two sons, one 11 and one 16) has been living and working in southern Illinois for the past three years. They are illegal Mexican aliens who voluntarily allowed us to photocopy their documents. The woman was unable to return to her native Michoacán in 1977 because of an automobile accident. Authorities charged her husband with drunk driving. During the winter of 1978-79 her husband was bedridden with his arm in a cast. He had overturned a tractor (which he had not been taught how to drive) and was severely injured. The family got through both winters on workmen's compensation checks. They had free rent and heat in an abandoned schoolhouse. They could not go to Florida to pick crops during the severe winter, as had been their custom. Today it is doubtful whether the husband will ever be able to work again. His workmen's compensation has run out and, because he is an illegal alien, he is not qualified to receive unemployment compensation. Some assistance may be provided him by the Illinois Migrant Council. The mother hopes to continue to pick fruit, but that will not support her family. These IMAs are stranded.

Debts and Economic Dependency

Eight single Mexican men live in relatively precarious housing in north Saint Charles County, Missouri, where they are employed in a vegetable and nursery operation. Their pay is slightly above the legal minimum agricultural wage of $2.90 per hour (as of 1979). Their average weekly pay is about $150, with only

Social Security deducted. Three of the men, while "single" in Missouri, are married in the Mexican state of Hidalgo. Their wives receive postal money orders for $100 twice monthly (with only an occasional skip of remittances). The men have an average of 15 persons each in Mexico who depend on their Missouri wages for food and shelter. These men are able to work year-round, although during December through March the work is light and their income is reduced. They have not seen their families for three years and more. Returning to Mexico might mean apprehension en route. It would certainly mean loss of pay and support, since the men are paid only for the hours they work. Remorse and anxiety have led them into alcohol abuse and violence with their fellow workers. They cannot return to Mexico because of the dependency of their families, and they cannot incorporate themselves into the broader society of eastern Missouri because they are illegal Mexican aliens. They are stranded.

Detention by Law Enforcement Authorities

Esteban Maldonado Tovar is serving a ten-year sentence in the state prison near Chester, Illinois, for his complicity in the shooting of a rural sheriff during the mid-1970s. His story, hidden here behind a pseudonym, involves his role as a smuggler of both aliens and narcotics from Chihuahua, Mexico. He was reputedly involved with the Chicago underworld. The real issue, however, is not just Maldonado Tovar. It is the two Mexican aliens who were detained with him and are also serving sentences. They had been employed in an East St. Louis, Illinois, industrial operation in which illegal aliens were used on a special night shift in order to camouflage illegal activity. When the two men were interviewed by authorities, their employer fired them as a reprisal for drawing police attention, telling them that they would be on a blacklist and unable to find employment in that area. Desperate financially, they involved themselves with the smuggler and ended up sharing his sentence. They are, indeed, stranded.

Conflicting Acculturation Patterns

Near Fenton, Missouri, a Mexican family lives in mixed legal and cultural circumstances. The head of household, a man approximately 55 years old, has 13 children. The youngest four were born in the United States and have unquestioned citizenship. Their father says he has papers — the "green card" that would legalize both his alien status and his employment. Some of his older children, however, are in the process of getting "papers," and it is not clear whether two of these children are really his sons or his nephews. In addition the man's two brothers live in the household, and they are admittedly illegal aliens. All of these people, including the mother of the 13 children, want to go back to Mexico as visitors to renew family ties, but they wish to live permanently in Missouri. Part of their dilemma is the questionable legal status of some members of the family. Another aspect is that the four youngest children are American citizens and appear to speak better English than Spanish. In their native village of Cherân, these people have all but lost their family and social roots since they crossed the Río Grande surreptitiously over ten years ago.

Loss of Personal Prestige or Loss of Face

In Washington Park, Illinois (on the fringe of East St. Louis), there is an often visible Mexican community, one in which it is very possible to make the mistake of assuming that someone is an illegal alien on the basis of "looks." A woman who claims to be a U.S. citizen, who speaks colloquial Spanish but better English, and reads English but cannot read Spanish lives on welfare. This includes Aid to Dependent Children, unemployment compensation, and Social Security benefits. She has children by several Mexican nationals whom she describes as "wets" or *mojados*. Jaime Tehandón Martí married her in 1979. Jaime, 12 years younger than his wife (who claims to be 30), told us he mainly wanted to get papers from the St. Louis INS office by means of a petition that his wife, a U.S. citizen, executed. He, in turn, agreed to give her his entire weekly paycheck of about $150 for two years. Jaime would live with the woman and her children so as to "constitute" a domicile for the purpose of justifying his permanent resident petition.

But Jaime liked younger women, especially white American ones, so there were regular fights with his wife. One day she called the police and denounced him as a wetback, and the police turned Jaime over to the INS. They, in turn, sent him back to Mexico with nothing but bus fare. Jaime called friends from Ciudad Juárez, asking for help. He could not return to his native San Luis Potosí and confront his family. He had written to them about the money he earned, and had promised to use his legal status to bring others to St. Louis. Jaime had lost face, and at last word was waiting for an opportunity to slip back into the United States to try to recoup his lost fortune. He had been extorted by a Mexican American who professed pride in being of the same background. Jaime was definitely stranded.

Observations on IMAs in an Industrial Environment

Our observations of the Mexican-American subculture in Arizona, and specifically the activities of the MANZO Area Council in Tucson, suggest that strong ties exist between many IMAs and some Chicanos in the American Southwest. To be sure, there are Latin American *barrios* elsewhere, as in Chicago, where the IMAs are spread out. But throughout the rest of Illinois and into Missouri it is harder to put one's finger on a distinct Mexican community. On weekends migrant workers with a Mexican cultural background from all over southern Illinois and eastern Missouri frequently converge on Fairmont City, Illinois. The principal attractions there are a Mexican restaurant and dance hall, and a small Spanish-speaking population. Mariachi bands are brought in from Texas, Arizona, California, and Chicago to provide entertainment. Law enforcement officials in the greater St. Louis area are in almost unanimous agreement that Fairmont City is not the safest place for a uniformed officer to go on Saturday night with the thought of apprehending "wets" (or anyone). The case of Fairmont City is stressed here because the principal owners of the Mexican atmosphere establishments there are said to be American citizens of Mexican-American background. One of them is influential in local politics.

On the basis of interviews with both Mexican aliens and law enforcement officials, it appears that one entrepreneur from Fairmont City has another business, that of renting sleeping space to illegal Mexican migrants who work in some of the nearby industrial establishments.[34] INS and Illinois police officers have found numerous illegal alien workers being charged, as a group, $650 per month for mattresses on the floor of a large room. The formula is to rent each mattress to two men, one who works a 12-hour night shift and another who works the 12-hour day shift at the same plant. When one man gets up, the other lies down. Aliens have stated that this is done in collaboration with a given industrial employer; when one laborer returns "home," he passes on work instructions to the man with whom he shares the mattress.

The plant in question has been charged by U.S. citizens with firing them in order to hire illegal Mexican aliens. This is believed to be related in part to the fact that illegal activity was conducted on the night shift (shredding of new cars). The illegal aliens could be counted upon to keep silent or lose their jobs. There, in and of itself, is a gross human rights abuse in legal terms. The IMAs were forced to become accomplices to illegal activity as a condition for keeping their jobs. This case has been documented elsewhere,[35] and several agencies within the Department of Justice are still investigating it.

But the human rights question is even more complex. On one shift the illegals are forced to work in a special metal-separating operation called the media building. There is an extremely high noise level in this building, so high that unionized American laborers have refused to work there. The Mexicans can be coerced into enduring the noise, even with permanent damage to their hearing, and to work on 12-hours shifts. During early 1979 one Mexican lost his thumb while working at this plant. After giving the man emergency first aid, the management fired him in order to avoid his receiving workmen's compensation. This was not only an abuse of the worker but a violation of the Illinois labor laws.

The slum landlord mentioned above is believed to have a permanent arrangement with the industrial plant to provide a continuous supply of illegal Mexican aliens to work in those hazardous conditions. The Mexicans must agree to sleep on the landlord's mattresses, to contribute to the monthly group rent of $650, and to work 12-hour shifts every day of the week. They are paid relatively good wages as an inducement to sacrifice their health and safety, and they are threatened with being turned over to the authorities if they complain about working and living conditions. Detained Mexicans from that plant have admitted this to INS and St. Louis authorities, and we have corroborated this independently.

Apparently there is a high level of physical exhaustion among these workers, which is often accompanied by anxiety and emotional distress, alcoholism, and violence. The IMA named Jaime, whose story involved loss of face, once worked there, and told us his story. The slum landlord once boasted to one of our alien respondents that if tenant IMAs should be arrested just two days after they paid the rent, that would be "great," because he could then collect a second rent for the same month from the next group of illegals to be brought in from Toronto, Detroit, and Chicago (where there apparently were more aliens than jobs) within a matter of days.

The St. Louis INS authorities cannot prosecute this landlord because of legal technicalities: he never refuses to allow the INS to inspect his facilities; he never tries to conceal the illegal aliens; and he is not their employer. Should the aliens' employer also maintain housing on the work premises, he would be in violation of Section 1324 of Title 8 of the U.S. Codes as it was interpreted by INS in the Kentucky court case cited at the beginning of the chapter. But it is still not illegal to rent to illegal aliens provided there is no concealment; it is not illegal to hire illegal aliens so long as there is no concealment; it is only illegal to be an illegal alien and for an employer to provide an illegal alien with on-premises housing. That is "the American way."

Flesh peddlers profit from this anomaly. Businesses and industries subject illegal workers to inhuman conditions, and deprive American citizens and legal resident aliens of work in the process. The illegal aliens working in industry pay both income and Social Security taxes. Few of the aliens so taxed ever enjoy the benefits they have paid for, although being in the United States illegally does not necessarily disqualify one from claiming Social Security benefits.[36] In a very real sense the illegals are subsidizing the U.S. Social Security system. This circumstance has been cited in several recent studies.[37] By leaving employment in Mexico and not being registered with Mexico's official labor conglomerate, CTM (Mexican Workers Confederation), those workers have also lost their social security and welfare benefits in their home country. Understandably this contributes to great personal anxiety when the prospect of losing one's job appears. There is clearly a human rights issue at the taxation level — taxation without benefits — plus the more basic issue of physical and emotional distress and economic uncertainty.

IMAs in an Agricultural Setting

Migrant agricultural workers have distinctly different roles and environments in eastern Missouri and southern Illinois. They do not have the easily identifiable neighborhoods that often exist in the large industrial urban areas, and thus it is difficult for them to blend into a Chicano or Latin American community. But in the region under study, the illegal Mexican aliens who work on farms have at least one support mechanism available to them, the Illinois Migrant Council.

Services from that federally and state-financed organization are readily available to IMAs in Illinois, but assistance is available to any migrant workers, legal or otherwise, who go into Illinois and ask for it. The Illinois Migrant Council offers state-financed placement services and limited federally financed health and welfare benefits, and makes its guidance and counseling facilities available to all migrant workers.[38]

The IMAs employed in agriculture generally do not have income taxes deducted from their wages, and to this degree they are "evading." Whereas their urban industrial counterparts in the greater St. Louis area are often exploited, yet well paid, the rural IMAs in this region are paid much less, and generally their living conditions are similar or even better. Whereas most urban industrial IMAs have jobs that many unskilled American citizens would take if the job conditions were better, the rural IMAs in eastern Missouri and southern Illinois are filling jobs that most Americans simply do not want. At the time of this writing, the Department of Labor offers a program designed to entice unskilled Americans into jobs that IMAs frequently take. A major feature of this program, called WIN, is federal payment of over half an unskilled laborer's salary, on a graduated scale downward, for three years to inspire both growers and "welfare livers" to join together fruitfully.[39] Early reports in the area indicate that the growers still prefer wetback labor, although many are trying to "convert" to U.S. citizens and recognize the merits of the Labor Department's new program.

The Mexicans who do seasonal work (picking fruit and vegetables) and those who take year-round agriculture-related jobs (including the processing of food grown out of state for wholesale distribution) are for the most part willing to be housed in circumstances that most American citizens would not accept. We inspected such housing near Cairo, Illinois, and Fenton, Missouri. The housing for married couples and families is generally decent but not pretty. The housing for singles is generally indecent, but there is a serious dispute over "who got it that way." We have seen evidence indicating fault on the part of growers, landlords, and aliens. We have also worked in enough slums in Mexico and Latin America to know that most poor housing in the St. Louis region is a paradise by comparison. So the Mexicans stay in circumstances most Americans would reject, and that gives them an advantage in work access over most U.S. citizens. They live close to the farms, in a bondage of fear and dependency.

Thus, there is an emotional dimension that should be considered. Since most American cities and counties do not have public transportation facilities that allow people great mobility without owning a vehicle, the IMAs tend to be stranded in the physical sense, and subsequently in the emotional sense. Not having independent transportation, they can either go shopping in the grower's vehicle occasionally or pay uncompetitive prices at the nearest source (a circumstance that some local merchants exploit). Again, lacking mobility for social purposes, the Mexican farm workers tend to pool their resources for a big weekend binge in Fairmont City, Illinois. In that location the local merchants are happy to profit from both urban and rural IMA workers with inflated entrance fees and relatively high prices. But this is practically the IMA's only way to enjoy a piece of the culture he could not bring with him. Many IMAs end up in jail on the return from these weekends and are turned over to the INS.

Naturally, such threats contribute to the alien's sense of cultural isolation. The alienation potential here is great. Anxiety is produced in lethal amounts. At some point most of these isolated workers undergo severe emotional traumata. But most of them are still sending money home to people whom they desperately want to see.

For the IMA it is a vicious cycle: surreptitious border crossing; living in relative cultural isolation; few mechanisms to discharge aggression and anxiety; an ultimate eruption of feelings that produces disorder and violence; the sudden decision to return to loved ones in Mexico, who receive him with mixed emotions because everyone wonders whether he can return to his job. The process takes its toll on human beings. The basic human right to physical and emotional inviolability has again been transgressed.

Quantitative Evidence and Conclusions

Table 3.4 contains a sample of the data that have been drawn from arrest and detention records (the I-213 forms) in the St. Louis office of INS for some 1,000 illegal Mexican aliens who were detained over a period of several years. It seems clear from the percentages in Table 3.4 that young IMAs (those under 25 years) are more likely to be apprehended and returned to Mexico, and that as age increases, the detention rate goes down. This is significant from the standpoint of frustration and disappointment among the younger IMAs. We do not know, of course, how many of the older IMAs had been apprehended and returned to Mexico before they gained enough insight and skill to avoid detention.

With a higher arrest rate for young IMAs, we can ask whether this fact may tend to segregate them, whether older IMAs might steer clear of the younger ones out of fear of apprehension. This raises the distinct possibility that the younger group is deprived of the moderating influence their more experienced seniors could provide and may, therefore, fall more often into precarious and anxiety-producing situations. Such has been our observation in Missouri and Illinois. We have no way of knowing to what degree this is representative of all IMAs residing in the United States. We have reason to believe, however, that the St. Louis area experience is typical of similar midwestern cities.

As the politics and policies of illegal immigration in the United States vacillate with changing demands and the passage of time, the rural illegal Mexican alien is a pariah in varying degrees of severity. This condition has been well stated by Ellwyn Stoddard:

Increasingly, local directives to law enforcement officials in Chicago, Kansas City, Denver, San Antonio, Los Angeles and San Diego told

TABLE 3.4
Time Spent in United States by Illegal Mexican Aliens in Greater St. Louis Area Before Apprehension, by Age

(N = 1,101)

Age		72 hrs.	4-30 days	1-6 mos.	6 mos.-1 year	1-2 yrs.	2 yrs. +	Not Ascertained	Row Total
To 19	Number	24	138	78	20	22	2	7	291
	Column %	30.4	28.6	24.8	24.7	21.4	15.4	25.9	26.4
20-25	Number	27	183	114	31	42	6	14	417
	Column %	34.2	37.9	36.3	38.3	40.8	46.2	51.9	37.9
26-30	Number	16	61	40	16	18	1	5	157
	Column %	20.3	12.6	12.7	19.8	17.5	7.7	14.8	14.3
31-35	Number	7	42	31	6	8	2	2	98
	Column %	8.9	8.7	9.9	7.4	7.8	15.4	7.4	8.9
36-40	Number	0	29	24	5	8	1	0	67
	Column %	0	6.0	7.6	6.2	7.8	7.7	0	6.1
41-50	Number	3	18	21	2	3	1	0	48
	Column %	3.8	3.7	6.7	2.5	2.9	7.7	0	4.4

51+

	Number							
Number	2	12	6	1	2	0	0	23
Column %	2.5	2.5	1.9	1.2	1.9	0	0	2.1
Col. Total	79	483	314	81	103	13	28	1,101
Col. %	7.2	43.9	28.5	7.4	9.4	1.2	2.6	100

Source: Kenneth F. Johnson and Nina M. Ogle, *Illegal Mexican Aliens in the United States* (Washington, D.C.: American University Press, 1978).

them to avoid arresting IMA's unless they had broken some law other than just being in the United States illegally. This will result in greater expenses for midwest farmers who, in the past, worked the illegal aliens during the harvest season and then, after helping to send their seasonal wages home, worked them in plain sight close to the highway where they would be picked up and transported back to the border at the government's expense. Now the farmers will have to pay the aliens' transportation themselves.[40]

The acculturation process of IMAs is anxiety-producing. In the process of crossing the border surreptitiously and installing oneself as part of an illegal subculture, the anxiety-to-neurosis process drives many illegal aliens from the pursuit of their socioeconomic goals to preoccupation with threats both perceived and real. The various escape mechanisms that are employed, including neurosis, geographic flight (even, and increasingly, according to our interview evidence, north into Canada), and deviant and violent behavior, all constitute losses in basic human rights. The IMAs must even assume false identities and face ideological conflicts within the Catholic Church, which once symbolized, at least in Mexico, a source of spiritual refuge.[41] The IMA not only finds the illegal subculture a threatening one, but cannot always count on Americans of Mexican origin for protection.[42] Ethnic politics in the United States are focused on the human rights of legal minorities. Given the important economic contribution of the illegal Mexican alien subculture to the United States, and the fact that many (if not most) of us would not be able to afford to eat vegetables year-round were it not for the migratory laborers from Mexico who are willing to toil under adverse human conditions, it will be a credit to human rights researchers and activists to embrace the cause of the IMAs for the betterment of all.

SUMMARY AND CONCLUSIONS

It has been argued that the American *bracero* program from 1942 to 1964 did more than anything else to activate the "magnet" that attracted contemporary illegal Mexican migration into the United States.[43] To this we could add that the Border Improvement Program thereafter and the *maquiladoras* (industries with plants on both sides of the border) created additional attractions for Mexicans who came to the border in greater numbers than any legal employment could absorb. Insistence by the Mexican government that *braceros* be protected by labor and human rights guarantees motivated some U.S. employers to go outside the law and hire the illegal "wetbacks," who could be housed poorly and treated shabbily. This practice grew, until in the 1980s hiring the illegals has become the near-slave base of much of America's agriculture.

The unique circumstances of American cities on the southern border make the illegal presence felt there more acutely than farther north. There is a borderlands culture shared by Mexico and the United States with great interdependency and joint demands for services. For example, El Paso, Texas, with a 1970 population of 322,000, would need to budget for parks, police, and recreation much the same amount as would such interior cities of the same size as Omaha, Tulsa, and Birmingham. But in functional terms El Paso must consider the additional 500,000 residents of Ciudad Juárez to the south as potential users of municipal services, as well as the thousands of illegal aliens who cross over.[44] Borderlands cultures are something of a magnet in themselves for illegal entrants, representing a transition zone where one's ethnic characteristics are less of a problem insofar as detection is concerned. Moreover, the relative affluence of the United States and the rising desperation of Mexico's growing population make illegal migration north a constant of contemporary life.

Some important moral and ethical issues have been raised in this regard by several border scholars who studied the "Tortilla Curtain" incident in late 1978, an affront to Mexico created by a special fence the U.S. government was building to keep out the illegal aliens.[45] Is it not hypocritical for the United States to build a fence to keep out workers whom U.S. employers deliberately recruit and legally hire? Can there be any justification for building a fence that is capable of maiming the innocent – or anyone, for that matter? If it is to remain legal to hire illegal aliens, then why not make it legal, safe, and dignified for them to receive social welfare and medical services? How can a nation pledged to human rights around the world ignore the rights of foreign migrant workers inside its borders? And "if the borders need protecting, why does the U.S. not have plans for a U.S.-Canadian fence along the populated regions of that binational boundary?"[46] In view of the evidence already presented about smuggling of aliens into the United States from Canada, the question about the northern boundary is a realistic one. Is America simply afraid to admit too many brown-skinned people from the south?

Canada, America's neighbor to the north, is not yet as seriously affected by illegal Mexican aliens, but it does have an overall illegal alien problem, as shown by the deportation figures. Canada, by allowing itself to become known as a stepping-stone into the United States, had inadvertently encouraged the immigration of visitors whose intentions are doubtful and who, in many cases, would be inadmissible to Canada were their true financial status and motives known. The Canadian practice of not placing visa requirements on tourists from most nations contributes further to the migration of persons who subsequently overstay their visitor permits. The fortunes of Canada and the United States are intertwined insofar as illegal migration is concerned. In the future it is also likely that we shall see more illegal Mexican migration crossing the United States en route to Canada, especially as the aftereffects of the economic recession in the early 1980s are felt. Some such migration now occurs. Thus it is probably more than coincidental that at some spots on the United States-Canada border, such as the bridge connecting Detroit with Windsor, Ontario, there are already established Mexican and Spanish-speaking communities that serve as jumping-off points for northward migration. Again, we must be cautious about attributing illegality, or potential illegality, to ethnicity.

The ethnic composition of Canada seems to be changing. It is becoming a "less British" country than it was in the past, with those of British origin declining from 40.5 percent to 36.1 percent during the 1960s and Canadians of French origin dropping from 30.4 percent of the total population to 28.7 percent.[47] This trend continued through the 1970s, and with European birth rates dropping also, it is people from the overcrowded Third World countries who are knocking at Canada's door. Yet there is some evidence of a prevailing racism, according to the Hudson Institute of Canada, and whereas Caucasian peoples will probably find it easy to immigrate to Canada, those from Jamaica, Colombia, and Mexico will have greater difficulty.[48] Whether it is racism in Canada, or the cold weather there, that country's reception of immigrants and visitors, genuine or otherwise, will probably affect the migration fortunes of the United States. Thus, an approach to hemispheric immigration that is genuinely that — hemispheric — within a community-of-nations concept, is the only realistic approach. Canada and the United States can work out their border-crossing problems in a spirit of friendship and without a fence. And they will surely do so. Collaboration with Mexico may not be so fruitful.

Some analysts believe that a deep recession could reduce the flows of illegal Mexican aliens into the United States, and potentially into Canada. If accompanied by increased enforcement, the reduction could be substantial. Statistical exercises have been invoked to test whether the U.S. recession of 1974-75 reduced the overall migration flow, particularly the illegal component. The evidence seems inconclusive, but it does suggest that the growing size of the Mexican labor force generates more clandestine migration: "An increase of one million in the Mexican labor force is associated with an increase of 186,000 in the apprehension of [illegal] migrants."[49] The same study presents additional statistical exercises showing that a substantial portion of the clandestine ("unsanctioned") migration becomes permanent, a finding based on the questionable assumption that the "number of successful unsanctioned entrants in each year is equal to the number of INS apprehensions."[50] On this basis one would be asked to believe that up to a million illegal migrants remained permanently in the United States in each of the years 1978, 1979, and 1980. A similar projection, on a reduced scale, could perhaps be made for illegal migration into Canada from Jamaica and Guayana.

But the outcome of these statistical exercises is no more valid than their underlying logic and the empirical validity of the data put into them. We are not prepared to take sides as of this writing, but the serious scholar should be aware of this statistical research that challenges the notion, popular in some circles, that illegal migration has no permanent effect on population growth nor on jobs or public services, since few or none of the illegals, it is argued, remain permanently in the host country. It is worth noting that some scholars believe that the clandestine Mexican migration adds a substantial number of new entrants to the already disadvantaged U.S. labor pool.

Illegal Mexican migration into the United States will not be reduced until the Mexican government controls its population, makes jobs for its work force, and helps to control clandestine emigration. The United States will need to provide a new guest-worker program with safeguards for the rights of the workers and to avoid the abuses of the *bracero* era.[51] It will need to strengthen border enforcement with realistic allowances for the borderlands culture to continue to thrive. The United States will need to impose severe penalties on those who employ illegal aliens and those who smuggle them. Border enforcement should be done with more consultation with the Mexican government, treating that government diplomatically as an equal, and without the appearance that tighter U.S. border controls constitute a punitive act with racist overtones. We can live, migrate, and work together in this hemisphere for the benefit of everyone, and we should!

NOTES

1. Sasha G. Lewis, *Slave Trade Today: American Exploitation of Illegal Aliens* (Boston: Beacon Press, 1979), p. 151. Neither the Mexican nor the American governments has been willing to take decisive action on the illegal migrants. During June 1980 the governors of all Mexican and American states sharing the border held a meeting, the first of its kind, and called on their central governments to take joint action (as reported in *Uno más uno* (Mexico), June 28, 1980.

2. The writer says that the illegal aliens are not a burden; "instead . . . it's the rest of us who are a burden to the aliens." See Stephen Chapman, "Let the Aliens in," *Washington Monthly* 9, no. 6 (July/August 1977): 43. He cites various studies in California where jobs vacated by illegal aliens could not be filled by U.S. citizens, implies that the INS should be recruiting people to fill the jobs that are left by deported aliens, and ignores the responsibility of the employers to make jobs sufficiently attractive so that Americans will take them. There is, of course, no legal responsibility, only the moral one that is easily forgotten in the haste to make money by paying low wages to illegal aliens. The same author, by suggesting that the United States ought to help more people escape various dictatorships around the world, ignores the bitter irony that U.S. foreign aid is bolstering many of these dictatorships and creating the very conditions that turn people into illegal migrants (consider El Salvador and South Korea, just to have contrasting cultural examples to compare).

3. Lewis, *Slave Trade Today*, p. 31.

4. Ibid., p. 32. Another indicator of the degree to which aliens generally are coming to be seen as a source of income for attorneys is the frequency of newspaper ads offering legal services. In many cases the assistance needed by the alien is available free from the U.S. government, but fear leads the alien to pay exaggerated fees in the belief that only someone with an "in" can make the wheels of government move. Increased attention has recently been paid by the Latin American press in the United States to Latin American aliens who have committed ethical violations of their status as visitors or recently naturalized citizens. One editorial in *Diario las Américas* (Miami), June 27, 1980, castigated Cuban and other aliens for abusing their freedom of speech during the exodus of refugees from Cuba.

5. U.S. Congress, Select Commission on Immigration and Refugee Policy, *Semiannual Report to Congress* (Washington, D.C.: U.S. Government Printing Office, March 1980), pp. 13-15.

6. Ibid.

7. Ibid., p. 14.

8. Edwin P. Reubens, "Illegal Immigration and the Mexican Economy," *Challenge* 14, no. 8 (November/December 1978): 14.

9. Ibid., p. 15. An excellent source on the Mexican agrarian problem is J. W. Barchfield, *Agrarian Policy and the National Development in Mexico* (New Brunswick, N.J.: Rutgers University Press/Transaction Books, 1978). Barchfield has taken the commendable role of policy-formation activist. He gave valuable testimony to the U.S. Senate in October 1979 concerning a proposal whereby Mexican guest workers coming to the United States would make a "good will deposit" with their own government as a guarantee that they would return to Mexico after their work in the United States was completed. Barchfield pointed out, correctly, why such a proposal wouldn't work, given the norms of Mexican politics and the realities of international labor exchange between the two countries.

10. Reubens, op. cit.

11. It is difficult to document the source of this proposal. One source would be (by implication) Robert L. Ayres, "Development Policy and the Possibility of a 'Livable' Future for Latin America," *American Political Science Review* 69, no. 2 (June 1975): 507-25.

12. The "dominant class" argument has been developed in Kenneth F. Johnson, *Mexican Democracy: A Critical View* (rev. ed.; New York: Praeger, 1978). It helps to explain the inability of the Mexican political system to solve the socioeconomic problems that underlie the illegal migration. Mexican writers are now recognizing their responsibility for this phenomenon. See, for instance, the article by Teresa Gil and Saide Sesín in *Uno más uno*, June 16, 1980, and one by Patricia Morales, ibid., June 28, 1980.

13. Joseph F. Krauter and Morris Davis, *Minority Canadians: Ethnic Groups* (Toronto: Methuen, 1978), p. 94.

14. Ibid., p. 95.

15. Ibid.

16. Ibid., p. 96.

17. Ibid. Traditionally there has been suspicion in Canada, especially in French Canada, with respect to any immigration policy that could increase the "preponderance of the English-speaking section of the population" over the French (Frinley Thomas, *Economics of International Migration* [London: Macmillan, 1958], p. 152). Migrants from India and certain nations of the Caribbean might be viewed with suspicion by French Canadians if they had English, even as a second language, but no French. Yet the Canadian economy, like the American, is capable of using these migrants as "new raw material" in the effort to keep profit margins high and operational decision making flexible as the United States and Canada continue to replace industrial Europe as population magnets. See Elsa M. Chaney, "Peoples on the Move: An International Perspective on Caribbean Migration," in Richard Millett and W. Marvin Will, eds., *The Restless Caribbean* (New York: Praeger, 1979), pp. 37-41, passim.

18. The deportation profile data for Toronto are part of a longer longitudinal study that is in progress with the collaboration of the Canadian government. The data are not classified in any diplomatic or military sense. The names of persons involved and their origins were never seen by the principal investigators (Kenneth F. Johnson and Nina M. Ogle), so there is no possible way that the civil rights of the deportees could have been violated. The motive of the study was a better understanding of the illegal alien phenomenon in a way that would be relevent academically and in policy-formation terms for the host government. We are grateful to Al Naylor of the Canadian Employment and Immigration Commission (Foreign Service liaison officer for the Toronto District) and to George H. Jeffs, district administrator of CEIC, Toronto, and his staff for their sincere collaboration. Our general feeling is that American immigration policy could profit much from a study of the Canadian experience, especially as regards the high degree of professionalism we have found among Canadian immigration officers and officials.

19. *Washington Post*, January 16, 1980.

20. Ibid.

21. According to FAIR, "The Border Patrol and Immigration and Naturalization Service now make over 1,000,000 apprehensions of illegal immigrants a year, as compared with under 100,000 per year in the early 1960's. Yet the Border Patrol Supervisors Association estimates that, with its present staff of 2,101 agents, the Border Patrol is now only 33% to 50% effective. At any one time, only about 350 officers are on duty on all U.S. borders." A Border Patrol study urged that by increasing the number of on-duty agents from the present 2,101 up to 5,500 over a period of three years, the Patrol could become 90 percent effective, providing the American government truly wanted to stop the illegal migration. See FAIR *Immigration Reporter* 1, no. 7 (1980): 2. But an important part of the implied Border Patrol equation is the attraction for and influence on illegal migrants of the Hispanic population already living inside the United States. According to one Mexican estimate "There are 20 million Hispanic Americans (*hispanoestadunidenses*) living inside the country, which means that the United States is the fifth largest Hispanic nation in the world" (from *Uno más uno* (Mexico), June 28, 1980).

22. Wayne A. Cornelius, *Mexican Migration to the United States: Causes, Consequences, and U.S. Responses* (Cambridge, Mass: Massachusetts Institute of Technology, Center for International Studies, 1978), p. 51.

23. Ibid., pp. 87-88.

24. See John Kendall's series of articles in the *Los Angeles Times*, January 9-27, 1977.

25. Los Angeles Police Department, "The Illegal Alien Problem and Its Impact on Los Angeles Police Department Resources," staff briefing paper, January 1977.

26. Ibid.

27. Part of this research was presented at the annual convention of the Rocky Mountain Council on Latin American Studies at El Paso, Texas, May 5, 1979, by Kenneth F. Johnson as "Stranded Mexican Aliens in Missouri and Illinois: A Spectrum of Livability and Human Rights Issues." Care is being taken to protect the confidentiality of the interview sources, but given the research circumstances, that is not possible at all times.

28. The title "Cilantro Experiment" comes from the cilantro plant, which many of the Mexican workers cultivate in small plots or trays so as to have a familiar taste in their food.

29. Alejandro Portes, "Labor Functions of Illegal Aliens," *Society* 16, no. 3 (September/October 1977): 31-37, passim. The same author also argues that "The more rights immigrants acquire and the more they come to resemble the native proletariat, the less useful they are as a defense against labor demands. It is for this reason that the objective interest of firms for which profit depends on a low-wage labor force is to import immigrants in the most legally tenuous position. Thus, illegal immigrants become the most vulnerable of workers. Their juridical situation deproves them of most civil rights and prevents their effective organization for making demands" (Alejandro Portes, "Toward a Structural Analysis of Illegal (Undocumented) Immigration," *International Migration Review* 12 [Winter, 1978]: 474). He considers the likelihood that the United States would either have to institute a "guest-worker" program or subsidize the salaries of U.S. citizens.

30. The case in point is that of the Horton Fruit Company (Lakewood Gardens) of Louisville, Ky., which was fined for the previously accepted practice of giving illegal aliens – indeed, all migrant workers – housing on the employer's property. While the federal government castigated one grower in Kentucky, other growers in southern Illinois operated federally approved and financed labor camps with no problem. This obvious contradiction raised the question of whether the "law" would be enforced so strictly in Texas, where the commissioner of INS had political roots, and in Airzona, where powerful interests (Goldwater's Arrowhead Ranch) benefited from employing and exploiting illegal Mexican aliens. See Kenneth F. Johnson and Nina M. Ogle, *Illegal Mexican Aliens in the United States* (Washington, D.C.: University Press of America, 1978), esp. Appendix A, and passim.

31. A perceptive comment on Kenneth Johnson's "Stranded Mexican Aliens . . ." was made by Miles Williams, who described the legal dilemma posed by the Kentucky alien housing case as a "legal Catch-22." He wrote: "You can hire illegals if you don't conceal them or don't bed them; and, you can bed them if you don't conceal them or hire them. The net effect is that employers and landlords are able to hold 'their civic responsibility' over the head of the illegals and exploit the hell out of them. Moreover, in so doing, they [the employers and landlords] seem to appear to be good law-abiding citizens . . . given the scenario you have described, INS law [*sic*] punishes illegals but to the benefit of no one in particular." Williams' informally written comment is probably much more valuable for the fact that he did not sit down and contrive it deliberately for an academic audience. His point should be patently clear: why punish the illegals when almost everyone, even the illegals, as most of them see it, are benefiting? Williams is right! And his observation, combined with those of Alejandro Portes concerning guest-worker programming and/or labor subsidies, should be considered very seriously by U.S. policy makers, if they are really serious about reforming U.S. immigration law, policy, and enforcement. A related irony in the above scenario is that if the federal government approves and/or finances a labor camp, then no issue is raised about "bedding" or "concealing." It comes down to the fact that in one part of the country you may bed and conceal the aliens as you please, while in a neighboring state you will be severely penalized for doing so. This is not uniform or fair law enforcement policy.

32. A theoretic basis for this observation is found in Christian Bay, *The Structure of Freedom* (New York: Atheneum, 1968), pp. 165-68. An economic basis for the anxiety-neurosis phenomenon is found in many writings on "superexploitation" of illegal alien workers. See, for instance, J. Craig Jenkins, "The Demand for Immigrant Workers: Labor Scarcity or Social Control," *International Migration Review* 12, no. 4 (1978): 514-35.

33. Ibid., p. 101.

34. Interviews with INS officers, March 31, 1979.

35. From Johnson, *Mexican Democracy*, and as reflected in a body of humanistic literature on the illegal Mexican aliens in the United States. See Carroll Norquest, *Rio Grande Wetbacks* (Albuquerque: University of New Mexico Press, 1972); and Grace Halsell, *The Illegals* (New York: Stein and Day, 1978).

36. David Carliner, *The Rights of Aliens* (New York: Avon Books, 1977), passim.

37. See Stanley Rose, ed., *Views Across the Border* (Albuquerque: University of New Mexico Press, 1978).

38. Interviews during 1979 with Steve Compton, director of the Illinois Migrant Council in Carbondale, Illinois, and with Arturo López, the IMC statewide director, in Chicago.

39. WIN means "work incentives."

40. Ellwyn R. Stoddard, "Illegal Mexican Labor in the Borderlands: Institutionalized Support of an Unlawful Practice," *Pacific Sociological Review* 19, no. 2 (1976): 187. Also see the argument on state complicity in the illegal alien worker phenomenon in Robert L. Bach, "Mexican Immigration and the United States," *International Migration Review* 12, no. 4 (1978): 536-58.

41. See Stoddard, "Illegal Mexican Labor . . . ," esp. pp. 196, 201.

42. As documented in Johnson, "Stranded Mexican Aliens . . . ."

43. In Arthur F. Corwin, "Causes of Mexican Emigration to the United States," *Perspectives in American History* 7 (1973): 557-635.

44. Ellwyn R. Stoddard, "Selected Impacts of Mexican Migration on the U.S.-Mexican Border," paper presented to the U.S. State Department Select Panel on U.S.-Mexican Border Issues, Washington, D.C., October 23, 1978.

45. See Ellwyn R. Stoddard, Oscar J. Martínez, and Miguel Angel Martínez Lasso, *El Paso-Ciudad Juárez Relations and the "Tortilla Curtain"* (El Paso: El Paso Council on the Arts and Humanities, 1979), esp. pp. 42-43.

46. Ibid., p. 43.

47. From *Globe and Mail* (Toronto), May 17, 1980.

48. Ibid.

49. This line of analysis is taken from Walter Fogel, "Twentieth Century Mexican Migration to the United States," in Barry R. Chiswick, ed., *Conference on U.S. Immigration Issues and Policies, Report* (Chicago: University of Illinois at Chicago Circle, 1980), p. 219.

50. Ibid.

51. See Richard B. Craig, *The Bracero Program: Interest Groups and Foreign Policy* (Austin: University of Texas Press, 1971). See the same author's "Human Rights and Mexico's Antidrug Campaign," *Social Science Quarterly* 60, no. 4 (1980): 691-701. The idea of levying a tariff on guest workers as a way of paying for social services to those workers is discussed in Larry C. Morgan and Bruce L. Gardner, "Potential for a U.S. Guest-Worker Program in Agriculture: Lessons from the Braceros," in Chiswick, *Conference on U.S. Immigration Issues* . . . , especially pp. 423-27. A valuable and broad survey on Mexican migration is Thomas Weaver and Theodore Downing, eds., *Mexican Migration* (Tucson: University of Arizona, Bureau of Ethnic Research, 1976). A related and important contribution is Milton H. Jamail, *The United States-Mexican Border: A Guide to Institutions, Organizations, and Scholars* (Tucson: University of Arizona, Latin American Center, 1980).

4

CLANDESTINE MIGRATION BETWEEN COLOMBIA AND VENEZUELA

The dispersion of ethnic or national populations from historic homelands (diaspora)[1] has been going on since the dawn of history. Originally the term "diaspora" referred to the dispersion of Jews, but it is now commonly applied to any identifiable group that emigrates for social, economic, political, or religious reasons.[2] In recent years the flow of migrants has generally been one of workers moving from the poorer countries to the wealthier, industrialized countries, and generally to the mutual benefit of both sender and receiver countries.[3] Since World War II still another category of population transfer has become important in the worldwide migratory network, the movement of people from poor countries to the better-off but still comparatively poor.

The sheer magnitude of the movement, and the declining selectivity of destinations by the migrants, are grim reminders of the growing desperation within the Third and Fourth Worlds. As recently as 1965 it was suggested that "International migration affecting Latin America is mainly of the past."[4] The recent literature and the cases examined in this volume clearly show that the pattern has not abated; on the contrary, population transfers within the Western Hemisphere have increased. The fact that the present proletarian diaspora to the Third World receiver states, as well as to the highly industrialized countries, continues to grow is an important clue to the gravity of the problem. This chapter examines one such case: the population transfer of Colombians to Venezuela.

EARLY MIGRATION PATTERNS INVOLVING VENEZUELA AND COLOMBIA

Early efforts to conquer and exploit the territory that is present-day Venezuela met with little immediate enthusiasm or financial success. Only with the

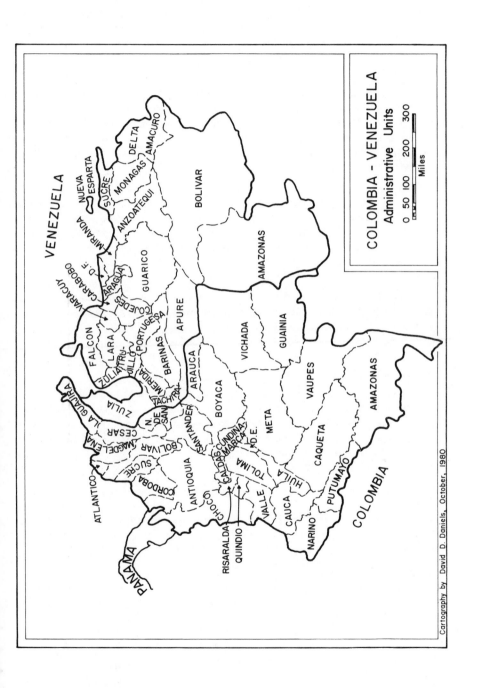

COLOMBIA - VENEZUELA
Administrative Units

0 50 100 200 300
Miles

Cartography by David D. Daniels, October, 1980

formation of the Caracas Company in the second half of the eighteenth century did Venezuela receive much interest from Spain.[5] The highly developed Chibcha civilization possessed the mineral wealth to entice the European adventurers, and its sedentary society proved vulnerable to Spain's expeditionary forces. While the Sabana de Bogotá and the entire Andean region of Colombia fell quickly to Spanish domination, the nomadic and seminomadic Caribs, Guajiros, Arawaks, Cumanagotos, and other indigenous groups in eastern Colombia and western Venezuela were less attractive financially and more difficult to subdue. In the sixteenth century the major population centers in Venezuela spread along an arch from Caracas to Lake Maracaibo, through the Andean region to San Cristóbal along the present border with Colombia. The principal means of communication and transportation between the more densely populated coastal region and the border region was by ship from Caracas around the Caribbean and down through Lake Maracaibo. At the southern point the passengers would disembark and follow the overland trails to Trujillo, Mérida, Tovar, and San Cristóbal, the largest city in the region by the nineteenth century.[6]

On the Colombian side of the border, near San Antonio and San Cristóbal, is Cúcuta. Founded in 1753, Cúcuta remained a comparatively unimportant city until recently. Perhaps its main claim to fame prior to the twentieth century was that the Congreso Constituyente met there on May 6, 1821, and the Republic of Gran Colombia was founded under the tutelege of Simón Bolívar. In the first third of the twentieth century, Cúcuta served as a regional commercial center. Luís Ospina Vásquez comments that a small-scale textile factory did develop there around 1929, but it was not particularly significant.[7] On the other hand, Colombia, particularly through Cúcuta, was of growing importance to Venezuela as a commercial center for legal and smuggled trade. In the early part of the twentieth century, Venezuela's less-developed economy made the border region important as a source of goods and work for Venezuelans.

As a legacy of the Viceroyalty of New Granada, Venezuela and Colombia shared a common nationality from 1821 to 1830 (along with Ecuador from 1826 to 1830) as part of the Republic of Gran Colombia. Today, Colombia and Venezuela share a border 2,219 kilometers long, a common language, a common ethnic background, and, to a great extent, a common historical experience. The national boundary separating the two countries has long been little more than a political fiction, particularly in the borderlands area. From the days of the conquest and colonization to the present, migration between Colombia and Venezuela has been constant, usually with one country having political or economic advantage over the other. Each country has provided sanctuary for the political refugees of the other, beginning with Bolívar's flight during the dark days of the wars of independence, continuing through the despotic periods of Venezuela's political history, and, more recently, as Colombians sought safety from *la violencia* in the 1940s and 1950s. Even so, most migrants have been economically rather than politically motivated. Until the late 1930s or early 1940s, the migrant flow was toward Colombia. The peso-dollar exchange in

1931 was 1.03 pesos to the dollar.[8] By 1980 the rate was 46.78 pesos to the dollar, and constantly deteriorating, while the Venezuelan bolívar had stabilized and actually gained against the dollar. Colombia has become the population sender and Venezuela the receiver.

For those living in the Venezuelan state of Táchira and to the south, the heritage has become more Colombian than Venezuelan. Radio and television stations from Colombia dominate the airwaves in many regions of western Venezuela. Colombian newspapers are readily available, stores have names that reflect the Colombian influence, pictures of Colombian presidents hang on the walls of many homes, and large numbers of families have relatives living in Colombia.[9] The general topography and settlement pattern clearly indicate that much of the borderland has historically ignored the question of national sovereignty. Comparatively free movement across the border was an accepted fact of life by both countries until the mid-1960s. The number of people along the border who have one Colombian and one Venezuelan parent is very large. Called venecos,[10] they carry identification cards from both countries, although that does not make them immune from deportation.

THE COLOMBIAN DIASPORA

In a 1975 speech to Colombians living in New York, President Alfonso López Michelsen expressed concern over the large and growing number of Colombians living abroad. He observed that "Few countries have so many workers living outside their borders under such different and frequently difficult conditions."[11] Colombian aliens do indeed live and work under a variety of circumstances. In recent years they have emigrated by the thousands. The vast majority have gone to Ecuador, Panama, the United States, and Venezuela, a growing majority of them living and working without the benefit or protection of legal status. A traditional receiver of aliens in Latin America, Colombia has become one of the major senders since the 1950s.

The change from receiver to sender status in Latin America is a reflection of both the deteriorating social and economic situation in Colombia and the improving climate for development in neighboring countries. This is evident in the changing exchange rate of the Colombian peso, the Venezuelan bolívar, the Ecuadorian sucre, and the Panamanian balboa. Aliens generally emigrate to earn a stake to start a business at home or simply to support a family, which they do by sending a large percentage of their earnings home at regular intervals.

Ecuador has traditionally sent more aliens to Colombia than it has received. Beginning in the late 1960s or early 1970s, however, the pattern reversed. By the mid-1970s Ecuador was complaining about the large number of *indocumentados* from Colombia. The change in the directional flow can be attributed to the discovery and development of petroleum reserves in Ecuador, and the corresponding impact that has had on the economy and the value of the

TABLE 4.1
Value of Four National Currencies Against the Dollar, 1960-80

Country	1960	1965	1970	1975	1980
Colombia	6.70	13.51	19.17	24.73	46.78
Ecuador	15.15	18.18	25.25	25.25	28.10
Panama	1.00	1.00	1.00	1.00	1.00
Venezuela	3.35	4.50	4.50	4.50	4.24

Source: Alfonso Arbeláez C., "El éxodo de colombianos en el período 1963-1973," *Boletín mensual de Estadística* no. 310 (May 1977): 43; for 1980, *Kansas City Times*, June 6, 1980, p. d-9.

Ecuadorian sucre (while the 1960 sucre was worth almost twice as much against the dollar as the 1980 sucre, the 1960 Colombian peso was worth nearly eight times as much as the 1980 peso). With the comparative weakness of the peso vis-à-vis the sucre, it has been estimated that the number of Colombian *indocumentados* in Ecuador is about 60,000.[12]

The migratory flow of Colombians to the former Colombian *departamento* of Panama is not as great as it is to Ecuador, Venezuela, or the United States, although it does appear to be growing. Colombians are not welcomed in Panama as they are in Venezuela, and the terrain separating the two countries is equally inhospitable. Moreover, employment opportunities in Panama, particularly in the border region, are less inviting. The attractiveness of Panama, the dollar/balboa, is a product of the Panama Canal, but employment opportunities there for Colombians are virtually nonexistent. Many Colombians who might reasonably be expected to go to Panama because it is close, generally tend to go to Venezuela, frequently entering in the vicinity of Maicao. By 1973 the Colombian government estimated that there were some 4,200 Colombian *indocumentados* in Panama,[13] probably a very conservative guess.

In spite of the great distance, there are more Colombians in the United States than in any other foreign country except neighboring Venezuela. The estimate of Colombians in the United States is 350,000, most concentrated in New York City.[14] Between 1951 and 1975, Colombians accounted for 35 percent of the legal migration from South America, and since the mid-1950s Colombia has sent more immigrants annually than any other South American country except for two years when Argentina led the way.[15] Colombians came to avoid *la violencia* in the 1940s and 1950s, but more recently the prospect of economic opportunity has lured even more.

In general there are striking similarities between the Colombian migratory patterns to the United States and to Venezuela. Highly skilled workers with visas go first, and unskilled workers without papers follow. Most have no intention of immigrating permanently and, according to Elsa Chaney, 65 percent going to the United States had migrated internally at least once before crossing international frontiers.[16] At the present time there is a growing number of unskilled workers, perhaps 60 percent without legal documents.[17]

Chaney also notes, with justified suspicion, that a large number of employers express a marked preference for Colombians over Puerto Ricans, asserting that Colombians are better workers, better behaved, "more obedient," and "more respectful."[18] There is a certain universality about this refrain, one that is frequently recited about illegal aliens, regardless of the setting. U.S. employers sing the praises of their hard-working "wetbacks," but when one is so vulnerable to all manner of exploitation, maintaining a low profile and adhering to a work ethic are to be expected. It is a fundamental reason why illegal aliens are constantly in demand. Puerto Ricans in New York have legal status and, therefore, legal recourse when they encounter wage and employment discrimination. The passive Colombian in New York illegally cannot be compared with the Colombian drug dealers in Miami or Toronto. Those self-employed entrepreneurs are anything but docile or law-abiding.

One additional similarity between the Colombian illegal in New York and his or her counterpart in Venezuela (or the Mexican in the United States) is that all are considered essential to the local, and perhaps the national, economy. Chaney comments:

> . . . many of those who cry out the loudest against the immigrants for political reasons must know very well, if the Hispanics who came to New York City in the past fifteen years suddenly were to depart tomorrow, the city would cease to function.[19]

The greatest number of Colombians living outside their homeland can be found in Venezuela. Estimates of the number of aliens — legal and illegal — vary greatly, although all agree that the number is staggering and growing. In the late 1970s the largest estimate was that there were some 1.5 million Colombians living in Venezuela without proper documents.[20] Assuming that the overwhelming majority are economically active — a reasonable assumption, since Colombia's Departamento Administrativo de Seguridad says that between 1963 and 1973 only 9.06 percent of the deported aliens were 15 years or younger,[21] — at least 10 percent of the Venezuelan labor force consists of illegal Colombian aliens.

Each person makes the decision to emigrate for personal reasons. Even so, it is not difficult to appreciate the fact that in Colombia the social and economic environment for the poor is dismal, and quite probably growing worse. Despite the agrarian reform of the 1960s, the concentration of farmland in the hands of the few is increasing; unemployment in the cities is probably between 40 and 50 percent if one includes the chronically underemployed; cities like Bogotá probably have surpassed their carrying capacity, and the prospects for the future do not look good. As bad as the urban picture is, the rural population continues to seek a better life in the cities. It is a widely accepted supposition that migration across international boundaries, especially by peasants, is an extension of the internal rural-to-urban migration pattern.[22]

Miguel Urrutia notes that in general the income distribution in Colombia did not change dramatically between the 1930s and the 1960s except in agriculture, where it grew worse (more concentrated in the hands of the few).[23] The situation in agriculture has grown worse even with the heralded agrarian reform. Commenting on the alarming level of unemployment in the country, the government's agrarian reform agency, INCORA, says:

> The concentration of rural property appears to be the principal cause of this situation since the absorption of manual labor is inversely proportional to the size of the farm operation; while farms less than five hectares accounted for 24.5 percent of the labor force (farming and ranching) and occupied 0.1 percent of the area, holdings of over 200 hectares or 55.1 percent of the total area accounted for just 17.2 percent of the agricultural labor force.[24]

INCORA goes on to point out that salaries went up 110 percent in the period 1962-68 but prices increased by 113 percent.[25]

While a recitation of aggregate statistics cannot truly capture the plight of Colombia's rural poor, the figures do illustrate that the conditions are bad and growing worse. For example, between 1960 and 1971 the number of farms in Colombia decreased by 2.7 percent; the average size of a holding increased by 13.4 percent; and, by 1971, 635 owners held over 7 million hectares and 1.4 million *campesino* families occupied just 6 million hectares.[26]

The push of the agricultural conditions and the pull of the cities have contributed to an extraordinary growth of Colombian cities, particularly the four largest, as Table 4.2 suggests. By 1980 at least three, and possibly four, Colombian cities had a population in excess of 1 million. Most Colombian social scientists claim that Bogotá's population has reached 5 million, over half of them born outside the city.

The push effect of the economically impoverished regions of Colombia is evident from the 1973 census data. For example, we found a -.63 correlation (Pearson's r) between those departments (states) with the highest percentage of the economically active population earning less than U.S. $43 per month (using the 1973 peso-dollar exchange rate) and net migration between 1964 and 1973, the two most recent census years. That is, the poorest departments were most likely to experience low immigration or high emigration. On the other hand, there appears to be little relationship between net migration and the services offered within the receiver departments. (Net migration was correlated with the percentage of dwellings having running water, .29; percentage having sewers, .09; and percentage having electricity, .34. In no case did p equal .05.) Either the migrants were less concerned with the amenities or they were not aware of the conditions. Perceived economic opportunity seems to be more important

TABLE 4.2
Population in Colombia's Four Largest Cities, 1905-73

Year	Bogotá	Medellín	Cali	Barranquilla
1905	100,000	53,936	30,740	40,115
1912	121,257	71,004	27,747	48,907
1918	143,994	79,146	45,525	64,543
1938	330,312	168,266	101,883	152,348
1951	648,324	358,189	284,186	279,627
1964	1,697,311	772,887	637,929	498,301
1973	2,855,000	1,100,000	923,000	662,000

Source: Departamento Administrativo Nacional de Estadística, data on twentieth-century Colombian censuses.

than comfort. The first choice of new residence for inhabitants of all departments except La Guajira and Córdoba was Bogotá, Cali, or Barranquilla.[27] According to the Colombian government's statistical agency:

> . . . 21 percent of the resident population in the departments was born in another geographical area. . . . In 1964 this percentage was only 18 percent. The net annual displacement within departments between 1951 and 1964 was approximately 79,000 people and between 1964 and 1973, it was 113,500 . . . , that is, there has been an annual increase of 43 percent between the two periods.[28]

Just as internal migration occurs as people perceive economic opportunity as justifying a move, regardless of overcrowding and poor living conditions in the target area, so international migration also occurs in the face of adversity. The rural-to-urban migrant experiences a lack of housing and social amenities, while the illegal alien suffers social, economic, and legal indignities resulting from his or her undocumented status. Both types of migrants are likely to perceive the economic opportunities as outweighing the concomitant discomforts.

VENEZUELA: THE "PULL" FORCES

Oil was discovered in Venezuela in 1913, and it would be difficult to exaggerate the impact it has had on the economy since then. 1920, 1930, and 1940, coffee and cacao constituted 92 percent, 15 percent, and 4 percent of the value of exports, respectively, while petroleum's contribution in the same period increased from 2 percent to 83 percent to 94 percent, respectively.[29] In recent years the importance of petroleum to the economy has increased, largely as a result of its skyrocketing price on the world market. Even before that, however, oil production increased by 300 percent and revenues soared eightfold in the period 1945-57. Venezuela has also been successful in using petroleum revenues to spur industrial growth. Between 1950 and 1957 industrial production increased at an annual rate of 12 percent.[30]

The rapid transformation of the Venezuelan economy has had an equally dramatic effect on the demography of the country, as Table 4.3 indicates. During the 1920s, 1930s, and 1940s, the petroleum states of Zulia, Anzoátegui, and Monagas received large numbers of Venezuelans from rural areas. The most directly affected states were those close by (Sucre in the Northeast, Falcón, Trujillo, Yaracuy, Lara, and Táchira in the West). In the 1950s, 1960s, and 1970s the attraction shifted to mining and the newly industrialized states of Miranda, Aragua, Carabobo, and Bolívar, all in the general region of the capital, Caracas. The essentially agrarian states of the South and West have consistently been the senders.[31]

The first major petroleum boom of the 1920s and the corresponding demographic impact created the atmosphere for a growing pro-immigration sentiment in Venezuela, one that continued until about 1958.[32] Many felt that Europeans should be enticed to "fill in" the countryside where internal migration created severe labor shortages. Europeans were likewise sought to assist in the development of the petroleum industry. Although resentment against foreigners never reached the proportions of the attitudes in Mexico prior to the revolution, there was, nevertheless, considerable hostility within Venezuela over the replacement of Venezuelans by foreigners who were supposed to upgrade the culture and skilled labor pool.[33] President Eleázar López Contreras (1935-41) was cautious, but the first pro-immigration laws were established in 1936.[34] A more aggressive immigration policy was adopted in the 1940s, particularly under the government of Marcos Pérez Jiménez (1948-58). Mary Kritz characterizes the policy as being more "open" than "selective," and the 1940s marked the beginnings of a notable population increase as a result of immigration.[35]

Although the pro-immigration policies have favored Europeans, Table 4.4 shows that only in one year, 1961, did any European country contribute more immigrants than neighboring Colombia. If *indocumentados* could have been included in the data base, the Colombian figures would no doubt have been far more impressive.

Kritz seriously questions the success of Venezuela's pro-immigration policy on several grounds. First, it was designed to increase the pool of highly skilled labor, which it did not. Second, it was designed to "fill in" rural areas where Venezuelans were short-handed because of internal migration, which it did not. Third, skilled workers tended to return to their country of origin, and no domestic training program was instituted until 1958. Fourth, the European immigrants were largely unskilled, although they ended up in the middle sectors of the social structure.[36]

TABLE 4.3
Estimated Net Migratory Flow in Venezuela, 1920-26 to 1961-71

Political Unit	1920-26	1926-36	1936-41	1941-50	1950-61	1961-71
Fed. Dist.	30,245	55,903	55,699	171,058	194,720	- 41,072
Anzoátegui	- 7,136	- 1,950	6,394	32,819	11,826	- 41,124
Apure	- 3,202	8,017	4,098	- 6,364	- 6,596	- 15,945
Aragua	-12,325	12,482	-10,268	19,949	39,455	86,877
Barinas	- 7,568	-10,552	- 1,356	2,416	18,777	13,583
Bolívar	- 2,447	- 4,405	660	5,190	22,447	52,828
Carabobo	808	782	5,572	7,962	39,192	103,845
Cojedes	-14,349	-47,502	- 5,274	- 3,507	- 1,166	4,819
Falcón	27,403	7,201	-13,598	-17,282	-38,214	- 40,804
Guárico	-13,684	-31,339	- 2,741	1,711	- 4,053	- 29,007
Lara	12,206	-24,643	363	-23,479	-16,857	2,693
Mérida	-55,887	4,374	-12,025	-18,293	-10,847	- 12,915
Miranda	-15,887	- 4,404	-20,229	12,748	131,592	258,036
Monagas	- 6,061	14,227	16,587	4,508	-14,136	- 47,627
Nva. Esparta	3,327	- 7,397	-14,787	- 6,045	- 8,967	2,110
Portuguesa	- 3,234	3,324	5,166	12,972	21,452	2,112
Sucre	39,378	10,356	- 8,821	-40,482	-55,854	- 69,465
Táchira	502	15,132	- 1,950	- 5,764	-25,698	65,670
Trujillo	7,808	-12,054	-13,412	-33,637	-31,264	- 28,995
Yaracuy	- 4,521	-19,017	-14,856	-16,618	- 2,004	- 12,418
Zulia	63,234	37,875	30,433	63,600	131,592	258,036
Territories	2,413	- 904	7,151	- 3,481	26	- 4,558

Note: Chen used the following formula: $\sum_{o}^{z} M = (I_z - E_z) - (I_o - E_o)$

Source: Chi-yi Chen, "Distribución espacial de la población Venezolana: Diagnóstico y Perspectiva," in *América Latina: Distribución espacial de la población*, Ramiro Cardona G., ed. (Bogotá: Editorial Canal Ramírez-Antares, 1975), pp. 222, 243.

TABLE 4.4
Distribution of the Foreign-Born Population of Venezuela, by Ethnic Origin, 1936-71
(percent)

Region/Country	1936	1941	1950	1961	1971
Americas	49.0	47.4	33.4	26.0	39.9
Colombia	41.3	34.0	21.8	18.1	30.0
Cuba	0.8	2.4	1.9	1.4	1.7
United States	4.7	7.2	5.6	2.4	1.9
Other	2.2	3.8	4.1	4.1	6.3
Europe	48.6	49.9	64.9	70.2	55.8
Spain	12.2	13.9	18.3	31.4	24.5
Italy	5.6	6.3	21.3	23.0	14.6
Portugal	0.1	1.3	5.3	8.0	11.4
Germany	3.0	3.4	1.8	1.3	1.0
Britain	14.4	11.0	4.4	1.1	0.3
France	7.4	6.3	3.5	0.9	0.7
Poland/Rumania	1.4	1.9	2.4	0.9	1.6
Other	4.5	5.8	7.9	3.6	1.7
Other	2.4	2.7	1.7	3.8	4.3
Total (percent)	100.0	100.0	100.0	100.0	100.0
N (thousands)	47	50	207	526	599

Source: Mary M. Kritz, "The Impact of International Migration on Venezuelan Demographic and Social Structure," *International Migration Review* 9, no. 4 (Winter 1975): 523.

Venezuela faced a number of crises growing out of the major petroleum finds. The oil boom had a negative impact on agriculture. As peasants sought the upward mobility of urban employment, Venezuela failed to benefit from a pro-immigration policy directed at the acquisition of a skilled labor force, and the new immigrants tended to compete, successfully, with the domestic unskilled labor force. Agriculture was particularly hard hit. As Howard Handelman points out, Venezuela has worked hard to increase production in the agrarian sector, but faces built-in limitations. There are only about 2 million hectares of good land and the best of it is already in production, while productivity per land unit has not improved much.[37] Moreover, as oil revenues trickle down, the demand for more and better foods increases. The population, two-thirds of which was rural in 1936, is becoming increasingly urban — approximately 80 percent by 1977. Production has not kept pace with demand, and the poor tend to be priced out of the market.[38]

Following on the heels of severe food shortages in 1972 and 1973, the government of Carlos Andrés Pérez embarked on a dramatic agricultural development program in 1974. Some of the major features of that program were canceling and/or favorable refinancing of agricultural debts; government subsidies for fertilizers and farm machinery; irrigation; massive credits channeled through private banks; price supports; and government subsidies to the poor to help cover the rising food costs.[39] As ambitious as the program has been, inefficiency, government red tape, and corruption have hampered the effort. One wealthy farmer reportedly took a low-interest, government-backed loan in excess of $250,000 and immediately invested it in Florida real estate.[40] The cost, paid by huge oil revenues, has not solved Venezuela's agricultural woes. Handelman concludes that production is up, although not enough to offset population increases. Furthermore, government claims of improved caloric intake by Venezuelans are misleading, in that much of the increase can be explained by the overconsumption among a small percentage of the population that has benefited from the oil bonanza while the poor are probably still undernourished and paying higher prices for that state.[41]

The soaring revenues from petroleum, the failure of Venezuela's pro-immigration policies, and the crisis in agriculture have created a favorable environment for Colombians who take to the *caminos verdes* (back trails) or *trochas*, and become *indocumentados* in Venezuela. From Venezuela's standpoint the Colombian illegals have been a serendipitous by-product of policy failures. The Colombian *indocumentados* make it possible for Venezuela to accomplish many of the agricultural production goals not achieved by the pro-immigration and agricultural programs. The infrastructure was set for greater productivity, but a stable labor supply did not exist. Not only have the Colombian *indocumentados* worked out better than the carefully devised and expensive government programs, at least in many respects, but the illegal migration gives Venezuela a certain amount of flexibility not possible through officially sanctioned programs. Where programs have the government's official blessing, there is also a responsibility to the immigrants and Venezuelan nationals who participate. Where the workers have no legal status, wages, social conditions, and even the demand for numbers of workers can be manipulated by employers. Miguel Soto Montiel, head of Venezuelan President Luís Herrera Campíns' special commission on illegals, admitted as much. He acknowledged the positive impact on the Venezuelan economy, especially in agriculture, and said that it was fundamental, even indispensable, for the economy. He also noted that those who were not making a positive contribution or who were considered undesirable would be deported.[42]

Since Colombians began to immigrate illegally in the 1940s, Venezuela and Colombia have entered into a number of agreements affecting the *indocumentados*, including the following: Estate del Régimen Fronterizo (Caracas, 1942), Treaty of Tónchala (Cúcuta, 1959), Commercial and Economic Development Agreement (Caracas, 1963), Act of Río Arauca (1966), Act of Caracas (1966), Declaration of Cochagota (1969), and various other joint declarations, including one on March 13, 1979, when Colombian President Turbay visited Venezuela.

Perhaps the most important of the agreements was the Treaty of Tónchala, which started a process of legalizing Colombians who had been in Venezuela since 1961 and instituted an agricultural work permit. The legalization of Colombians without proper papers has been changed a number of times – in 1969 and 1975, for instance. On those occasions the length of time in the country necessary to gain legal status was changed to facilitate the improved position of Colombians.

It can be argued that the program to legalize the status of Colombians is more cosmetic than substantive, however. In 1974 the Bogotá daily *El Espectador* prepared a list of Venezuelan requirements to gain legal status. It included a current passport, a citizenship card, a police certificate from the Colombian security police known as D.A.S., a birth certificate accepted by the Venezuelan consulate in Colombia, legal proof of the length of residency in Venezuela, a current health certificate, a certificate of prior police record, written evidence of medical prescriptions, a letter offering employment, two letters of recommendation from Venezuelans on *papel sellado* (a document containing the government seal), birth certificates of children who are Venezuelan citizens, a list of family members who are residing in Venezuela and their identification numbers, payment of a tax of 7 bolívars, and legalization of all documents by the Venezuelan consulate, accompanied by payment of 15 bolívars in the Office of Identification and Foreign Relations.[43]

To meet these requirements the Colombian had to return to Colombia, identify family members living legally or illegally in Venezuela, gather a great deal of documentation, and place himself/herself at the mercy of the Venezuelan government to accept or reject the application without having to spend the time or money to deport. Moreover, it assumes that the Colombian has the ability to read and has acquired the needed expertise to deal with government bureaucracy. Needless to say, most Colombians continued to accept their illegal status, which the Venezuelan government undoubtedly expected.

The "flow of Colombian *indocumentados* into Venezuela appears to have become the largest human migration in South America's history."[44] The jobs are there, particularly in agriculture; the pay is far greater than can be earned in Colombia; the value of the bolívar offers a solid hedge against Colombian inflation. There is also a certain spirit of adventure that attracts youth, much the same as we discovered in the clandestine migration affecting the United States, Mexico, and Canada.

THE INDOCUMENTADO: A PROFILE

It is difficult if not impossible to describe the "typical" Colombian *indocumentado* in Venezuela, since the total population cannot be identified. As with the Mexican illegal alien in the United States, more is known about those who are caught and sent back than about those who avoid detection, and it can be

TABLE 4.5
Reasons for Migrating to Venezuela

Reason	Number	Percent
Earn more money	118	57.8
Look for work	38	18.6
Visit family	19	9.3
Adventure	29	14.2
Total	204	99.9

Note: Tables 4.5-4.10 are based on interviews in Cúcuta with 204 deported Colombians between January and September 1975.

Source: Secretariado Nacional de Pastoral Social, Colombia, "Estudio sobre deportados colombianos 1973-1975," ch. 1, p. 47. (Mimeographed.)

argued that those who are caught are not typical. For example, most deported Colombians are male; but the conventional wisdom on both sides of the border is that there are at least as many, if not more, women residing in Venezuela without papers. It is also true that most of those who are deported are under 35 years old, a group that tends to be more visible and, therefore, more vulnerable. It is generally agreed that taking to the *caminos veredes* is the business of the young, and most *indocumentados* are young, but the older alien is probably underrepresented among the ranks of the deported. Furthermore, studies have shown that most deportees are unskilled, uneducated, and marginal workers in Venezuela. This too is predictable, for Venezuela's policy is to deport only those Colombians who are considered undesirable or are not deemed important to Venezuela's development.

Venezuela, like the United States, relies on unskilled foreign labor in agriculture. Also like the United States, it has adopted a practice that has the effect of discouraging the legalization of these workers. When Colombians enter Venezuela with documentation, they generally carry one of four kinds: *permiso fronteriza*, a border permit that allows them to cross, but not for extended periods or to work; *visas transuentes*, one-year work permits that can cost as much as 1,000-1,500 bolívars; *visas colectivas*, a group visa and work permit that obligates the alien to travel in a group and to work for a specific employer; or a *tarjeta agrícola*, a permit that allows the holder to work during the harvest season.

The *permiso fronteriza* may be used to enter, but the holder becomes an *indocumentado* when he or she stays on to work. The *visa transuente* provides legal status but is too expensive for most migrants. On a daily wage of 14-20 bolívars for unskilled workers, one would have to work two or three months merely to pay for the cost of entry, leaving absolutely nothing to live on. The *visa colectiva* is widely disliked by Colombian workers because it ties the worker to a particular employer under conditions of virtual slavery. The *tarjeta agrícola* is not very common, nor does it appear to have much appeal. Of the four basic types of documents, the *visas collectivas* and *tarjetas agrícolas* are technically designed to allow migrant agricultural workers to enter the labor market. While both add a sense of legitimacy to the foreign agricultural work force, they are difficult to get and provide difficult conditions for the workers.

Rather than encouraging legal entry, they promote illegal crossings.[45] One suspects that this may be by design. Some deported aliens told us that they were promised an attractive wage in Colombia and were paid a lower wage on arrival. The practice of turning in the illegals just before payday is not unknown, nor has it been uncommon in the United States. Bishop Pedro Rubiano Sáenz of Cúcuta feels that the emphasis on deportation declines during election periods; *indocumentados* are sometimes given *cédulas* (identification cards) and instructed to vote for particular candidates. Foreign workers with legal status could not be exploited in this manner.

The high cost of the *visa transuente* makes such a document practical only for the highly paid, skilled work force whose legal status is not discouraged. One has only to look at the long lines in front of the Venezuelan consulate in Cúcuta to appreciate the problems and irritations for those seeking legal entry. The lines consist not only of Colombians, but include Ecuadorians, Peruvians, Brazilians, Panamanians, Spaniards, and Portuguese. More and more one finds Europeans, although it is unlikely that the Europeans seeking entry and proceeding from Colombia possess marketable skills. Unskilled Europeans may travel to Colombia and attempt to get visas from Cúcuta, while skilled Europeans apply for visas from the Venezuelan consulate in their home country.

When asked why one does not seek to obtain the required papers to work in Venezuela, the common response is that it would take too long and cost too much, and the papers could be revoked before they were used. If the visa were revoked before used, the foreigner would be out not only the time and effort involved, but the financial investment as well. Of those recently deported Colombians with whom we spoke, not one suggested that he or she would try to get the required documents if entry were attempted again. One deported Colombian interviewed by Oscar Martínez claimed to have had a worker's permit, but authorities did not accept it and he was deported.[46]

The *indocumentados* come from all parts of Colombia, enter at various points along the extensive border, and find a wide variety of jobs in all parts of the country. Most Colombians make the decision to cross on their own, but a substantial number are recruited by Venezuelans and/or their Colombian agents. Puerto Santander, a small village south of Cúcuta, has institutionalized the process. There are hotels full of Colombians whose bills are paid by Venezuelan recruiters. The soon-to-be *indocumentados* are collected and sent into Venezuela by river.

TABLE 4.6
Department of Residence in Colombia of Colombian
Aliens Deported from Venezuela, 1973-75
(N = 11,547)

Department	Percent
Antioquia	3.05
Arauca	0.19
Atlántico	1.46
Bogotá, D.E.	2.53
Bolívar	2.39
Boyacá	8.43
Caldas	1.14
Caquetá	0.23
Cauca	0.91
César	0.61
Chocó	0.36
Córdoba	2.16
Cundinamarca	1.26
La Guajira	0.35
Huila	0.57
Magdalena	1.10
Meta	0.08
Nariño	0.58
N. de Santander	35.94
Putumayo	0.04
Quindío	0.81
Risaralda	0.70
Santander	26.48
Sucre	1.62
Tolima	1.83
Valle	5.04
Other countries/areas	
Ecuador	0.10
Peru	0.02
Brazil	0.01
Africa	0.01

Source: Secretariado, *Estudio sobre deportados*, pt. II, ch. 1, p. 22.

The youngest, the least skilled, and those residing nearest the Venezuelan border are the most likely to cross without assistance or any firm plan (see Table 4.6, and note the number of deportees from the Norte de Santander area). They simply seize the opportunity and make the trek along the *camino verde*, walking an average of three days before reaching a destination where work can be secured. The trip is grueling and full of uncertainty. Since they have no well-conceived plan, the probability of detection is greatest, and because they tend to be particularly poor, they lack the resources to bribe the Venezuelan National Guard into looking the other way. Those with a plan and the resources to carry it out have a greater chance of making it. Norman Gall cites a Venezuelan journalist's conversation with a Colombian *indocumentado*:

> I entered this time via Cúcuta. I took the long bus ride from Rioacha on the coast south into the mountains to Cúcuta because I went with some *paisanos* who had entered that way before, who knew the trails, so there were no problems. You have to cross a river and pay the man who takes you in his canoe ten pesos [U.S. $.50]. Then you take another trail to avoid the National Guard post, because if the National Guard catches you they will take you prisoner or charge you 20 or 30 *bolívars* to let you pass, whatever you have.[47]

Some pertinent demographic and socioeconomic status characteristics of Colombian undocumented aliens returned from Venezuela appear in Tables 4.6 and 4.7.

The reader will note some sharp discrepancies between the data from Bermúdez's survey and that of Cúcuta. There are a number of possible explanations, including the limited nature of both samples. Aside from that, however, it should be noted that the Cúcuta survey was of deported Colombians and the Bermúdez survey, conducted on the Atlantic coast of Colombia, was of Colombians who had lived and worked in Venezuela but who had not necessarily been deported. While the sample size and method of choosing respondents preclude any claim of representativeness, the data are interesting because they include "successful" undocumented workers. Three glaring differences can be seen: (1) a substantially higher percentage of women were included in the Bermúdez study; (2) a far lower percentage of those from the Bermúdez study had some secondary education; and (3) a far greater percentage of the respondents in the Bermúdez study were married. Without claiming statistical significance, one could speculate that the sex distribution in the Bermúdez study is a more accurate representation of undocumented workers in Venezuela.

Virtually all the people we spoke with told us that there are more female Colombians than male Colombians illegally in Venezuela, but that they are less likely to be deported. Many work as domestics in Caracas and a large number are prostitutes, neither category a target for deportation. Virtually no deported women admitted to prostitution in Venezuela, although on a visit to the

TABLE 4.7
Profile of Colombian Undocumented Aliens
Returned from Venezuela
(percent)

	Cúcuta Survey (n = 204)	Bermúdez Survey (n = 100)	Official (n = 5,629)
Age			
15-19	24.5		14.6
20-24	27.4		33.0
25-29	22.1		23.1
30-34	11.3	79.0	12.3
35 and over	14.7	21.0	17.0
Sex			
Male	79.1	47.0	71.0
Female	20.9	53.0	14.0
			(minors, 15.0)
Education			
Illiterate	6.4	55.0	
Primary	70.4	38.0	
Secondary	23.2	7.0	
Marital status			
Single	85.3	25.0	
Married	14.2	74.0	
Widowed	0.5	1.0	
Occupation in Venezuela			
Farming			45.07
Construction			14.92
Services			8.71
Carpenter			1.81
Mechanic			6.00
Commerce			0.89
Other			1.74
Services (women)			17.45
Other (women)			3.41

Sources: 1975 survey of 204 deported Colombians from Cúcuta; Secretariado, *Estudio sobre deportados*, ch. 4; S. D. Bermúdez, "La migración campesina a Venezuela" (Senior Thesis, department of anthropology, Universidad de los Andos, 1976); Secretariado, *Estudio sobre deportados*, ch. 4.

Colombian Center for Deported Colombians in Cúcuta, we learned that the center was alerted to expect the arrival of some 300 prostitutes by bus from Puerto la Cruz. Our field observations in Caracas reveal a conspicuous presence of Colombian women in the "oldest profession."

Domestics in major cities usually have a comparatively comfortable and protected life. The wages are substantially higher than can be earned in comparable work in Colombian cities and the living quarters are far better, frequently a private room with a television set. Domestics are rarely allowed to get legal papers, however, because they then leave for better-paying jobs. Thus, they are held under conditions of quasi slavery.

The higher percentage of married respondents in the Bermúdez survey may also be a function of the type of respondent surveyed. Unmarried aliens are more likely to go for the adventure or without adequate planning, and therefore are more vulnerable to detection by Venezuelan officials. Since the Bermúdez sample included a high percentage who returned of their own volition, one might expect to find more married respondents. It is difficult to explain the educational differences between the samples, although it may be a function of the way questions were formulated and of the rapport established by Bermúdez over the lengthy contacts with her respondents.

Bermúdez describes the complicated process for illegal entry in her study. The individual first secures a loan from a loan shark in the community. Along the Atlantic coast there are many people who specialize in such loans. Typically the person borrows about 2,000 pesos (this in 1975), to be repaid within a month at an interest rate of 20-25 percent. Half of the money is left with the family to live on, and the other half is used for the trip. Approximately 150 pesos (about $5) is used for passage; another 850 pesos, for food and shelter. Some migrants employ *tratantes*, guides to assist them in crossing. The family that remains behind serves as the *fia*, the guarantee that the loan will be repaid. The migrant travels by bus to the appropriate crossing point (from the Atlantic coast this usually means the region around Maicao). From that point the migrant takes to the *camino verde* for a one-to-three-day walk to the destination. Many have relatives in Venezuela, and the trip for them is easier.[48]

The lengthy border separating Colombia and Venezuela is even more difficult to patrol than the frontier between Mexico and the United States. The terrain is particularly inhospitable, sparsely populated in most areas, and watched by a comparatively small number of Venezuelan National Guard. And the remoteness of many border areas creates its own set of problems – for instance, the distance between the point of entry and available employment. A long, hard trek must be undertaken once the border is crossed. Most undocumented workers probably prefer the more heavily guarded, and more accessible, areas. Such is not always the case, however. One 16-year-old girl was taken from the home where she and her mother worked, and was deported. In Cúcuta she said that she planned to work a few months to get enough money to return. Determined to rejoin her mother, she said that she could make it "through *las materas*, that is, through the mountains that only Colombians know."[49]

TABLE 4.8
Method and Place of Entry into Venezuela:
A Sample of Deportees at Cúcuta
(percent; N = 204)

Place of Entry		Method of Entry	
Maicao	11.27	Car and trail	36.77
Puerto Santander	18.63	Taxi	54.90
Cúcuta-S. Antonio	52.46	Bus	6.37
Cúcuta-Urena	2.45	Canoe, trail, car	1.96
Arauca	8.33		
Arauquita	1.96		
Saravena	0.98		
Delicias	3.92		

Source: Secretariado, *Estudio sobre deportados*, ch. 1, p. 49.

Colombian *indocumentados* almost universally hate and fear the Venezuelan National Guard. In addition to the problem of coming up with enough money to bribe Guardsmen, a common practice, there have been many reports of brutality. Perhaps the most widely reported incident occurred in January 1979. Three Colombian peasants were reportedly killed by Venezuelan National Guardsmen in the Zulia and Táchira regions. The Bogotá daily *El Tiempo* asserted that more than 400 Colombians have been killed in similar incidents.[50] The deaths produced outrage in Colombia, and the Association of Retired Colombian Military Officers (ACOREO) directed a strong protest to Colombian President Turbay. The concern was presented to the Venezuelan government, which promised to investigate. The incident was not the first, nor will it be the last.

The position of the Venezuelan government has been not to sanction such brutality, but it says it is not its policy to permit unrestricted entrance of *indocumentados*. In 1971, Venezuelan President Rafael Caldera said:

Nobody has ever thought of expelling these hundreds of thousands of Colombians, although juridically it would be unobjectionable. . . . But the flow of those entering illegally has been until now uncontrollable. If from 1960 to 1970 the number of illegal immigrants, known as *indocumentados*, is calculated at several hundred thousands, this means that tens of thousands have come each year; and when one speaks of expelling 70 to 100 or 200 of them that continue penetrating, these are those who pretend that Venezuela is committing inhuman deeds.[51]

Excesses, whether or not a result of official policy, do occur. The very magnitude of the problem contributes to frustration and overreaction. On June 12,

TABLE 4.9
The Colombian Indocumentado's Experience in Venezuela:
The Cúcuta Survey
(percent; n = 204)

Time in Venezuela		Time Detained Before Deportation		Treatment Received from Officials	
Less than 1 mo.	33.83	1- 5 days	37.35	good	11.27
1-6 mos.	22.18	6-10 days	35.79	fair	31.37
7-10 mos.	5.91	11-15 days	8.32	bad	57.36
1-4 yrs.	19.21	16-20 days	7.35		
Over 4 yrs.	18.70	21-30 days	8.82		
		over 30 days	1.47		

Source: Secretariado, *Estudio sobre deportados*, ch. 3, pp. 52, 53, 57, 58. Due to rounding errors, percentages do not total to 100.

1978, for example, the Bogotá daily *La República* reported, in an article with a Rio de Janeiro dateline, that Venezuela had plans to deport some 75,000 Brazilians working in the state of Bolívar for "reasons of security."[52]

Not all Colombians are entering Venezuela completely of their own volition, however. One recently deported Colombian told us that even as he was being deported, he met a Venezuelan recruiter on his way to Colombia to get 40,000 farm workers to go to southwestern Venezuela. Others who deal with the *indocumentados* tell of particularly offensive recruitment practices by some Venezuelans. We were told that some Venezuelan recruiters go to the Putumayo region to recruit young Indian girls for domestic service in Caracas. They tell the girls' parents of the high pay and pleasant working conditions. To further persuade the parents, they offer 200 to 500 pesos as "compensation for lost services" that are suffered as a result of their daughters' departure. Some 60 to 70 recruits are then secured and taken to Venezuela. Since the girls have no papers, they are particularly vulnerable, and frequently are forced into prostitution. Stories also surface of young girls from secondary schools in the Colombian department of Boyacá who are recruited to tutor children of rich Venezuelan families. They, too, often find themselves forced into prostitution.

Venezuelan recruiters seeking farm workers are active in the Colombian departments of Valle and Antioquia. Workers from these areas frequently have experience in mechanized farm operations and are seen as especially desirable.

Men generally work as farmhands, in construction, as mechanics, as semi-skilled factory workers, or as street vendors. In an informal, unscientific sampling of deported workers, it appeared that the more skilled and in demand the job, the better the treatment received from the employer. The unskilled, "expendable" laborers complained of being treated like slaves.

In Venezuela the *indocumentado* generally maintains a low profile. Those who work in agriculture usually stay close to the farm where they work, even in their free time, so as not to be caught and deported. Venezuelan employers are obviously aware of this and play on the fear. A worker who fears deportation is less likely to look for a better job or to complain about wages or working conditions. On the other hand, *indocumentados* seem to have developed a remarkably good network of information about working conditions and employers in Venezuela. A farmer who attempts to defraud his workers risks a "boycott."

The risk of detection and deportation lies not only with unscrupulous employers or accidental encounters with the National Guard, but also in trying to send a money order home. Obviously the worker who goes to the bank to buy a money order and then mails it home from a nearby post office runs a greater risk than one who sends it home with a friend (a common practice) or who can find some other method of "laundering" it. The traffic back and forth is sufficiently heavy that some workers engage in a lucrative business smuggling goods back and forth and serving as couriers. There, too, the risks are great, for those who are caught frequently have their money taken from them. A thriving black market in currency exchange operates in many parts of Venezuela, and many Colombians do business involving money and contraband.[53]

The growing symbiotic relationship between the *indocumentados* and their Venezuelan employers is one in which myths, suspicions, and stereotypes thrive. Venezuelans are characterized by Colombians as lazy, arrogant, and notoriously poor farmers. Colombians frequently describe their Venezuelan employers as having a slave-owner mentality. The National Guard is seen by many as sadistic and brutal. Colombians, on the other hand, are frequently described by Venezuelans as ignorant, dirty, and thieves by nature.

When the alien is caught, the deportation process is frequently unpleasant. While many Colombians attribute their poor treatment to Venezuelan sadism, at least part of the problem stems from a lack of organization and funds in the deportation process. For example, when illegals are picked up, they are sent to the border by bus. While the average time spent on the bus is two or three days, it can be much longer if the person is apprehended in Caracas or some other point far from the border. Some told us that a person caught in Caracas can expect to spend two weeks in detention while enough aliens to form a group are gathered. The trip can be circular, depending on the number of stops that are made to pick up aliens. One illegal alien told of passing through the same town three times. Conditions on the buses are less than ideal. There is very little opportunity to sleep or go to the bathroom, and the food is poor and inadequate, consisting of a bowl of soup a day. The end of the journey in Venezuela is San Cristóbal, a few miles from Colombia. Once at San Cristóbal, they are held until the paperwork can be completed for the Colombian D.A.S. to pick them up and return them to Colombia. Those arriving at San Cristóbal typically have had little sleep or food, and are housed in cells approximately four feet by eight feet. Nights in San Cristóbal are frequently quite cool, and some *deportados* complain that there is water on the floors of the cells. Thus, their final night in Venezuela is spent in cold, damp cells where sleep is virtually impossible.

The five deported aliens interviewed by Oscar Martínez were unanimous in their criticism of the Venezuelan jails. Freddy Gary Valverde, an Ecuadorian, said that he was picked up and driven around for several hours while the authorities looked for other illegals. In jail the food is poor and insufficient. According to Martínez's account, prisoners eat the food, placed on pieces of paper, with their fingers. The food consists of rice and clear soup. No provision is made for sleeping, and one fears the other prisoners. After spending four days in La Planta, "the worst jail in Venezuela," Valverde was taken to the Foreign Office, and the deportation process was begun.[54] That is the general pattern: one is held, frequently for several days; is taken to the Foreign Office; is bused to the border and turned over to the Colombian government, even if one is not Colombian, as was the case with Valverde.

The Colombian government is not very helpful either. When D.A.S. is ready to pick up the deportees, the Venezuelans take them to San Antonio, the city across the border from Cúcuta. D.A.S. does not always collect them immediately, and sometimes the wait can be several days. When they are picked up, they are taken to the Reception Center for the Deported, which is operated by the Catholic Church without assistance from the Colombian government. The reception center feeds them, gives them medical assistance through the Red Cross, debriefs them, offers them a clean bed, and even pays for their transportation home. Usually this means a bus trip, but on some occasions the distance is too great and an airline ticket is provided.

In addition to looking after the deportees' physical needs, the center tries to offer counsel and, on occasion, even assists them in locating employment in Colombia. Since 1976 the Colombian government's National Employment Service (SENALDE) has had border offices to help locate jobs, provide information on conditions in Colombia and Venezuela, and generally assist the migrant worker.[55]

IMPLICATIONS FOR COLOMBIA AND VENEZUELA

Any "accounting" procedure designed to tabulate the cost-benefit factors of population transfers must include the qualitative implications for the individuals involved as well as for the larger societies. It is clear that the illegal migration of Colombians to Venezuela is not a zero-sum situation. Neither country clearly gains or loses. The same might be said of individuals, particularly the poor on both sides of the border. The Colombian *indocumentado* is better off in the sense that he or she may make more money, but worse off because the migration entails leaving home, traveling to another country, and frequently facing all manner of indignities. The Latin American peasant is often characterized as fatalistic — not possessing the "Protestant ethic" — but when he or she does make personal sacrifices to get ahead economically, treatment as a criminal results. The severe treatment received by Colombians in Venezuela raises strong human rights questions that cannot, and should not, be ignored any more than the treatment of Mexican illegal aliens in the United States can be dismissed. Moreover, the Colombian government, like the Mexican government, is guilty of duplicity for failing to deal with the conditions that give rise to illegal alienage.

At the same time, the Venezuelan peasant suffers too. The presence of even poorer peasants from Colombia may tend to depress wages and force migration to urban areas. The massive petroleum exploration in Venezuela was both the cause of migration by Venezuelans and an intermediate factor that contributed to still more migration from Colombia. Venezuelan peasants migrated to the petroleum areas to seek a better life, thereby leaving the rural areas short of labor and opening the way for Colombian migration. On the other hand, the flow of Colombian labor depressed wages and probably forced many remaining peasants to migrate.

John Armstrong describes the "proletarian diaspora" as an "essentially disadvantaged product of modernized polities." No doubt this is true, particularly in cases like the Mexican illegal entering the highly industrialized United

TABLE 4.10
The Venezuelan Residence of Colombian
Undocumented Workers, 1975
(n = 204)

State	Percent
Táchira	42.65
Miranda	13.24
Barinas	10.79
Zulia	6.86
Mérida	4.41
Caracas, D.F.	3.43
Carabobo	1.47
Portuguesa	1.47
Trujillo	0.49
Apure	0.49

Source: Secretariado, *Estudio sobre deportados*, ch. 2, p. 51.

States. On the other hand, population transfers from poor countries to relatively poorer states constitute a different form of "proletarian diaspora" with different consequences. Where the receiver state is highly industrialized, one is likely to find a highly developed social welfare program. Farmers in the United States frequently argue that they cannot get enough domestic farm labor because the marginal utility of working for low wages is insufficient to lure those collecting unemployment or welfare benefits. Farmers claim, correctly or as a rationalization, that they cannot pay enough to satisfy the potential domestic workers. In some cases they opt for mechanization, and in others they employ illegal aliens who will work for the wages offered.

Where the receiver country is not highly industrialized (as is true in Venezuela), the dislocation of domestic workers is potentially great. Some farming operations do mechanize, but in other instances domestic workers who might otherwise work for low wages are displaced by *indocumentados* who will work for even less. Some policy planners would argue that forcing the country people into the cities, to work in industry, is beneficial to the society as a whole and to the individuals in it, at least in the long run.[56] In that sense the population transfer caused by Colombians forcing Venezuelans to the cities could be beneficial.

Venezuela, like most comparatively poor societies in the Third World, is developing unevenly. While revenues from petroleum are high and the industrialized sector of the economy is growing at a rapid pace, many problems characteristic of Third World countries persist. Not only is income distribution still a problem, but the backward agricultural sector is unable to keep pace with the rapidly growing population. Not only has Venezuela been unable to control the population explosion resulting from lower infant mortality and high immigration, but prospects for the future do not look good. Unlike the United States, Venezuela is surrounded by poor countries. While the highly industrialized societies of the world are approaching zero population growth, Venezuela's population growth soars. The finite amount of land is not producing at higher rates, partly because the influx of cheap labor makes improved production techniques economically infeasible.

Certainly the availability of Venezuelan employment has been a short-term benefit to Colombia, providing a safety valve for unemployed persons and contributing positively to the balance of payments through the money Colombians send or take home. On the negative side of the ledger, the safety valve encourages Colombian policy makers to avoid dealing with unemployment and the balance of payments. The population beachheads established by Colombian nationals living abroad probably form a "critical mass"[57] for still more immigration. These beachheads established, some Colombians have developed a massive drug operation that corrupts both the sender and receiver countries and leaves the Colombian economy in shambles. The money from drugs, now thought to be two to three times as much as earned from coffee, is of course illegal, and must be laundered and invested in legitimate business. The influx of such sums of money into the economy has resulted in artificially high prices on the Colombian stock exchange, in real estate, and in the everyday necessities purchased by poor Colombians. Political corruption in Colombia resulting from the drug traffic is unprecedented, and the Colombian Congress recently considered legislation to legalize drugs in order to tax and otherwise regulate the traffic.

One can point to short-run benefits to Venezuela from the flow of *indocumentados*, such as a ready source of cheap labor and lower food prices, but the long-range implications are mostly negative. The bishop of Cúcuta speculates that as much as half of the Venezuelan labor force is foreign-born, consisting of legal residents and *indocumentados* from Colombia and other Latin American countries.[58] While this figure may be high, it is apparent that Venezuela has little, if any, control over its population growth or the size of its labor force. Colombians may generally work in agriculture at first, but they later find their way to the cities as well, where they eventually compete with Venezuelans for all sorts of jobs. Corruption is also a growing problem in Venezuela. The agricultural sector has not been too successful, and smuggling (cattle in particular) and corruption by business and government officials alike threatens to undermine the fabric of society.

Lelio Mármora says that Colombia was the first country in Latin America with substantial emigration to develop a systematic immigration policy.[59] The cornerstone of that policy involves the flow of internal migrants during the harvesting of such crops as cotton. By attempting to correct the supply and demand imbalances within Colombia, SENALDE, the National Employment Service, hopes to make staying in Colombia more attractive. The program is admirable, and no doubt has been useful, but given the magnitude of the unemployed and underemployed labor force, it is doubtful that it will be able to solve the problem. SENALDE has also worked with the Venezuelan Ministry of Labor to provide seasonal workers,[60] but it has not substantially reduced the number of undocumented laborers. Beginning in mid-1976, SENALDE established regional offices along several borders: Arauca, Cúcuta, and Maicao with Venezuela; Ipiales with Ecuador; and Leticia with Peru and Brazil.[61]

Countries bordering Colombia, particularly Ecuador and Venezuela, have worked with Colombia in recent years to control the problem. The Andean Instrument of Labor Migration was ratified by the Board of Accord in Cartegena and by the Venezuelan and Colombian governments in 1977 and 1978.[62] The program hopes to develop a more comprehensive plan to utilize labor on a regional basis. One could envision a program of guest workers similar to that existing among European Common Market members, although the problems are different, in that none of the Andean Pact members is highly industrialized.

Like Mexico, Colombia would like to be in the position of not being forced to push its workers beyond its national borders to find employment; and like the United States, Venezuela would prefer to be able to rely on domestic labor supplies to meet its worker requirements and profit objectives. The realities are harsh, however, and senders and receivers alike find it expedient to emphasize the benefits of illegal migration through their practices while ignoring the social, economic, and political costs to the individuals and societies involved.

NOTES

1. The term "irredenta" might also apply. Although Italian in origin, the Colombian settlements in western Venezuela, like the Mexican immigration to the American Southwest, may constitute an irredenta.

2. See John A. Armstrong, "Mobilized and Proletarian Diasporas," *American Political Science Review* 70, no. 2 (June 1976): 393-408.

3. Kingsley Davis, "The Migrations of Human Populations," in *The Human Population* (San Francisco: W. H. Freeman, 1974), pp. 53-65, cited in Elsa M. Chaney, "The Colombian Diaspora in New York City: Linkages in the Colony and to the Homeland," paper prepared for the Workshop on U.S. Immigration: Research Perspectives, National Institute of Child Health and Human Development, Washington, D.C., May 16-18, 1977.

4. Artur Hehl Neiva, "International Migrations Affecting Latin America," *Milbank Memorial Fund Quarterly* 43, no. 4 (October 1965): pt. 2, p. 129.

5. John D. Martz and David J. Myers, ed., *Venezuela: The Democratic Experience* (New York: Praeger, 1977), p. 3.

6. Chi-yi Chen, "Distribución espacial de la población venezolana: diagnóstico y perspectiva," in *América Latina: Distribución espacial de la población*, Ramiro Cardona G., ed. (Bogotá, Editorial Canal Ramírez-Antares, 1975), p. 219.

7. Luís Ospina Vásquez, *Industria y protección en Colombia, 1810-1930* (Medellín: Editorial La Oveja Negra, 1974), p. 479.

8. *International Financial Statistics*, International Monetary Fund, August 1971.

9. Charito Rojas, "La incontrolable invasión colombiano," *Momento*, August 1971.

10. Hector Villamizar V., oral history interview no. 319, by Oscar Martínez, May 22, 1978, Cúcuta, Colombia. On file at the Institute of Oral History, University of Texas at El Paso.

11. Alfonso López Michelsen, "Homenaje de la colonia colombiana," in *El presidente de Colombia en los Estados Unidos* (Bogotá: Secretaría de Informacion de la Presidencia de la República de Colombia y USIS/Colombia, 1976).

12. Elsa M. Chaney, "The Caribbean on the Move: Undocumented Workers in the Hemisphere," paper prepared for the Study Group on Immigration and U.S. Foreign Policy, Council on Foreign Relations, New York City, May 15, 1978, p. 21. Lelio Mármora says that most Colombians come from the departament of Nariño and work in the bordering provinces of Carchi and Esmeraldas. Mármora, "Labor Migration Policy in Colombia," *International Migration Review* 13, no. 3 (Fall 1969): 444.

13. Alfonso Arbeláez C., "El éxodo de colombianos en el período 1963-1973," *Boletín mensual de estadística* no. 310 (May 1977): 39.

14. Chaney, "The Caribbean on the Move," p. 22.

15. Ibid., p. 20.

16. Ibid., citing Carmen Inés Cruz and Juanita Castaño, "Colombian Migration to the United States," in Ramiro Cardona, project dir., *Elements for a Comprehensive Model of International Migration: The Case of Colombia and the United States* (Bogotá: Corporación Centro Regional de Población, 1976). This would seem to contradict (or perhaps update) Neiva, who asserts that migration across borders is essentially rural to rural. Our own research has found that international migration from Colombia is frequently a two-step process; internal rural to urban, and then urban to urban or urban to rural across borders.

17. Elsa M. Chaney, "Colombians in New York City: Theoretical and Policy Issues," in *Sourcebook on the New Immigration*, ed. R. S. Bryce-Laporte et al. (New Brunswick, N.J.: Transaction Books, 1980), pp. 285-94.

18. Ibid.

19. Ibid.

20. This estimate was offered by Miguel Soto Montiel and his special commission appointed by Venezuelan President Luís Herrera Campíns. The Venezuelan commission admitted that the exact number is unknown. See *Diario las Américas*, April 4, 1979.

21. Arbeláez C., "El éxodo de colombianos . . . ," p. 38.

22. Mary M. Kritz, "The Impact of International Migration on Venezuelan Demographic and Social Structure," *International Migration Review* 9, no. 4 (Winter 1975): 526; Paulo Singer, "International Migration and Development," in *International Migration World Population Year* (Paris: CICRED, 1974); Chaney, "The Colombian Diaspora in New York City."

23. Miguel Urrutia M., "Income Distribution in Colombia," *International Labour Review* 13, no. 2 (March/April 1976): 209.

24. INCORA, "La reforma agraria," *Boletín mensual de estadística* no. 234 (January 1971): 65.

25. Ibid.

26. S. D. Bermúdez, "La migración del campesino a Venezuela: Estudio socioeconómico en dos comunidades de la costa atlántica: Guacamayal y Manatí" (senior thesis, department of anthropology, Universidad de los Andes, 1976).

27. D.A.N.E., "La migración interna y el proceso de concentración de la población de los departamentos," *Boletín mensual de estadística* no. 314 (September 1977): 47.

28. Ibid., p. 9.

29. Chen, "Distribución espacial . . . ," p. 220.

30. Saskia Sassen-Koob, "Economic Growth and Immigration in Venezuela," *International Migration Review* 13, no. 3 (Fall 1979): 455-74. Between 1972 and 1974 state revenues increased by 250 percent, primarily because of petroleum.

31. Chen, "Distribución espacial . . . ."

32. Sassen-Koob, "Economic Growth and Immigration . . . ," p. 456.

33. Kritz, "The Impact of International Migration . . . ," pp. 513-43.

34. Ibid., p. 519. Kritz notes that in 1929, in response to growing discontent among domestic workers, Juan Vicente Gómez kicked out many West Indians contracted by the oil companies.

35. Ibid., p. 521.

36. Ibid., pp. 541-43.

37. Howard Handelman, "Scarcity Amidst Plenty: Food Problems in Oil Rich Venezuela," *American Universities Field Staff Reports* no. 42 (September 1978): 2, 12.

38. Ibid., pp. 11-13.

39. Ibid.

40. Ibid., p. 11.

41. Ibid., pp. 11-13.

42. *Diario las Américas* (Miami), April 4, 1979.

43. Bermúdez, "La migración del campesino . . . ."

44. Norman Gall, "Los indocumentados colombianos," *American Universities Field Staff Reports* 16, no. 2 (December 1972): 2.

45. It might be noted that during the *bracero* program in the United States, the flow of illegal aliens also increased.

46. William González Aparicio, oral history interview no. 315, by Oscar Martínez, May 22, 1978, Cúcuta, Colombia. On file at the Institute of Oral History, University of Texas at El Paso.

47. Gall, "Los indocumentados colombianos . . . ."

48. Bermúdez, "La migración del campesino . . . ."

49. Inez Morales Agredo, oral history interview no. 316, by Oscar Martínez, May 23, 1978, Cúcuta, Colombia. On file at the Institute of Oral History, University of Texas at El Paso.

50. *Diario las Américas* (Miami), March 15, 1979.

51. Gall, "Los indocumentados colombianos . . . ," p. 2.

52. *La República* (Bogotá), June 12, 1978. In the early days of 1981, long after the completion of this research project, the Venezuelan government announced a new amnesty program for illegal aliens. While it is too early to determine the seriousness of the offer, it is bound to be received with skepticism. The Venezuelan government further stated that should the illegal aliens fail to accept the offer of legal status, a vigorous effort to expel them would be made. Colombians, Brazilians, Peruvians, Ecuadorians, and Dominicans would be among the nearly two million illegal aliens affected.

53. Gall, "Los indocumentados colombianos . . . ," p. 4.

54. Freddy Gary Valverde Avellon, oral history interview no. 314, by Oscar Martínez, May 22, 1978, Cúcuta, Colombia. On file at the Institute of Oral History, University of Texas at El Paso.

55. Mármora, "Labor Migration Policy in Colombia," pp. 440-54.

56. Lauchlin Currie, *Accelerating Development: The Necessity and the Means* (New York: McGraw-Hill, 1966).

57. Chaney, "The Caribbean on the Move," p. 9.

58. Based on a personal interview. Sassen-Koob says that in October 1977, there were 1.2 million foreigners with residence visas in Venezuela, out of a population of 13 million. Sassen-Koob, "Economic Growth and Immigration . . . ," p. 463.

59. Mármora, p. 440.

60. Ibid., p. 446.

61. Ibid., p. 447.

62. Ibid., pp. 448-49.

5

CLANDESTINE IMMIGRATION INTO ARGENTINA AND WITHIN THE SOUTHERN CONE

MIGRATORY PATTERNS IN THE SOUTHERN CONE

In contrast with Mexico and Colombia, it is claimed that Argentina is an underpopulated country. One does not get this impression when visiting the capital city, Buenos Aires, where (in the Federal District and surrounding Buenos Aires province) nearly half of Argentina's 27 million inhabitants lived in 1980. The capital city's congestion is due to the centering of import-export functions there, to the fact of great absentee landholding that extracts agricultural wealth from the provinces and deposits it in the capital, to the "Little Europe" cultural environment that attracts the international intelligentsia, and to clandestine migratory patterns. To a certain degree the entire north of Argentina acts as a magnet that attracts population movement from the neighboring countries. Because of the vast, irregular border across which the migration takes place, it is difficult for the Argentine government to gather population movement statistics. For the same reason it would be extremely difficult to stop such migration via the "curtain" tactics that were discussed in Chapter 3 in connection with Canada, Mexico, and the United States. A glance at the map reveals the extent of Argentina's borders. The northeastern province of Misiones is almost totally surrounded by other countries. The capital city and Buenos Aires province constitute the principal population magnet whose drawing power reaches north to Bolivia via an extensive system of railroads and highways. These have their underground counterparts for clandestine migration.

Argentina's 1980 estimated population will not double for at least 53 years, and is projected to be at some 33 million by the turn of the century.[1] When compared with Mexico's population growth during the same projected time frame (Mexico will double its population by 2000), Argentina emerges as a

Argentina

probable target nation for population transfer in the coming century; this assumes that livability strategies for status quo population containment in the hemisphere have not been set in motion by that time. In contrast, Argentina's neighbors will experience the following demographic change: Chile's 1980 population is estimated at 11.2 million, and should increase to 15.1 million by 2000; Uruguay's 1980 population is 3 million, and should increase to 3.5 million by 2000; Bolivia has 5.2 million in 1980, and should have 8.9 million by the end of the century; Paraguay has 3.9 million in 1980 and will increase to 5.3 million by the century's end; Brazil, bordering more than half of Argentina's Misiones province, has some 119 million inhabitants in 1980 and is projected to have a population of 205.2 million in 2000. This means that of Argentina's neighbors Chile and Uruguay will take 43 and 63 years, respectively, to double their populations, while the remaining countries will double theirs in from 22 to 25 years. The doubling of Brazil's huge population may be a crucial factor in the course of demographic change within the Southern Cone. Argentina, Chile, and Uruguay seem the likely recipients of population shift. Considering the small size of Uruguay and the mountainous character of much of Chile, it appears that Argentina holds out the greatest migration receiving potential in the Río de la Plata area.

Argentina is the second largest South American nation in area and is the seventh largest in the world. Its annual population growth is 1.5 percent, and although Roman Catholicism is the official religion of state, the use of birth control devices and family planning techniques is widespread, especially within the large middle class. It might be said that the "quality of life" ethic discussed in Chapter 1 has operated, along with geography and climate, to keep Argentina an immigrant-receiving nation. Since the turn of this century, Argentina's population has changed from approximately 50 percent urban to more than 80 percent urban in 1980.[2] The urban character of northeastern Argentina, and the corresponding demand for building trades workers, help to explain much of the clandestine migration in recent years, just as the seasonal sugar and tobacco harvests in northern Argentina explained such migratory patterns in the past. The population of Argentina, as noted before, is unevenly distributed, with nearly half the total living in and around Buenos Aires province. Population densities range from over 14,000 per square kilometer in the Federal District to less than one per square kilometer in the southern provinces of Chubut and Santa Cruz.[3]

It is not known precisely how many illegal aliens now reside in Argentina, but government estimates suggest that there are several million and that their number is growing each year. These clandestine migrants, by and large, have little to do with the political turmoils of the nations in the Southern Cone. True, all of these nations do trade political exiles at an impressive rate. But they are only a handful out of the total population flow, and are often counted among the legal immigrants. This is not true of the proletarian classes, however, whose exiles are usually not political but economic. These we will characterize as clandestine migrants.

ILLEGAL MIGRATION INTO ARGENTINA

On the basis of interviews in Buenos Aires during 1980, plus special tabulations from the national immigration archives, we have developed some rough indexes of clandestine migration. We should note that Argentine officials prefer to avoid use of the term "illegal," not because of ethnic sensitivities, as in the case of the Mexico-United States interface, but because under the fluctuating interpretations of Argentine law, it is not always illegal to be a clandestine migrant.[4] Evidence of this circumstance was presented in Chapter 2, in the discussion of amnesty proposals and experiments. It comes down to the fact that a nation like Argentina, whose government uses its public media to tell the undocumented and unsanctioned immigrants that they are welcome and that they should sign up and be "regularized," should hardly be mounting a parallel campaign against the illegals.

The contrast here with North America is striking. Argentina absorbs the clandestine migrants from surrounding countries without difficulty, and publicly welcomes them. If the U.S. government made such a public announcement, it might empty out Mexico and Central America in a matter of weeks (President Carter's amnesty proposal, when discussed publicly, provoked a wave of clandestine northward migration). But wages are not so continuously high in Argentina, nor are social services in that country so generous, as to provoke major immigrant streams. Treatment of the undocumented migrants in Argentina is often severe, as in the micro view of a *villa miseria* that is presented below. Argentine governmental officials freely admit that policing their borders for clandestine migrants is all but impossible. It is known that along these same borders one can find residents who profess national allegiance as convenience dictates, and many of them honestly do not know which is the country of their birth. In such an environment the concept of clandestine or informal migration takes on greater significance.

With the above caveats entered, we can proceed to examine some very rough indicators of clandestine migration in Argentina. Table 5.1 shows the Argentine government's official figures on legal immigration and emigration during the mid-1970s.

From this it can be seen that Argentine citizens constituted the principal departure group for the years in question. For the nearly three-year period there was an official total immigration of nearly 300,000 persons. That is only a fraction of the number of Mexicans deported from the United States in any one of the recent years, so at least at the formal level it would seem that there is not a mass invasion of Argentina by legal immigrants. But, of course, our testimony from Argentine government officials indicates that their nation is not exactly being inundated by illegal migrants. Argentina receives, according to our testimony, just enough informal immigrants to satisfy its labor force deficiencies. There is, however, more to the official Argentine view, as shown in Table 5.2.

TABLE 5.1
Argentine Migratory Trends, 1973 to Mid-1975

	Total	Argentines	Foreigners
Entries	4,307,900	1,475,200	2,832,700
Departures	4,052,800	1,506,200	2,546,600
Balance	255,100	-31,000	286,100

Source: República Argentina, Ministerio de Economía, Secretaría de Estado de Programación y Coordinatión Economica, Instituto Nacional de Estadística y Censos, *Boletín estadístico trimestral* July-September 1979, p. 8.

TABLE 5.2
Principal Foreign Migration Affecting Argentina, by National Origin, 1973 to Mid-1975

Entrants		Departees		
Nationality	Number	Nationality	Number	Balance
Germans	56,800	Germans	57,900	- 1,100
Bolivians	98,500	Bolivians	76,800	21,700
Brazilians	288,100	Brazilians	275,000	13,100
Chileans	471,800	Chileans	396,800	75,000
Spaniards	89,500	Spaniards	102,600	- 13,100
Italians	106,500	Italians	115,800	- 9,300
Paraguayans	333,400	Paraguayans	207,600	125,800
Uruguayans	912,900	Uruguayans	832,100	80,800
Others	475,500	Others	482,500	- 7,000

Source: República Argentina, Ministerio de Economía, Secretaría de Estado de Programación y Coordinatión Economica, Instituto Nacional de Estadística y Censos, *Boletín estadístico trimestral* July-September 1979, pp. 10-13.

The above statistics are admittedly incomplete, at least according to what we were told by Argentine government officials. They admit that persons who entered Argentina legally may have left clandestinely, and vice versa. A breakdown of the above figures shows, for instance, that some 10,000 Bolivians entered Argentina by plane in 1973 and almost the same number departed by plane. But the bulk of the clandestine migrants from Bolivia couldn't have afforded a plane fare! Looking at the land entries, in the same year some 22,000 Bolivians entered Argentina legally across its frontiers, and only 16,700 exited in the same way. That could be a vague indicator of visa overstays, but it will be objected that 1973 was a troubled year for both nations. The 1974 figures indicate that 24,500 Bolivians entered by land and only 13,400 exited the same way. This confirms the tendency for Bolivians to stay in Argentina, but it proves nothing definitive about clandestine migration in a broad sense. Still, the pattern of migration is suggestive. In all European categories there was a net loss, whereas a net gain was registered in all Latin American categories.

Inspecting the entry figures for Uruguayans coming into and leaving Argentina by land proves nothing; they balance nearly perfectly. However, the figures for Paraguayans entering Argentina in 1973 and 1974 combined show some 24,000 coming in and some 7,000 leaving. This makes sense in the context of political and socioeconomic realities of those countries. Moreover, the figures reveal that officially some 204,000 Paraguayans entered Argentina by river travel during 1973-74 combined and that 125,700 left in the same manner. Again, this does not prove that the remainder stayed on as illegal aliens. But our expert informants believe that they did. They may very well have left by other means, or they may have died in the political violence that was rampant in Argentina during those years. Indeed, in the context of Argentina's tumultuous politics, in which violence seems to play a constant role, it would not be surprising to discover apocryphal migration statistics; in point of fact, it is a wonder that the Argentine government is able to generate any reasonable-sounding figures at all, given the political chaos in which the statistical work is done. In all fairness, we should say that we were well received by the severely understaffed Argentine agencies, and it appears that they were doing their best to clarify a highly confusing immigration situation.

Inspection of other official statistics revealed little about clandestine migration at the time of our research, with one possible exception. We were allowed to make a special tabulation of hand-kept records from the Argentine government's migration control center located in a naval base on the Avenida Antártida Argentina, no. 1355. The data were kept in a loose-leaf binder at the immigration statistical center, and we were told that they had not been previously published. Considering the size and importance of Argentina within Latin America, it appeared to us that the statistical records on immigration were being given very low priority by the Argentine government. The data we copied were from 1970-74, overlapping the second Perón era (1973-76). These figures do not include the present regime, which came to power through a coup in March

1976. Our understanding is that the incumbent regime probably will not want to release its immigration/emigration figures until after its principals are out of office, in view of the raging international controversy over political repression and human rights violations in Argentina as the 1980s begin.

Looking only at Argentina's bordering countries, the statistical picture of legally sanctioned migration is shown in Table 5.3.

From the table it can be seen that there is a marked tendency for more people from the bordering states to enter Argentina than to depart. This may be a reflection of the manner in which Argentina's immigration law is enforced. However, one Argentine immigration official told us that the above table "proves" that many legal visitors overstay their visas and become illegal aliens. In this case, he said, it is correct to call them illegals because they did not enter clandestinely and abused their status only after their permits expired (usually from 30 to 60 days). Our experience over more than ten years of traveling to Argentina and its contiguous states makes the above explanation questionable. It is possible for Brazilians to enter the province of Misiones without inspection, and nothing is done to prevent their movement into the interior of Argentina. The same is true on the borders Argentina shares with Paraguay and Bolivia. There is less ease of clandestine entry from Chile because of the Andes, but even there surreptitious entry can be accomplished.

An immigration official provided the estimates in Table 5.4 concerning deportation of illegal aliens (understood here as foreigners who had become offensive or inadmissible to the Argentine government for reasons that were not specified at the time of the interview).

The existence of states of siege in Argentina, a nearly perpetual fact of that country's political life, makes it difficult to gather data from official sources. No data were available to us on any deportations out of Buenos Aires province (where about half of Argentina's total population is concentrated). That region, including the Federal District, is the scene of some of the most violent confrontations between the military government and popular revolutionary forces. Worldwide attention has been focused on the disappearance of thousands of Argentine citizens. One journalist told us that instead of deporting people, "they" just make them "disappear." The notion of political deportation is most notable in the cases of former revolutionaries from Uruguay and Chile. Yet many Argentines have also "disappeared" only because they knew someone who might have been subversive. The personnel manager of a bank told us that his enterprise often hired exiled persons from Uruguay who were admitted legally to Argentina and were trying to arrange their residency papers, only to be picked up during the night by government agents and never heard from again. Thus the international politics of human rights and international migration may be overlapping, and this phenomenon has attracted attention in North America:

> Hundreds of well-known Argentine writers, politicians, clergymen and businessmen published a newspaper advertisement Tuesday calling on

TABLE 5.3
Migration Affecting Argentina from Bordering States, 1970-74
(in thousands)

	Bolivians		Brazilians		Chileans		Paraguayans		Uruguayans	
	Ent.	Exit	Ent.	Exit	Ent.	Exit	Ent.	Exit	Ent.	Exit
1970	23.5	14.8	47.6	46.3	154.8	144.2	79.5	58.0	223.8	322.7
1971	26.0	19.2	56.7	54.5	114.4	112.8	76.8	58.5	261.9	259.2
1972	34.8	29.1	115.9	106.1	106.6	98.5	143.2	98.8	247.2	246.0
1973	33.7	27.7	114.2	108.6	113.2	109.5	115.2	70.0	296.6	286.8
1974	40.0	29.0	96.8	89.8	205.3	173.5	144.7	93.4	427.4	386.4

Source: From a special tabulation of official records made by Oscar F. Risso and Kenneth F. Johnson during June 1980; Ministerio del Interior, Dirección Nacional de Migraciones, *Resumen de estadística migratorio año 1974* (administrative archive files).

TABLE 5.4
Selected Deportation Data, by Argentine Province and Country of Origin

	Deported to					
	Uruguay	*Brazil*	*Paraguay*	*Bolivia*	*Chile*	*Time Period*
Deported from						
Entre Ríos	2,500					1970-75
Corrientes		2,700				1973-74
Misiones		1,600	N.A.			1973-74
Chaco			N.A.			
Formosa			6,200			1970-75
Salta				7,000	N.A.	1970-75
Jujuy				2,300	N.A.	1970-75
Mendoza					7,400	1971-75

N.A. = not available.

Source: Interviews by Kenneth F. Johnson during June 1980 in Buenos Aires, Argentina.

147

the military government to account for thousands of their countrymen who have disappeared over the last four years. Human rights groups have estimated that between 5,000 and 15,000 people have disappeared in the anti-terrorism campaign that the government waged after it took power in March, 1976.[5]

One military spokesman, Gen. Roberto Viola, claims that the human rights groups have lists of disappeared "subversives" who may have emigrated clandestinely from Argentina or who were liquidated in fights with their fellow guerrillas.[6] This excuse makes it possible for the government to claim that the disappearance phenomenon is caused by the subversives themselves. The testimony we obtained in Argentina during 1980 revealed a different interpretation: that many political refugees who could not get out of Argentina took refuge in the slums (*villas miserias*) that encircle Buenos Aires. This version contends that since those *villas* are populated with large numbers of undocumented foreign immigrants (mostly Bolivians and Paraguayans), the search for political refugees in them has served as a justification to bulldoze whole slums, driving the people into other provinces, and as a justification for persecution of foreign residents among the urban proletariat. The government's hard-liners are willing to end "godless subversion" at any price, even though each disappearance may be a seed of future revolutionary violence.[7] It is also believed, according to our testimony, that reports of the many disappearances during the late 1970s served to reduce all immigration into Argentina, both legal and clandestine.

Not being able to show deportation profile data for the capital city area is a major deficiency. In that area the number of deportations of aliens who have become inadmissible or illegal is certain to be higher than at any other location in Argentina, given the large foreign population in Buenos Aires city and Buenos Aires province. According to the 1970 census the foreign resident population of the total nation was 2,210,400, and over 70 percent was in the Buenos Aires metropolitan area.[8] Since World War II the number of immigrants arriving by sea has diminished to the point of little importance. The *Boletín estadístico trimestral* for July-September 1979 shows that the great bulk of immigration from the eight countries listed in Table 5.2 entered by air or land. Although exact figures were not available on how many migrants from each country went to each province, we were told that the bulk of all immigration is still directed to the Buenos Aires area. Table 5.5 gives an overview of the immigration into the various provinces for 1960-70 (unfortunately, this still leaves unknown how many immigrants from which nation immigrated into which province).

The data in Table 5.5 are, of course, official tabulations of the migration of legal resident aliens in Argentina. These can be compared with some of the estimates given in Table 5.4 of deportations of illegal (inadmissible-unwelcome) aliens. The northern province of Salta shows a very high number of foreign immigrants leaving. That province also had a relatively high deportation estimate

TABLE 5.5
Immigrants to Argentina, by Province, 1960-70

Province	Immigrants
Buenos Aires metropolitan area	107,992
Remaining districts of Buenos Aires province	13,595
Catamarca	- 180
Córdoba	1,998
Corrientes	- 1,060
Chaco	- 2,517
Chubut	4,054
Entre Ríos	- 421
Formosa	2
Jujuy	- 5,447
La Pampa	- 1,068
La Rioja	324
Mendoza	- 691
Misiones	2,144
Neuquén	4,533
Río Negro	9,629
Salta	- 9,272
San Juan	-1,073
San Luis	- 339
Santa Cruz	5,986
Santa Fé	2,046
Santiago del Estero	- 454
Tucumán	- 1,822
Tierra del Fuego	1,766

Source: Instituto Nacional de Estadística y Censos, *La migración interna en la Argentina 1960/70*, p. 32.

for 1970-75. The story in Jujuy is similar. It can be noted also that several Patagonian provinces — Río Negro, Chubut, and Santa Cruz — had strong positive foreign immigration figures, reflecting the recruitment campaign to populate those sparsely settled areas and to develop their vast natural resource potential. Even the frigid Tierra del Fuego territory had a positive foreign input. Generally, then, the northern provinces of Argentina are unable to absorb more people and their foreign immigrants are migrating to other areas, principally the federal capital. This means that the greatest concentration of foreign residents is to be found in Buenos Aires city and province; thus it is likely that illegal resident aliens will be attracted there as well. Although we lack hard figures, our interviews during 1980 support such a contention. Therefore, Buenos Aires becomes a good place to observe the local impact of Argentina's illegal aliens.

LOCAL DIMENSIONS OF ILLEGAL ALIEN IMPACT: THE CASE OF VILLA RETIRO

During 1976 a study of immigrant Bolivians living both legally and illegally in Argentina was undertaken by Kenneth F. Johnson.[9] Many of the findings supported the contentions about labor exploitation that were cited in Chapter 2.[10] Illegal immigrants from Bolivia and Paraguay made up the largest part of the unskilled workers in the building trades in Buenos Aires, with the Bolivians tending to work with bricks and cement and the Paraguayans specializing in woodworking. Employers in the Buenos Aires area wanted a large and mobile labor pool, workers who would accept great uncertainty in their working hours and locations. These workers were expected to sit by without pay while foremen and managers decided whether and where they would work. Argentine citizens by and large will not work under those conditions.

We should point out that Argentina has a large middle class, almost on the same scale as the United States and Canada, at least in the Buenos Aires metropolitan area. The presence of large numbers of relatively affluent middle-class citizens with high mobility desires results in a thriving building industry that profits from the availability of large groups of unskilled laborers willing to live in precarious conditions. Middle-class Argentines invest in apartments, especially in vacant apartments they have no intention of renting or occupying; this is to validate their status claims and to guard against inflation. Real estate in the Buenos Aires area is one of the best investments for those not wishing to see their money lose its value through the inflation rates, which usually top 100 percent annually. Inflation and the Argentine myth of status through property ownership combine to create a vigorous demand for labor.

Attention has been paid to the psychology of spending and status among *porteño* (Buenos Aires area) Argentines by a number of writers in various disciplines.[11] The balance sheet comes down to this: Argentines (especially the *porteños*) need to feel and herald their claim to a superior culture (borrowed in part from Europe); this superiority depends in part upon ostentatious domination of others; one dominates by speculating in empty apartments, not only to show off one's business prowess but also to control the behavior of others who would like to rent or buy. The less fortunate must be kept in their place; it is the special fear of *porteños* that someone might think they have become mongrelized by mixing with the Indians (Bolivians, Paraguayans) or with the blacks (Brazilians). Therefore, the domination of Bolivians, Paraguayans, and (occasionally) Brazilians who do the dirty work of building construction in Buenos Aires is a reassurance to the *porteño* in search of status. (*Porteños* have even incorporated into their *lunfardo*, or jargon, such disparaging word usages as *muy boliviano*, or "very Bolivian," to describe someone who is lazy or slow.) It also is well to maintain the migrant workers in ghettos so as to avoid the unsightly appearance of the rural folk (called *cabecitas negras*, or "black heads") mixing too freely with the superior European society.

The migrant laborers, thus, depend for their living on the status whims of the European *porteños*, who in turn keep the dependency cycle going with their financial investments and discriminatory social norms. This is a sad relationship, but both the exploiters and the exploited need to continue that relationship in order to survive. For the middle class *porteños* the principal commodity is self-esteem vis-à-vis others: the celebration of status and deference values through investment and conspicuous consumption. For the migrant workers the principal commodity is security-food-shelter, obtained through physical work.

Johnson's 1976 study began with a poor slum district in Buenos Aires and a priest who organized the slum dwellers into a relevant political movement. The priest, Father Carlos Mujica, lost his life while working to improve the circumstances of life for the itinerant poor. The slum in question, known formally as Villa Comunicaciones de Retiro, had railroad tracks on one side, the Buenos Aires naval yards on another, and a major post office center on a third. The overall slum was informally called Villa Retiro. The term *villa* ties in with the expression *villa miseria* ("miseryville"), which means "slum" in Argentina. About 1,200 families lived in the Villa Retiro neighborhood under study. Nearly 85 percent were from Bolivia, and of these at least half were reported to be living and working illegally in Argentina. During the course of the study, the Argentine military invaded the area several times looking for subversives, weapons, and illegal aliens. Just about anyone could be picked up as an illegal alien, despite the amnesty that had been declared and the program of legalizing illegal aliens. In fact, the Villa Retiro slum existed in the shadow of the very naval base where the Argentine national immigration center was then housed.

It was the habit of the illegals to form colonies within the slums where it would be clear that "Bolivians live in this sector" and "Paraguayans live over there." New migrants were recruited by mail. People arrived every week in Villa Retiro and asked where the Comunicaciones subdivision (that closest to the postal facility) or *barrio* (neighborhood) was. The caretaker priest of the neighborhood had set up a help center, a place with volunteers to aid persons newly arrived from Bolivia who needed a place to live and some food. Many of the migrants could not read. Many had no documents of any kind, but called themselves Bolivians and knew their place of birth.

Those who came with documents often had been robbed of them; in Buenos Aires, as in most international centers, there is a flourishing business in stolen travel documents. A few Bolivians admitted having sold their identity papers while traveling in order to eat. Later, they regretted having done so, especially when an employer asked for identification as a requisite for getting paid. Such requests occurred frequently when an unscrupulous foreman suspected that a worker was new, lacked Argentine friends to help him, and had no documentation. In fact, one of the most frequent complaints of the workers in Villa Retiro was that their illegal status could be used as a pretext for low wages and, ultimately, for not paying at all. Firsthand impressions of the Argentine slum showed few people who appeared to be starving, at least in comparison with the wretchedness one finds around Mexico City or in Colombia or Peru. Argentina has always prided itself on being the land where everyone eats meat, regularly and generously. The itinerant Bolivians in the slum did seem to be eating at least adequately.

Father Carlos Mujica had created a church called Chapel of Christ the Worker and a medical center where limited care was available. Government funds had been secured for a teacher and a school. University student volunteers maintained a day-care center in the chapel. But when Father Mujica was assassinated in May 1974, the spirit of change in this slum parish began to diminish. The Argentine establishment was fearful of the power of organized workers. The General Confederation of Workers, part of the populist apparatus created by President Juan Domingo Perón, was part of that establishment. While one group of Peronists preached an appeal to the illegal alien workers, competing groups feared erosion of their power. The Peronist tradition of *descamisados* ("shirtless ones") proclaimed that all the poor and itinerant were welcome, but the fact of Peronist political life was that skilled Argentine workers (and not a few unskilled ones) saw the Bolivians as a threat should they become organized by anybody, even by a priest. Organized labor in Argentina had become something of a closed society. The dirty jobs were left for the Bolivians and Paraguayans. Any attempt to organize them, even without the intention of forming a syndicate, was suspect. And then there was the matter of ideology, Marxist ideology in particular.

The Peronist movement had split into at least two general sectors that can be roughly labeled as fascist and Marxist (this oversimplification is needed simply to lay the basic outline of what happened), with the former based in the old-line Peronists of the first Perón era (1945-55) and the latter sector growing out of the newer Peronist generations, those whose first real triumph as activists was realized in the second era (1973-76). Father Mujica and his slum dweller organization, Villeros de Perón, belonged to what was nominally the Marxist sector, although Mujica himself was not a Marxist. Some of his collaborators in the Villa Retiro project were members of a guerrilla band calling itself Montoneros. Late in 1973 the Montoneros decided to merge with another organization, and embraced Marxism as their official ideology. Montonero leader Mario Firmenich told the slum dwellers to choose between his organization and the sector that Father Mujica represented. The *villeros* chose Father Mujica. Soon thereafter Mujica was murdered. It was an unpopular act, and in an era in which almost every political assassination was publicly acknowledged by someone, his death remained a mystery. But it is no mystery that he had successfully organized the slum dwellers, many of whom were illegal aliens from Bolivia. And they had rejected Marxism, not at all what one would have predicted after listening to the stories of "red hordes" from the north threatening to engulf Buenos Aires in "mestizo communism."

The first Perionist, Juan Domingo Perón, had been ousted by a military coup in 1955 and forced to spend 18 years in exile. A court-martial board had found him guilty of murder, rape, robbery, and other acts "unacceptable" for an Argentine president. It took 18 years of coups and bad public management in Argentina for people to forget what Perón had done, and in late 1972 and early 1973 he appeared as a unity symbol to many. His homecoming meant the beginning of the great national accord. On his first visit to Argentina since his exile, he visited Father Mujica's slum parish, an impressive symbolic gesture. Mrs. Perón, who succeeded her husband in the presidency in 1974, had entered the Mujica chapel in Villa Retiro. When she left, the *villeros* presented her with the flag of Argentina and a flag of Bolivia. The *villeros* of Father Mujica had dual national loyalties.

Peronism's second era collapsed in March 1976, when the military intervened in what had become administrative chaos and near political anarchy.[12] One of the first things the military junta did to Villa Retiro was to bulldoze it and relocate all the aliens at the periphery of Buenos Aires. Some aliens were given publicly financed apartments, but most were simply abandoned to construct other *villas* with whatever they could find. From our interviews in Buenos Aires during 1980, we learned that many of the former *villeros* had been deported to Bolivia, and that the remainder continued the work patterns of the past. Argentina's economic boom in 1980 had meant employment opportunities for migrant workers, in contrast with the recession that was ripping North America.

What was the impact of the Villa Retiro alien community on the greater Buenos Aires area from 1973 to 1976, roughly the period under study? The 1,200 families averaged slightly over two laborers per household (counting sons, brothers, and uncles within a family unit). They helped to construct over 400 apartment buildings in Buenos Aires, according to one former community leader. They paid millions of pesos in taxes. They made social welfare contributions and often were charged union dues without ever receiving the benefits that were implied.

Had Father Mujica's project continued as planned, these workers would have received their benefits, and perhaps Argentine citizenship as well. We were told in 1980 that the military government that replaced the Peronists was uncomfortable with the great Retiro slum alongside its naval establishment and train depot; moreover, it was sometimes visible from the upper floors of the recently built Sheraton hotel — and was unsightly. The *villeros* had to go, and they went. Most important, probably, they had yielded up their "surplus value" in order that Argentines might continue their self-indulgence, conspicuous consumption, and looking down on the *cabecitas negras*, the illegal alien workers who had made it all possible.

PARAGUAYAN EMIGRATION: THE EXPATRIATION OF WORKERS AND INTELLECTUALS

The 1980 estimated population of Paraguay is 3.0 million, a figure that may double within 22 years and reach some 5.3 million inhabitants in 2000. Paraguay's birth rate is high, 3.1 percent annually.[13] Throughout much of its recent history Paraguay has been an emigrant country; domestic turmoil, dictatorship, repression, and war have united to drive the people of the Guaraní nation away from their home. In his study of the Paraguayan "brain drain" Andrés Flores Colombino notes that one cannot study the real flow of Paraguayans into the surrounding countries on the basis of official figures; these yield low migratory profiles because the preponderance of the Paraguayan emigration is clandestine and unsanctioned.[14] The number of clandestine migrants from Paraguay and the other countries bordering Argentina who, according to Flores Colombino, came forth and regularized their situations in Argentina in 1964-67 is shown in Table 5.6.

TABLE 5.6
Legalized Resident Aliens in Argentina
from Neighboring Countries, 1964-67

Nationality	*Number*
Chilean	49,108
Bolivian	42,673
Brazilian	4,795
Paraguayan	54,469
Uruguayan	4,336
Total	155,381

Source: Andrés Flores Colombino, *La fuga de intelectuales: Emigración paraguaya* (Montevideo: Editorial del Autor, 1972), p. 42.

Obviously, during those years Paraguayans were far more numerous than any other national group in the total of clandestine migrants who gained legal status. Flores Colombino assumes that the figure above is an impartial and proportional reflection of the overall clandestine residency of nationals of those five countries in Argentina; if that is true, it can be claimed that Paraguay, having the next to smallest population of the five states, has contributed more than any of the others to Argentina's population. A glance at the map reveals the geographic circumstances that would favor such migration. After Argentina it is Brazil and Uruguay that have "received the human richness of Paraguay."[15] History has been cruel to the people of Paraguay; like the Irish they are often found in greatest abundance outside their homeland. Because Flores Colombino's study of their flight, often clandestine, is unique in the genre, we have elected to make a special case of it here.

Paraguayan émigrés are described as uprooted people in the best of their productive years, attractive and virile, natural farmers and builders, and perpetually nostalgic for their native soil. They are people of honor who possess a simple but sincere culture that is transmitted orally in the Guaraní language. They are people to be proud of, but lamentably they are in difficulty with the authorities of neighboring countries. This is "for lack of documentation, because the Paraguayan exile is an errant pariah, persecuted, who has entered clandestinely into the country of refuge; later, in the fiestas and patriotic affairs which the exiled Paraguayans celebrate as subcultures, you will hear native Guaraní orchestras and see their fireworks at the time of Christmas."[16]

Paraguay emerged from the disastrous Chaco War of the 1930s with thousands of citizens homeless. In 1936 the February Rebellion created another wave of émigrés. Another violent change of government in 1940 provoked additional emigration that helped to establish 11 new towns in the northern Argentina province of Formosa.[17] Much of the colonization of northern Argentina in those years can be laid to the forced, yet unsanctioned, emigration of Paraguayans. In the provinces of Misiones, Corrientes, Formosa, and Chaco the Paraguayans provided agricultural and forestry workers, ranch hands and some ranch foremen, river port workers, and some urban professionals. A few Paraguayans established businesses. There also emerged a special kind of Paraguayan immigrant called *inmigrante golondrina*, a worker who goes here and there, like a swallow who crosses the Argentine (or Brazilian) border each year to work at temporary labor and who returns to Paraguay with his earnings.[18] They are similar to the migrant Mexican workers in the United States and Canada whose yearly itinerary is almost predictable.

Some of the Paraguayan migrants are known to have several "homes" away from home, and the yearly cycle takes them to all of these; they ultimately return to Paraguay if all goes well. The existence of such cyclic migratory patterns constitutes something of an infrastructure for the continued clandestine migration of other Paraguayans — a kind of "underground railway" like the one used by the clandestine Mexican migrants in North America. Flores Colombino notes that the infrastructure so constituted "offers aid that is both emotional and economic to the new members of the transplanted culture, thereby producing a higher degree of personal adaptation. This appears to be the basic mechanism of the Paraguayan migration. This facilitates not only the clandestine exodus of workers but of students who also go with well defined interests and goals."[19] Students migrate toward Buenos Aires when the academic year opens there, just as the field hands go to northern Argentina to harvest cotton and to work on the sugar plantations.

Another internal rebellion in 1947 sent still more waves of Paraguayans, estimated to total some 400,000, into the neighboring countries. Beginning with 1947, it is possible to speak with greater clarity about Paraguayan migration into Argentina. There was a constant increase in registered migrants into Argentina between 1947 and 1955, the year when the Stroessner dictatorship in Paraguay consolidated its power. In this period more than 20,000 persons migrated annually from Paraguay into Argentina, and in 1958 some 32,400

Paraguayans were registered. In 1964 the figure rose to 34,700 émigrés from Paraguay. It is assumed that these "legal" figures have an "illegal" counterpart that is at least as great, and probably greater. It is believed, then, that in the 1950s and 1960s perhaps 100,000 Paraguayans moved legally into Argentina. If at least the same number entered illegally, then roughly 250,000 of Paraguay's population had been driven by want or persecution beyond its borders, a migratory phenomenon without historical precedent in that region.[20] Flores Colombino estimated that as many as 400,000 illegal Paraguayan aliens could be residing in Argentina in 1967, making the total migration well over 500,000.[21] His estimates are sufficiently cautious, and his access to Argentine governmental archives and immigration personnel sufficiently generous, to lend credence to the estimates he gives. By 1972 he could speak in terms of 1 million Paraguayans living in Argentina:

> The Argentine Republic, that regional superpower which absorbs voraciously our population more so than does any other neighboring country, determines of and by itself (now and to the extent that Paraguay should remain in its present relatively under-developed state) the future direction of Paraguayan emigration . . . and this is interesting to contemplate given that the Argentine government maintains that it still has great immigration possibilities, that some 80 percent of its territory is insufficiently inhabited.[22]

But Flores Colombino believes that Argentina's neighbors are themselves underpopulated, and should they ever achieve government by enlightened social planners, they would need their own policies for attracting back the population they have lost over the years to Argentina, Brazil, and Uruguay. To a certain degree, also, it would appear that the development of Argentina has benefited from the sacrifices of Paraguayans and others who were expelled from their native lands, for whatever reason, and whose underpaid toil was in a major contribution to Argentina's economic growth.

Out of every 100 students who enter primary school in Paraguay, only 6 can expect to reach high school. Only a tiny fraction of the population, thus, can realistically think of going to college. Paraguay has two universities, one Catholic and one run by the state. In practice there is no academic freedom of the sort needed in the social sciences — indeed, the social sciences scarcely exist. Veterinary medicine, agronomy, and pharmacy are among the major fields of study offered. Politically "dangerous" fields are closely controlled. Students in search of free-inquiry programs could traditionally go to Uruguay until that country's democratic freedoms were ended by a military fist in 1973. So long as one stayed out of the politics of Argentina, it was possible there to enjoy considerable freedom of inquiry in sociology, economics, and related fields. "In Argentina there is no limit on student enrollment, although some Argentine universities have qualifying entrance exams but usually they are easily passed. That is the country where the great majority of the expatriated Paraguayan students go, given the superior cultural development of Argentina and the common language shared with Paraguay."[23]

Paraguay can expect to generate few university students if the university is a real option only for offspring of the upper classes. Paraguay's upper class was some 4.6 percent of the population in 1972 (compared with 3 percent in Haiti and 4 percent in Honduras), in contrast with 35 percent in Argentina and Uruguay.[24] University careers, along with military service, were and are traditional avenues for upward socioeconomic mobility for the small middle class in Paraguay. They are also avenues for the small upper class to preserve its elite status. For this reason little effort is made to offer the university to the lower classes. By going to Argentina and Uruguay, however, it has been possible for "poor students" to gain at least a touch of intellectual stature. Again, recent political developments, especially in Uruguay, make it uncertain to what degree Paraguayans can profit from emigration if they have university careers in mind. Uruguay in 1980 was under such a hard military rule that little academic freedom was possible.

In 1966 there were 595 Paraguayan university students studying in various Argentine universities, 280 in Brazil, and 140 in Uruguay. There were, in contrast, 18 in the Soviet Union and 25 in the United States.[25] Of the Argentine total some 400 were in the Buenos Aires area. The number in Uruguay had been drastically reduced by 1980. No figures in 1980 were available there or in Argentina, but at least the latter country's universities continued to be open to Paraguayans without regard to the legality of their status. Paraguayans could still be seen as university subcultures in both Argentina and Uruguay. Flores Colombino cites Darcy Ribeiro, the Brazilian anthropologist and one-time politician, to the effect that the dominant groups in Uruguay and Argentina were European transplants, maintaining their "ethnic profile, their language and original culture," against whom the Paraguayans would stand out as a "subproduct" that had resulted from their miscegenation and acculturation over the centuries with Indians, blacks, and various Europeans.[26]

Some 4,000 Paraguayan students at all levels were residing in Uruguay (about half in Montevideo) at the time of Flores Colombino's research, and it was possible to generalize their socioeconomic and political impact as a subculture, using their various organizations as a key. It was believed that the Uruguayan experience reflected university student integration in Argentina as well, keeping in mind that the military dictatorship imposed in Uruguay from 1973 on had restricted the functioning of university students' organizations.

In 1972 the Paraguayan students in Uruguay were involved in seven professional unions (*asociaciones gremiales*) having the word Paraguay in the title — for instance the College of Exiled Paraguayan Lawyers. Included in the seven groups was a center for exiled Paraguayan students, which served many clandestine migrants. In addition there were six social institutions, four cultural organizations, one Paraguayan news agency in exile, twelve political parties that were both Uruguayan and Paraguayan in scope of action, nine political movements (the distinction between parties and movements here remains unclear), and three Uruguayan institutions pledged to support Paraguayan causes. In all this meant some 42 socioeconomic and political influence groups that were active on behalf of Paraguayans in Uruguay at the beginning of the 1970s. It is not known how many of their members or clients were also illegal aliens, but certainly many were. By joining forces with other student exiles, the Paraguayans contributed to student solidarity drives of an international scope. Although there are no hard figures, it was believed that nearly half of the Paraguayan exiles had emigrated clandestinely in order to avoid being readily located by agents from their "home" government.

The basic settlement unit of the exiled Paraguayans was the group. Accommodations were frequently rented in the name of a group. This facilitated a tie-in with the "underground railway" of clandestine migrants and spared many students the anxiety of finding themselves alone in an unfamiliar environment. It also helped the new arrivals to locate jobs, which was especially critical for those whose families in Paraguay were unable to send regular financial support. Some 53.5 percent of the students in Flores Colombino's study would have had difficulty in obtaining the necessities of life in Uruguay without some outside income.[27] Most of them suffered a period of longing for home and even paranoia, especially when they encountered the familiar points of social attention in Buenos Aires — which had meaning for Argentines but little social significance for the Paraguayans[28] but still reminded them that other such symbols existed at home. This was an easier problem to overcome for the student who emigrated legally, was not exiled, and therefore had the option of returning to Paraguay. The sense of alienation that went with clandestine emigration was and is undoubtedly greater, thus the great importance of the network of settlement groups established in Argentina to assist the new migrants who came clandestinely.

In the Montevideo study Flores Colombino found that 51.1 percent of the Paraguayan students who completed their university education did not return to Paraguay.[29] This included both sanctioned and clandestine migrants. The intellectual loss to Paraguay is obvious. If there is a positive side, it is stated in terms of potential: those émigrés who later return can place Paraguayan reality in a realistic comparative perspective that may eventually become a force for progressive change. That is a slim hope, especially where professional talent is concerned.

It was the contention during the 1970s that Paraguay had a total of 3,607 professionals (doctors, engineers, teachers), of whom 2,877 were concentrated in the capital city Asunción. This meant that 78 percent of the nation's professionals concentrated their attention on only 15 percent of the total population. This, combined with an annual population increase of more than 3 percent, plus the "brain drain" into other countries, meant that Paraguay's university system could never hope to keep up with the national need for professional training.[30] In light of this, the clandestine emigration of professionals would be serious unless compensated for by a corresponding emigration of citizens who would need those professionals' services. Emigration of all kinds out of Paraguay has been remarkable, but it seems not to have alleviated the pressing need for trained professionals.

Perhaps most serious was the ratio of doctors to patients. In 1970, Paraguay had 0.4 doctors per 1,000 inhabitants.[31] That ratio would require a truly mammoth emigration of population, with little or no emigration of physicians, to improve the balance significantly. As Argentina now experiences its own "brain drain" of physicians to the more developed countries, there is an attraction for Paraguayan doctors to migrate to Argentina. True, most of the emigration of medical doctors is not clandestine, but with the massive clandestine popular migration out of Paraguay and into Argentina, it is not surprising for the doctors to follow their potential patients. The overall loss to Paraguay is patent. Nor will it change so long as Paraguayan state support for professionals depends upon "that rigid and deplorable law/custom which, for more than the last twenty years, has made acquisition of public office depend upon one's adherence to and support of the incumbent political regime."[32]

In broad terms are there any positive consequences of the flight of intellectuals from Paraguay? To the degree that the émigrés engage in creative endeavors outside Paraguay that contribute to the general store of knowledge that can later be applied for the benefit of Paraguay, there is some indirect or residual benefit. But few of the advances achieved elsewhere can be applied over the short term in so backward a country as Paraguay. And of all the sorts of emigration that can occur, that of the intellectuals is perhaps the most lamentable, since they are the best prepared to lead Paraguay toward socioeconomic and political change. A nation that exports its trained specialists is destined to be governed by the worst who remain behind.[33]

CONCLUSIONS ON MIGRATORY PATTERNS IN THE SOUTHERN CONE

For most of the region under study, the direction of change in Argentina is the key to migratory trends. Were Argentina effectively to block the clandestine migration of Bolivians and Paraguayans across its borders, this would surely place enormous social and political pressures on the regimes that dominate the two countries. Closing the border between Argentina and Brazil would have little effect anywhere except in Misiones province, and stopping the clandestine migration from Chile would have negligible importance to the latter country's regime. Bolivia and Paraguay are surely the countries to be more strongly affected should migratory access to Argentina be blocked. Insofar as the "brain drain" out of Argentina may attract a "brain drain" from the surrounding countries to fill that void, any change in the flow of professionals from Argentina could affect neighboring countries. To the degree that legal migration of professionals becomes more difficult, the illegal migration of professionals and intellectuals may be encouraged.

In 1977 the Argentine government mounted a campaign to attract its expatriate professionals home. A decree law signed by the president, General Jorge Videla, offered duty-free entry on a wide range of capital goods (excluding automobiles) to expatriate Argentines who could prove they had lived outside the country for at least one year.[34] This was later expanded to give special preference to those whose specialty was considered critical in Argentina and to those who would be willing to relocate to one of the provincial areas where population input was needed. Should this program, or others like it, become highly successful, it could put limitations on the legal migration of professionals into Argentina and stimulate their clandestine migration. An economic collapse in Argentina, one adversely affecting the building trades, could produce a similar result insofar as unskilled migrant workers are concerned.

If the main course of international migration in the Southern Cone depends principally upon the absorptive capability of Argentina, and barring some catastrophe such as a war between the South American superpowers, then we must look to internal changes in the remaining countries that will affect migration, both legal and clandestine. Revolution against the military regime of Chile could provoke new waves of outward migration. Should Bolivian politics become involved in the internecine warfare of drugs, as has happened in Colombia, then new migratory exile groups could appear from that direction. Economic collapse in Uruguay, which is a distinct possibility, would undoubtedly send thousands more south into Argentina and north into Brazil. The collapse of the Paraguayan dictatorship could have various migratory consequences for all neighboring countries. But what about the people who cannot flee Paraguay?

We have not talked about them because they do not constitute clandestine migrants in the international context of this book. But in another and distinct cultural context they should be mentioned, if only briefly. These are the traditional hunting and gathering societies that still exist not only in Paraguay but also in Brazil, Bolivia, and elsewhere. The Aché Indians of Paraguay are being systematically exterminated, in the sense of ethnocide and genocide, by forced emigration out of their traditional sacred forests and lands. They have been placed in concentration camps where they are dehumanized, deculturized, starved, and exterminated. According to all the reasonable laws of nature, the forced alienage of the Aché is an illegal and immoral migration that is imposed upon these peace-loving people by the Paraguayan regime and its foreign friends. These include the governments of the United States and Israel, plus a host of multinational companies. The tragedy of the Achés is well documented. And it could be considered directly relevant to the phenomenon of clandestine migration in the Southern Cone.[35]

How can a regime that directs the annihilation of its own people, in order to take their valuable forests, be expected to create a social and economic infrastructure capable of caring for and absorbing its own people so that they won't be forced to emigrate clandestinely? How can one appeal to social science to solve the problems of the Aché, or those of the clandestine migrants, when "social science, in striving to be value-free, recognizes no joyous or suffering humanity, only the play of ghostly abstractions emptied of sentient and needful men."[36] In violating the Aché we all lose something of the world's cultural heritage. If preservation of culture is a requisite for the good life, how can we possibly pretend to solve such complicated problems as clandestine migration when the people we must appeal to are in the business of exterminating culture — ethnocide? This leaves us with few alternatives other than massive and violent revolution. One approach may be a hemispheric community/regional government concept. But how can that be instituted, in time to protect the Aché, in time to rescue the Bolivians sentenced to life in a *villa miseria*? The United States and Canada, with their enormous hemispheric influence, could be instrumental in this quest before it is too late for peaceful means to work.

NOTES

1. Population Reference Bureau, *1979 World Population Data Sheet* (Washington, D.C.: Population Reference Bureau, 1980).

2. Federación Argentina de la Industria Gráfica y Afines, *Argentina: Un país latino-americano* (Buenos Aires: Editorial FAIGA, 1977), p. 12.

3. Ibid., p. 13.

4. Interviews by Kenneth F. Johnson with C. Garrido, Argentine national immigration center, Buenos Aires, 1980.

5. *St. Louis Post-Dispatch*, August 13, 1980.

6. *Globe and Mail* (Toronto), March 15, 1980.

7. Ibid.

8. Instituto Nacional de Estadística y Censos, *La migración interna en la Argentina 1960/70* (Buenos Aires: Instituto Nacional de Estadística y Censos), p. 31.

9. Kenneth F. Johnson, "Life and Death of Carlos Mujica," *Latin American Digest* 11, no. 1 (Fall 1976): 8-12.

10. See *International Migration Review* no. 44 (1978) and no. 47 (1979).

11. For instance, H. Ernest Lewald, *Argentina: Análisis y autoanálisis* (Buenos Aires: Editorial Sudamericana, 1969), passim.

12. Background for this is in Kenneth F. Johnson, *Peronism: The Final Gamble* (London: Institute for the Study of Conflict, 1974).

13. Population Reference Bureau, *1979 World Population Data Sheet*.

14. Andrés Flores Colombino, *La fuga de intelectuales: Emigración paraguaya* (Montevideo: Editorial del Autor, 1972).

15. Ibid., p. 43.

16. Ibid., pp. 45-46.

17. Ibid., p. 71.

18. Ibid., p. 73.

19. Ibid., pp. 73-74.

20. Ibid., p. 76.

21. Ibid., p. 79.

22. Ibid., pp. 79-80.

23. Ibid., p. 125.

24. Ibid., p. 131.
25. Ibid., p. 133.
26. Ibid., p. 136.
27. Ibid., p. 148.
28. Ibid., p. 153.
29. Ibid., p. 158.
30. Ibid., p. 181.
31. Ibid., p. 184.
32. Ibid., p. 210.
33. Ibid., pp. 233-34.
34. Ministerio del Interior, Argentina, *Texto del decreto del poder ejecutivo nacional no. 464, sobre programas especiales de radicación e instalación de extranjeros* (Buenos Aires: Poder Ejecutivo Nacional, 1977). Pamphlet of decree law made available by the Dirección National de Migraciones.
35. A more rational (but by no means less sinister) way of looking at the tie between the clandestine emigration of displaced Paraguayans and the persecution of the Achés is as follows: Poverty and repression force much of the available labor force to emigrate clandestinely. This leaves a void in the labor pool that is partially filled by enslaving the Achés and other aboriginal peoples to make them fill that void; in the process the valuable lands of the Indians, especially their hardwood forests, are taken from them. The question is whether stopping the clandestine emigration would save the Achés.
36. See Richard Arens, ed., *Genocide in Paraguay* (Philadelphia: Temple University Press, 1976), p. 56 and passim.

6

EXTRALEGAL POPULATION TRANSFERS: CONCLUSIONS AND POLICY DEVELOPMENT

INTRODUCTION

Western industrial democracies generally boast of their large middle classes and the virtual nonexistence of a subsistence working class. A close look at the illegal migration to the United States and receiver countries in Latin America has revealed that the subsistence level has not disappeared but, rather, has developed into a large clandestine stratum. The demand for cheap labor to do the unpleasant and unskilled jobs continues in the industrialized and industrializing societies, but the prevailing wage structure and the social welfare benefits available to the domestic work force are such that it has become difficult to find an adequate supply of exploitable labor within the domestic population. The marginal laborer in industrial societies like the United States is unlikely to find the low wages and poor working conditions in labor-intensive agriculture or the urban sweatshops a sufficient incentive to abandon the social-welfare benefits available to the chronically unemployed. In the industrializing receiver states of Latin America, the illegal alien finds a demand for his or her services in the low-paying tertiary sector or in agriculture to replace the upwardly mobile domestic population. In sum, industrialization has not eliminated the demand for marginal workers, only the supply of those willing to work for subsistence wages.

The illegal aliens have become the new lumpenproletariat of industrialized societies and, like the lumpenproletariat of the presocial-welfare state, are social outcasts. In times of prosperity and high employment they are encouraged to "fill in" the unskilled labor market, but during hard times they are the scapegoats for the economic woes that plague society. Illegal aliens allow the economy the luxury of reducing unemployment (or at least seeming to do so) by reducing the supply of labor rather than by creating new jobs. The benefits of illegal population transfers to the receiver country are many. They provide a

163

ready source of cheap labor, lower food costs, elasticity in the supply of labor, and an uncomplaining work force to do the unpleasant jobs.

Likewise, the sender country acquires certain important benefits. The significance of an employment/population safety valve is difficult to overstate. A restless, unemployed population has an alternative to starvation and revolution that is mutually beneficial to the worker, his or her dependents, and the government of the sending country. Cornelius (see Chapter 3) estimated that over 20 percent of the Mexican population was directly dependent on the earnings of Mexican nationals working illegally in the United States. Comparable estimates for Colombia, El Salvador, Bolivia, the Dominican Republic, Haiti, and other sender countries are not available, but it seems fair to assume that the figures there would also be high. For example, if one takes the figure of 1.5 million Colombians working illegally in Venezuela, and many more working in Ecuador, Panama, the United States, and elsewhere, then a very high percentage of Colombia's 30 million citizens must also depend on the illegal workers. There are, of course, costs to both the sender and the receiver countries, but they tend to be long-term or ethical, or to be incurred by the aliens; these are not the kinds of concerns that prompt policy decisions.

The ethical costs to the societies involved are associated with the inevitable human rights violations that the receiver countries may visit upon the aliens and the humiliation that the sender countries (should) experience in not being able to provide jobs for their own citizens, thus forcing them into degrading, slavelike living and working conditions. Illegal aliens are always vulnerable to social, economic, and legal exploitation, yet they continue to find the conditions more tolerable than those at home. The preceding chapters have documented a wide variety of human rights violations experienced by the illegal aliens, and the evidence shows striking similarities in those violations, be they in Canada, the United States, Paraguay, Venezuela, or elsewhere. The receiver society rationalizes that the treatment of aliens is not all that bad, since they continue to come and, after all, they are lawbreakers. The sender society masks its humiliation with frequent indignant statements about the inhuman treatment *paisanos* suffer abroad, adding that all people have a right to work for a living.[1]

The long-term costs to the sender society are substantial. The employment safety valve and windfall foreign earnings encourage the sender society to avoid making the hard policy decisions concerning wealth redistribution that are so critical to the development of a "livability strategy" for the future.[2] Since the sender society is dependent on the loose enforcement of immigration laws in the receiver state, a policy shift within the receiver state could throw the sender society into social, economic, and political chaos. What would happen, for example, if the United States were to deport 2 or 3 million Mexican nationals or Venezuela were to deport 1.5 million Colombians? For the receiver country the long-term costs are also great. The presence of illegal aliens tends to depress wages in some areas and results in artificially low prices for some food and clothing items. The availability of illegal alien workers for low wages understandably discourages many on welfare from seeking employment, while the society develops an ever greater dependency on the new lumpenproletariat. What would happen if Mexicans, Colombians, Haitians, Bolivians, and illegal aliens from other countries just stayed home?

Finally, the rights of the illegal alien are ignored. Treated as a criminal in most receiver states, his plight is generally of little consequence to policy makers. A memorable comment made by a large farmer to Edward R. Murrow in the famous 1960 "Harvest of Shame" television documentary summed it up: "In the past we owned our slaves, now we just rent them." Yet in some respects the illegal is worse off legally and economically. Under slavery the owner had a moral and legal responsibility for his "chattels," even though he did not necessarily live up to those responsibilities. Illegal aliens, as "free" men and women, are seldom considered to be the responsibility of employers, or anyone else.[3]

In sum, extralegal population transfers in the Western Hemisphere have been responsible for the symbiotic relationships between the poorer sender states and the wealthier receiver states. The magnitude of the population transfers appears to be directly related to the degree of interdependence. The costs of sustaining the relationship are easily ignored because those who must immediately bear them are not politically powerful. Moreover, politicians who concern themselves with abstract ethical issues or the long-term dangers generally find little political consideration. But, as we have tried to show throughout this study, the illegal alien phenomenon is symptomatic of much deeper social, economic, and political problems. Everyone recognizes that there is chronic poverty in the Western Hemisphere, but few seem willing to admit that the structure of that poverty is such that several states may no longer be capable of carrying even the destitute. That is, the carrying capacity[4] of several states has been exceeded, and only three possibilities exist under those circumstances: a sharp and immediate population reduction to a level that can be supported (genocide); a drastic and immediate increase in the state's carrying capacity (revolution or reforms that allow for better wealth distribution and lower expectations); immediate population transfers that reduce the population size to a supportable level.

It is extremely difficult to pinpoint a "threshold" at which a state's carrying capacity can be said to have been surpassed. The survival instinct in humans is strong, and most will not wait until extinction is imminent to react. Therefore, it seems reasonable to assume that extralegal population transfers occur before the threshold is reached. Perhaps the real danger is that the problem is defined in legalistic terms, whereas carrying capacity is determined by biological considerations. To the poor, survival may take precedence over laws, treaties, and executive agreements that legally define the population transfers, but policy makers operate within the framework of the sanctity of the sovereign nation-state. Not only does this hamper efforts to find answers for the pressing problems of population transfers, but it makes it extremely difficult for policy makers to recognize the real questions.

The most fundamental question is whether the population transfers in the Western Hemisphere are an indication that the poor are now seeking the promise and upward mobility of the industrial world, or a signal that the ability (or willingness) of some nation-states to support the existing population is being severely strained. A definitive answer is not yet known, and much more work needs to be done. On the basis of our investigation, however, we are inclined to believe that extralegal population transfers are an indicator that the existing and growing population is not being supported. The pattern of the extralegal population transfers and the policies that have been devised in response lead us to conclude that we are heading for a major crisis.

PATTERNS AND POLICIES

The clandestine nature of extralegal population transfers makes it difficult to gather data scientifically on the illegal alien. But profiling illegal aliens is a necessary first step, even though it is fraught with methodological risks. Interviewing those who have been apprehended is useful, but one should not assume that this group is "representative." Such interviews may tell us little more than what kinds of people are caught, but on the other hand generalizing about the universe of apprehended illegal aliens may be valuable in and of itself. Our study does in fact include the entire universe of deportable aliens in Toronto and St. Louis within a specified time span. Gathering data on illegal aliens where they work, or after they return to the sender country without being apprehended, is likewise useful, but a caveat should be observed. Accessibility is limited in either case, and the representativeness of the sample is suspect. We have gathered data from statistics on apprehended aliens in various parts of the hemisphere, and have supplemented them with interviews of deported aliens and illegal aliens at their job sites, particularly in eastern Missouri and southern Illinois. While recognizing the data limitations, we feel that the patterns that emerged justify generalizations about the nature of the problem and the appropriateness of the policies being applied. A detailed examination of the universe of illegal aliens will be possible only with a truly representative sample.

It is apparent that illegal migration is primarily the business of the young. Commonly between 16 and 25 years of age, the illegal alien is only infrequently over 35 years old. This conventional wisdom is generally accepted by scholars and public officials alike, meaning that the older illegal has a distinct advantage. He or she is better able to mingle in the host country without detection, and is probably underrepresented in official reports of apprehended aliens. Moreover, the older alien is likely to have established employment and proven techniques of illegal entry. Even so, it seems safe to assume that the vast majority of illegal aliens are young, even if our data on age cohorts are "soft." The consequences of the age distribution are significant for many reasons. It means that the most productive members of the sending society's work force, particularly in the agricultural sector, are abandoning the land and leaving the country to the older, less productive members of society. Second, if young, marriage-age workers emigrate on a permanent or long-term basis, they may well have an impact on the population growth of both the sender and receiver societies, potentially decreasing the rate in the former and increasing the rate in the latter.

The vast majority of illegal aliens in the United States are male, although in Venezuela, and perhaps other regions of Latin America, the number of males and females is nearly equal. Again, our information may reflect a sampling bias. It is possible that women, particularly in the United States, go undetected because the stereotypical image of the illegal alien is that of a young male. Hence, like older males, the female arouses less suspicion and is therefore under-represented among deportees. It is also possible that fewer women are detected because of the nature of their employment. The garment industry sweatshops in New York and California obviously employ thousands of illegal female aliens; but since their employment is not as seasonal as agricultural labor, they are less likely to be reported. Moreover, working in large cities within Hispanic communities affords greater protection. Female illegals of course work in agriculture as well, but their numbers are fewer and they generally work as part of a family unit. Still other female illegal aliens work as domestic servants in the United States, particularly in the major cities and along the border, where they can commute. The nature of their employment gives them a low public profile and reduces the probability of detection.

Female illegal aliens in Latin America tend to suffer the same difficulties as rural-to-urban female migrants. That is, the opportunities for unskilled employment are highly limited. Unfortunately it is true that the two greatest prospects for employment are as domestic servants and as prostitutes. The demand for domestic servants is particularly high in Latin America, where domestic appliances – refrigerators, washers and dryers, power lawnmowers, vacuum cleaners – have not replaced the convenience and status of domestic servants for the middle and upper classes. Moreover, the minimum-wage laws have not limited the affordability of such labor in Latin America as it has in the United States.

Most illegal aliens have comparatively little education and no vocational skills that are marketable. This would logically be the case, since those with education and/or skills are less likely to feel forced to migrate. Migrants with education or skills do migrate, but they find it easier to obtain visas. The low educational attainment of the illegal alien has important consequences for both the sender and the receiver society. Where the magnitude of the population transfer is large, the sender society benefits by the reduction in the level of illiteracy and the size of the unskilled labor force looking for work. The receiver country inherits these problems. There is, therefore, a transfer of ignorance.

Most illegal aliens cross the border without their families. This is partly a function of the age of the migrant and partly of the task's being so difficult and risky that comparatively few wish to try it. Still another factor is the fact that a very high percentage of illegal aliens view the move as temporary. Those who do leave relatives behind generally send a portion of their earnings home to support the family.

Most illegal aliens seem to prefer to cross the border without legal papers. This was particularly true outside Canada and the United States. The difficulty, expense, and time involved in securing permission are major considerations, but beyond that illegal aliens feel that legal papers offer no guarantee of status nor of protection from deportation. On the basis of information we gathered, their skepticism is frequently justified. As a consequence of this clandestine migration, however, it is virtually impossible to know the magnitude of the illegal alien population or its impact on employment or social services. The method of crossing the border is highly individualized. Some cross alone without assistance, some in groups without assistance, and many cross alone or in groups with the aid of a smuggler (coyote). Alien smuggling seems to be a growth industry throughout the hemisphere, although it is unquestionably larger in the United States than elsewhere. In the United States it is so large and relatively unrisky that many specialize by nationality. Along the Mexican border, for example, one finds many who handle nothing but OTMs (other than Mexicans). As the business has grown, so has the tendency to branch out. If one can success-fully smuggle aliens, then why not drugs? Taking that one step further, if one smuggles aliens and drugs, why not aliens with drugs, thereby cutting down the risk to the smuggler?

The probability that an illegal alien will be caught varies greatly from country to country and from alien to alien, depending on his or her personal characteristics, economic prospects, and method and place of entry. The ones most likely to be caught are those entering the United States, young males, those who are crossing for the first time, those who do not enlist the help of a smuggler, those who have not been recruited, and those without a skill in high demand. The longer the illegal alien avoids detection, the lower the probability that he or she will be detected. Most are apprehended within 48 hours and near the border they crossed.

HUMAN DIMENSIONS OF ILLEGAL MIGRATION

Certain patterns of illegal migration in the Western Hemisphere may yield insight into comparable phenomena in other cultural settings. We know, for instance, that poor and deteriorating economic conditions within many Latin American countries are at the root of illegal migration today. Conditions are particularly favorable for such population transfers where (at least compara-tively) rich and poor countries share a common border. Argentina tends to pull illegal aliens from Bolivia, Paraguay, and other neighboring countries; Venezuela draws illegal aliens from Brazil and Colombia; and the United States attracts illegal aliens from Mexico.

The relationship between migration and distance has never been perfect, the Chinese migration to the United States in the nineteenth century being a case in point, although distance barriers in recent years have been all but shattered. The United States attracts increasing numbers of Haitians, Dominicans, Jamaicans, Colombians, and other illegal aliens from all parts of the Western Hemisphere, as well as from Africa. Canada has recently become a large and growing receiver country for illegal aliens, and Venezuela now must contend with illegal aliens from all parts of Latin America and southern Europe. As population pressures increase and economic conditions deteriorate further, perceived opportunities will be of far greater importance than the distances the migrant must travel.

It is of course possible to differentiate between "push" forces and "pull" forces on the migrant, at least in a theoretical sense, but in the final analysis they are usually two sides of the same coin for the destitute. "Pull" forces are more likely to exist, independently, for those who can afford the luxury of dreaming of upward mobility. There is a conservatism of the destitute that generally represses such adventuristic impulses as migration. Desperation, on the other hand, pushes people to seek survival where they can find it. Throughout the hemisphere one finds such desperation. The land available for subsistence farming is insufficient, not only because a disproportionately high percentage of the land remains in the hands of a few, but also because population growth automatically forces many peasants off the land. The "pull" factor is most likely to become important in the selection of a destination or when *enganchadores* (labor recruiters) actively pursue potential illegal aliens with promises of good money.

The deterioration of rural life has pushed peasants into the cities, where they face unemployment, inadequate housing and social services, inflation, and the other pressures of life in urban centers whose population growth far exceeds industrial development and economic capacity. Thus, international migration becomes an extension of the rural-to-urban migration pattern. As population pressures continue to force peasants off the land and as the already overcrowded cities continue to grow without corresponding economic opportunity, illegal migration becomes an increasingly attractive option.

Political repression, which is frequently the handmaiden of economic failure, is a second major correlate of illegal migration. Tens of thousands of Mexicans came to the United States in the first third of the twentieth century to avoid the consequences of backing the "wrong" revolutionary; Colombians fled to Venezuela in the 1940s and 1950s to escape the ravages of *la violencia*; and countless thousands have since left Argentina, Chile, Cuba, El Salvador, Haiti, Nicaragua, and other countries for similar reasons. Such are the more obvious examples of the perception of political repression having resulted in massive exile (ousted leaders receive invitations from sympathetic governments; supporters are left to fend for themselves). On the other hand, a government whose policies exacerbate the poverty, such as Rafael Trujillo's

Dominican Republic, Anastasio Somoza's Nicaragua, or François Duvalier's Haiti, constitute a form of political repression in their own right. That is, where the corrupt governmental administration devises and implements policies that consciously benefit an economic elite at the expense of the masses, it is difficult to make a meaningful distinction between economic and political refugees.

In describing the illegal alien phenomenon in the Western Hemisphere, we have frequently been forced to rely on numbers (body counts if you prefer) to express the magnitude of the population transfers and the suffering that goes with them. We have relied more heavily on statistics in those cases likely to be less familiar to most readers, such as Colombians in Venezuela. Where partic16ipant observation and other forms of qualitative research have been useful, we have tried to avoid an overreliance on numerical evidence. The more one reduces such phenomena to numerical totals, the easier it becomes to dismiss the human dimension. Indeed, this is the heart of the problem, for if human compassion were a thousand times more deeply felt for the injustices suffered by a thousand than for the agony of a single individual, there probably would not be an illegal alien problem, since neither the sender nor the receiver society would tolerate conditions that force the destitute to emigrate under such dehumanizing circumstances.

Unfortunately it seems to be human nature that compassion and empathy are more nearly in inverse proportion to the number of victims. Entire towns can "adopt" Cambodian refugees in the name of humanity but remain tolerant of the threatened extinction of the Cambodian people. One Cambodian is real, with a face, a name, and a personal history of suffering, whereas the Cambodian people are an abstraction. As Phillip Crane puts it, everything beyond the borders of the United States is an "abstraction."

Each alien migrates for personal reasons and because of individual experiences. The stories they tell are similar, but few generalize their experiences beyond themselves and the small circle of illegals with whom they have contact. Most say that they want to provide a decent life for themselves and their families, get enough money to start a business at home, or purchase a house and pay off some outstanding debts. Elsa Chaney relates a conversation she had with an illegal Colombian alien on a flight from New York to Bogotá that illustrates the personal side very nicely. The woman had worked as a maid in the United States for six years. She was on her way home voluntarily. In response to Chaney's question concerning the likelihood of returning, she said:

> Go back to the United States? Ayyyyy, no, señora! I'm 46 years old, and I'm never going back even for a visit. Well, since I was there for so many years without a visa they aren't going to let me in anyway. But I don't care. If my brother and sister want to see me, they'll just have to come to Colombia. I'm never ever again going to leave my family, or my house, or my town.[5]

The woman had left her husband and children to go to New York to work. With the money she sent home, she bought the family a house and furnished it completely, including a television set and a sewing machine – on a salary of $95 a week. Like so many illegal aliens she confessed to being afraid and extremely reluctant to leave her family, but she felt compelled by circumstances to leave her homeland until she could earn enough money to build a better life at home.

To summarize, the poor and deteriorating economic condition of numerous countries in the Western Hemisphere has contributed greatly to the increase in illegal migration in recent years. Having said that, however, it should be pointed out that economic deprivation alone has not produced the large and growing number of illegal migrants. The dynamics of the illegal migration include a number of interrelated factors, among them the following: First, the rapid growth of population has created a critical shortage of agricultural land over and above the scarcity caused by the prevailing latifundia system. Second, the shortage of farmland has pushed a large segment of the rural population into urban areas that cannot provide sufficient jobs, adequate housing, education, or basic social services. Third, where subsistence farming ceases to be possible, economic deprivation is replaced by the struggle to survive. Per capita income has always been a highly misleading measure of poverty. A per capita income of $150 a year, for example, is feasible where one works the land and barters agricultural products for nonagricultural necessities. When that same person is forced off the land and into the money economy, survival at $150 per year becomes impossible.

Fourth, as political and economic elites have sought to modernize their countries' economies through industrial development, they knowingly or unknowingly have exacerbated the problem for the *minifundista*. The cities have taken on the appearance of modernization without the industrial infrastructure. The pull of the cities, combined with the push in the rural sector, has created a large and growing pool of cheap labor that has led to massive unemployment and underemployment. The political and economic elites, taking a cautious business approach to the problem of economic development rather than a "livability strategy," have opted for multinational connections in corporate development and financial dealings that widen the gap between the rich and the poor.

Fifth, the highly industrialized countries in the hemisphere, faced with a perceived need for cheap labor, a supply of which is not readily available in the social welfare state, have welcomed much of the surplus labor of neighboring poor countries (openly or clandestinely), giving further impetus to the extralegal population transfers. Sixth, the growing interdependence of rich and poor countries and their political and economic elites has contributed greatly to strong, frequently violent political reaction within the poorer country (such as Nicaragua) and has been met with strong political repression, further contributing to the alien flow. Seventh, the importation of technology and the improvement of health care has had the unfortunate consequence of contributing to ever greater population growth (through the decline of mortality rates) while limiting the need for more new labor. Eighth, the improved communications and transportation between sender and receiver countries, coupled with the establishment of illegal alien "beachheads," encourages even greater extralegal population transfers.

Treatment of illegal aliens varies throughout the hemisphere. Those with whom we spoke in Canada, the United States, Argentina, and Venezuela were generally rather positive about their work experiences, yet abuses were noted. It seemed that in most cases the treatment of the given alien in his or her country of origin (the "sender" country) was so bad that by comparison the circumstances in the host country seemed favorable. Still, it is clear that employers are generally attracted to illegal alien workers because they are less likely to protest long working hours, poor working conditions, or low wages. In the final analysis the vulnerability of the illegal alien to deportation encourages all manner of exploitation. An illegal alien is in no position to insist on the right to collective bargaining or to contest the outrageous rent and prices that must be paid for food (frequently food must be purchased from the employer). Not surprisingly, throughout the hemisphere employers like illegal aliens because "they don't mind hard work," or "they are better workers than the locals," or "they aren't troublemakers." The obvious common denominator throughout the hemisphere is the vulnerability of the illegal alien. It is fair to generalize that employers welcome the illegal alien, and equally accurate to say that the exploitability of the aliens (either with or without malice) is a fundamental attraction.

The strong symbiotic relationship that has grown between the sender and receiver societies does not benefit the alien, nor does it improve the treatment he or she is likely to experience. While the receiver society has become dependent on a source of unskilled labor, it does not rely on specific laborers. In the flower fields of Encinitas, California, for example, we frequently observed employers hiring large numbers of illegal aliens in the morning, with the intention of choosing among the afternoon survivors for regular employment. Similar practices are common elsewhere, particularly in Venezuela.

It is more difficult to generalize about public reaction to the presence of illegal aliens. As one would expect, those most directly affected by the presence of illegal aliens are the most vocal proponents of a hard-line policy: unskilled laborers, ethnic minorities who may be direct competitors for jobs, and school boards and local governments in areas of high alien density who must provide costly services for a large alien population.

The political influence of the unskilled worker and the ethnic minorities has been low historically, and the potential influence of local officials tends to be canceled out by influential business interests who benefit from the presence of the illegal alien. The *bracero* program experience in the United States during the late 1940s offers instructive examples (see the appendix). The impact of, and need for, the continued presence of illegal alien workers in the United States have drawn cyclical negative reactions from politicians and administrators over the years. Occasional strong protests over the presence of illegal aliens have been voiced in Latin American receiver states as well. Most Latin American states have lacked a strong pluralist political tradition, however, and political leaders have been even less responsive than has been the case in the United States. Consequently we find that in Latin American receiver states, illegal aliens are even more openly invited to work in the marginal jobs.

IMMIGRATION: THE POLITICS OF NONDECISION-MAKING

Richard Craig's *The Bracero Program: Interest Groups and Foreign Policy* presents an excellent analysis of the competing interests that affected the *bracero* program of the 1940s, 1950s, and 1960s.[6] As Craig shows, the numerous ethnic, labor, and business interests actively lobbied the U.S. Congress and administrative branch of government intensively. The resulting policies in the period of the various contract labor programs were frequently vague, sporadically enforced, and sometimes deliberately ignored. Commenting on the 1948-51 period of the *bracero* program, Craig says:

> In contrast to the preceding period, braceros were contracted directly by United States employers with the aid of government officials from both nations. Fulfillment of contract provisions was not guaranteed by the host government. In this and in many other respects the postwar bracero program was the responsibility of United States employers and their representatives. Government interference was held to a minimum. The years 1948-1951 constituted the *laissez faire* era in Mexican migratory labor policy.[7]

Put more bluntly, the government of the United States adopted a policy of "nondecision-making." Peter Bachrach and Morton S. Baratz describe the ambience of nondecision-making as a situation in which the "dominant values, the accepted rules of the game, the existing power relations among groups, and the instruments of force . . . effectively prevent grievances from developing into full-fledged issues which call for decisions."[8] Immigration laws were passed but only selectively enforced. The laws satisfied ethnic groups or labor organizations when they were restrictive, and agricultural interests when they were not; and they were ignored when doing so would pacify certain groups (see appendix for a concrete example).

The politics of nondecision-making seems to be a general pattern in receiver countries. Venezuela, for example, abandoned its pro-immigration stance when it was more profitable and less politically costly to assume a hands-off approach concerning illegal aliens. Canada has generally avoided the issue by not developing a comprehensive policy on visas, although a guest-worker program does exist. Argentina, on the other hand, publicly welcomes undocumented aliens from surrounding countries and privately "regulates" the type and number of such aliens through a practice whereby many are allowed to "disappear," along with thousands of Argentine citizens who oppose the government. Clearly the policy of nondecision-making is one of the most insidious options open to a receiver country, in that it gives tacit consent to myriad human rights violations while postponing the hard decisions that must be made.

POPULATION TRANSFERS AND A "LIVABILITY STRATEGY"

If policies to respond successfully to extralegal population transfers are to be developed, both senders and receivers must respond to the underlying causes rather than merely to the symptoms. Thus far such policies have been formulated as though illegal migration were a result of "pull" forces even though it is generally accepted that "push" forces are more important. For example, receiver countries have stressed tighter border enforcement and greater penalties for those who violate immigration laws (the aliens, those who smuggle aliens, and those who employ the aliens). The general assumption seems to be that if the attractiveness of the receiver country can be reduced — the "pull" force lessened — the aliens will stop coming. Sender countries that argue that the prevention of illegal migration is primarily the responsibility of the country whose laws are being violated seem to be saying the same thing. Of the sender countries we examined, only Colombia has made anything like a concerted effort to provide an alternative to illegal migration. Colombia's border employment offices that attempt to place workers and offer the migrants counsel show at least a token acceptance of responsibility for the migrant's plight, something yet to be observed from the governments of Bolivia, El Salvador, Mexico, Paraguay, and the other sender countries of Latin America.

In the final analysis, large-scale illegal migration is compelling evidence that the society has exceeded its carrying capacity — it is unable to support the existing population within the social, economic, cultural, and political context. In general terms it can be said that such a circumstance can be brought on because the resources cannot support the society's chosen lifestyle, or because its policies reflect an unwillingness to redistribute the resources throughout the society. Catherine Maserang comments:

> The carrying capacity of nation-states, like those of other kinds of human societies, are affected by the interaction between their cultural systems and their environments. . . . Since no countries are isolated, their environment includes the whole world, but their carrying capacities are affected by more specific cultural and environmental factors, such as their level of industrialization, geographical size, climate, type of political system, and historical background.[9]

A society's carrying capacity can be and usually is, altered through adaptation. In modern times industrialization and the concomitant technological advances have tended to increase the carrying capacity of many societies. As this has happened, an increased interdependency of societies has developed: "The more countries have industrialized, the more their carrying capacities have become affected by patterns in other countries."[10] Raw materials are bought and sold, markets are established, political interaction increases, and population transfers occur. The states that industrialized first developed a comparative advantage, in that what they had to exchange was more in demand than what nonindustrialized societies were offering. André Gunder Frank makes the point that the developed were never "underdeveloped," although they were perhaps "undeveloped".[11] Underdevelopment came with industrialization, as capitalism passed through various stages. The countries that lagged behind were underdeveloped and remained dependent on the industrialized states. Hunting and gathering societies of premodern times were not underdeveloped. The simple lifestyle and the modest strain on resources did not result in artificial pressures on their carrying capacities. That would come with the industrial revolution and competition for limited resources.

As the land has ceased to provide an adequate living for the growing population in Latin America, people have sought refuge in the cities, where individual self-sufficiency is replaced by group interdependency. But the industrial development that was supposed to permit adaptation, and thereby increase the society's carrying capacity, had not succeeded. Not only is Mexico unable to provide for its constantly growing population, but it can be argued that the country is more dependent on foreign money, technology, and markets today than it was when the revolution opposed Porfirio Díaz and his "scientific" approach to modernization. The carrying capacity has not increased as rapidly as population growth. The cultural adaptation has been one of extralegal population transfers. The experience throughout the rest of Latin America has been similar. It is a bitter irony that while industrial development has failed to sufficiently increase the carrying capacity of most Latin American countries, it has contributed to the population growth (lower infant mortality rates, greater life expectancy), which places greater strain on the resources.

As extralegal population transfers increase, it becomes clear that the planet, and not merely the nation-state, is the arena for society's struggle to adapt to its carrying capacity. Survival is the fundamental socioeconomic and political issue facing all societies, not merely those belonging to an artificially contrived political unit in the poorer regions.

As noted above, it is difficult to determine a society's carrying capacity empirically because the human population is constantly making adaptations that will affect it. Massive population transfers may be one such adaptation. Table 6.1 suggests a series of empirically testable hypotheses that would, if accepted, add further evidence and provide a framework for policy development.

Table 6.2 contains recent population projections and demographic characteristics for the Western Hemisphere that must be related, where applicable, to the testing of hypotheses on clandestine migratory trends. One of the most

TABLE 6.1
Inventory of Hypotheses Linking Extralegal Population Transfers and Carrying Capacity

If Extralegal Population is Associated with Carrying Capacity, Illegal Migration Should Be Correlated with	Implications of the Hypotheses
1. High population density (HPD)	Each of these circumstances could understandably contribute to economic deprivation for large numbers of people. The critical factor relating to illegal migration is that they also tend to physically displace the poor.
2. A low ratio of arable land and rural population, given HPD	
3. A high concentration of arable land in the hands of a few, given HPD	
4. A high ratio of the rate of urban growth to population growth, given HPD	
5. A low ratio of industrial growth to urban growth, given HPD	In addition to the physical displacement, these conditions are such that the poor cannot retreat to subsistence agriculture, as has been the case historically.
6. A disproportionately high percentage of population under 25 years old, given HPD	
7. A high incidence of political repression and wealth concentration, given HPD	

glaring conditions is the shortness of time in which the Latin American and Caribbean nations will double their population (given current trends unimpeded) compared with the United States and Canada. The latter nations will surely be targets for intense clandestine migration during the coming two decades, given current population and wealth differentials.

In Chapter 1 we spoke of a "lifeboat ethic" of survival and a "quality of life ethic." The former holds that survival in the developed states may not be possible except at the expense of those who would cling to our "lifeboat," thereby sinking it. William E. Colby, former director of the Central Intelligence Agency, seemed to be advocating the adoption of a lifeboat ethic when he said, "The greatest danger of violence and difficulty in the world is between the 'haves' and the 'have nots' — them against us." According to Colby, the threat from countries such as Mexico and its illegal aliens is greater than the threat from the Soviet Union.[12] The "quality of life ethic," by contrast, argues that a redistribution of the wealth offers the only acceptable answer. The comfort of the few must be at least partially sacrificed for the survival of all.

As human beings we confess a distinct preference for an ethic that would advocate the survival of all. As social scientists we are not at all convinced that this will be the choice if in fact a decision has to be made. No political or economic elite can forever ignore the pressures on their society's carrying

TABLE 6.2
Population Projections for the Western Hemisphere

	Canada	United States	Middle America	Caribbean	Tropical South America	Temperate South America
Population Estimate Mid 1979 (millions)	23.7	220.3	89	30	193	41
Birth Rate*	16	15	41	29	36	23
Death Rate*	7	9	7	8	9	9
Rate of Natural Increase (annual percent)	0.8	0.6	3.4	2.0	2.8	1.4
Number of Years to Double Population	87	116	20	35	25	50
Population Projection to 2000 (millions)	29.0	260.4	171	43	332	51
Infant Mortality Rate†	14	14	72	70	99	57
Population under 15 Years (percent)	26	24	46	40	42	30
Population over 64 Years (percent)	8	11	3	5	3	7
Life Expectancy at Birth (years)	73	73	63	63	60	67
Urban Population	76	74	58	49	60	80
Physical Quality of Life Index	95	95	72	73	67	83
Per Capita Gross National Product (US $)	8,450	8,640	1,030	1,100	1,280	1,560

*Births/deaths per 1,000 population.

†Number of deaths to infants under 1 year of age per 1,000 live births.

Source: Population Reference Bureau, *1979 World Population Data Sheet* (Washington, D.C.: Population Reference Bureau, 1980).

capacity or that of others, and reasonably expect to remain unaffected. Within the developed world the "lifeboat ethic" will have considerable support. It is theoretically possible to build a great wall around North America and defend it militarily while diligently working to expel those illegal aliens who slip in. Such an approach might work if implemented in concert with other developed nations in the world, particularly in the area of resource pooling.

But therein lies the fallacy of the "lifeboat ethic." In a world of increasingly scarce resources (much of which is located in those areas against whose clandestine migration we are trying to fortify ourselves), cooperative ventures are difficult. If called upon to join us in this venture, it is highly doubtful that western Europe and Japan would go along. The experience of recent petroleum crises seems to support this. Moreover, not all countries face the same problems at the same time. The problem of extralegal population transfer may well become significant in Europe and Japan in the future, but now it is comparatively inconsequential. Given the growing U.S. dependence on the rest of the world for scarce resources, only a major change in lifestyle would permit a "Fortress America" or "lifeboat ethic" approach.

The "quality of life ethic" is certainly more morally uplifting, but it is likewise flawed. We see no evidence to suggest that American generosity extends to the point of a conscious sacrifice in standard of living for what remains to most an abstract humanitarian ideal. Most members of the U.S. Congress find it politically safe to vote against foreign aid bills (a mere pittance compared to what would be required if the "qualtiy of life ethic" were adopted) when the public clamors for cuts in government spending.

A "livability strategy" within the Western Hemisphere does not appear to be on the horizon. If and when it does materialize, it will probably come only after the carrying capacity of Latin American states has been so far exceeded that the mere trickle of illegal aliens becomes a virtual flood. At that point the issue will no longer be a mere abstraction to most.

Robert L. Ayres offers one of the more thoughtful proposals for a livability strategy in Latin America.[13] He observes that in the past, development models, such as import substitution and industrial growth, have failed in most respects. He also questions the value of the Soviet model in small, limited-resource countries. For Ayres a livability strategy recognizes the economic limitations of countries in the hemisphere and works within the framework of what is realistically attainable. The proposal's cornerstone is an emphasis on greater economic equality rather than a "trickle down" effect from high growth. Ayres is right. The destitute are not served by an extraordinary increase in per capita income (assuming that is possible) if the median income does not keep pace. Rapid growth is generally accompanied by high inflation, and frequently by greater wealth concentration; together they result in a more impoverished populace. The emphasis must be on an increase in the real median income. Realistically this is likely to mean that the median income must increase much faster than the mean income, thus leading to a redistribution of the wealth toward greater equality.

Ayres's approach deemphasizes the transfer of technology as being too expensive and inappropriate for a society that is not highly industrialized. As was argued above, misplaced efforts to achieve a high level of industrialization have been part of the problem. Ayres also stresses a new emphasis on agricultural development, not only to regain self-sufficiency in food but also to stem the tide of rural-to-urban migration, which is strongly correlated with illegal migration. Urban decentralization should be a goal, with small, labor-intensive industries established in satellite cities and in the rural areas. To support the new economic emphasis, a policy supporting nonformal education is proposed. Ayres notes the need for restructuring bilateral and multilateral assistance to support this livability strategy while recognizing that it will require a change in philosophy by the lenders as well as the debtors.

Many of Ayres's proposals are not new — some have been tried and have failed. The failures should not be seen as confirmation that they will not work, however, only that they will not work if there is not a commitment to a redistribution of the wealth. The commitment and burden of this redistribution will not fall entirely on Latin American countries. If it is to work, the developed world will have to lower its trade barriers, over the protests of domestic business interestst that will charge unfair competition, and probably will have to continue to absorb a measured number of the sending countries' workers, despite protests from domestic labor.

Ayres's livability strategy addresses itself to many of the causes of illegal migration and it, or one philosophically similar, may offer the only hope if a "quality of life" ethic is to be implemented. Unfortunately, Ayres's concluding remark is telling:

> Elites that are likely to perform such a feat are unlikely to be neatly classified as reformists, socialists, authoritarians or populists. What they should be called, *if indeed they ever appear*, is still an open question.[14]

Whether such policy makers do appear seems to depend in large part on a general acceptance of the artificiality of the nation-state where the survival of all is at stake. A complete political and economic integration of some states would be desirable. Countries like Haiti, El Salvador, Honduras, Bolivia, and Paraguay are simply not viable. Realistically, however, the prevailing climate of nationalism precludes this. Indeed, during the summer of 1980 the Latin American Free Trade Area (LAFTA) formally collapsed for lack of cooperation. Even so, some economic integration does not seem totally out of the question; and some states, such as Mexico and the United States or Colombia and Venezuela, could benefit. This would expedite the flow of raw materials and labor, and would open up the needed markets for those countries attempting to adjust to a new livability strategy.

Alternatively, Steve Mumme suggests a Hemispheric Migration Council (see epilogue) as a multinational approach to dealing with the problems of population transfers. These proposals cannot alone provide a long-term solution to the problems. Unless and until rapid population growth can be brought under control, we are merely postponing the day when the carrying capacity of the hemisphere — indeed, of our planet — is jeopardized.

Surely a "community of nations" concept at the hemispheric level is one place to begin working against disaster. Realistically, only a crisis of major proportions is likely to generate serious multinational consideration of these proposals. Such a crisis is possible, and one can only hope that before it materializes, we will have taken the courageous steps necessary to avoid the ultimate "lifeboat strategy" and have opted, instead, for a strategy that will permit survival with dignity.

NOTES

1. Newspapers in Colombia and Mexico, in particular, frequently carry banner headlines outlining the atrocities committed by the police and employers in the receiver countries. The stories are justified on the ground that they discourage citizens from illegal migration, a doubtful claim. In reality one suspects that they are an expression of shame and humiliation.

2. Robert L. Ayres, "Development Policy and the Possibility of a 'Livable' Future for Latin America," *American Political Science Review* 69, no. 2 (June 1976): 393-408.

3. We refer the reader to Chapter 3 and the discussion of the law that allows an employer to hire, but not to house, an illegal alien, and a landlord to house, but not employ, that person.

4. For our purposes, carrying capacity is the optimal population level that a society can support and still maintain its traditional lifestyle. For other definitions and discussion of carrying capacity, see Robert L. Carneiro, "On the Relationship Between Size of Population and Complexity of Social Organization," *Southwestern Journal of Anthropology* 23 (1963): 234-43; and Catherine H. Maserang, "Factors Affecting Carrying Capacities of Nation-States," *Journal of Anthropological Research* 32, no. 3 (Fall 1976): 255-75.

5. Elsa M. Chaney, "The Caribbean on the Move: Undocumented Workers in the Hemisphere," paper prepared for the Study Group on Immigration and U.S. Foreign Policy, Council on Foreign Relations, New York, May 15, 1978, p. 4.

6. Richard B. Craig, *The Bracero Program: Interest Groups and Foreign Policy* (Austin: University of Texas Press, 1971).

7. Ibid., p. 63.

8. Peter Bachrach and Morton S. Baratz, "Decisions and Nondecisions: An Analytical Framework," *American Political Science Review* 57 (September 1963): 641.

9. Maserang, "Factors Affecting Carrying Capacities of Nation-States," p. 256.

10. Ibid., p. 271.

11. André Gunder Frank, "The Development of Underdevelopment," in *Dependence and Underdevelopment*, James D. Cockcroft, André Gunder Frank, and Dale Johnson, eds. (Garden City, N.Y.: Anchor Books, 1972), p. 3.

12. *Los Angeles Times*, June 6, 1978.

13. Ayres, "Development Policy and the Possibility of a 'Livable' Future for Latin America."

14. Ibid., p. 525 (emphasis added).

EPILOGUE

"To govern is to populate," declared the Argentine Juan Bautista Alberdi in the middle of the nineteenth century. Alberdi's dictum, which then framed the demographic problems of managing a vast, underinhabited continent, today stands in distinct contrast with the population problems confronting governments throughout the Western Hemisphere. The Argentine philosopher could hardly have imagined that the realization of his demographic vision might impair the bodies politic within the hemisphere rather than contribute to their vitality. What he failed to foresee was that the standards of government would alter along with demographic parameters. Thus, in the late twentieth century the overburden of human population is evaluated in terms of its implications for social welfare and human rights, goals that constitute a standard in the measurement of good government. It is against this standard that the performance of governments in the Western Hemisphere is to be rated vis-à-vis the phenomenon of illegal migration.

Illegal migration throughout the region, perhaps more than any other issue, implies degrees of failure of regimes to govern and provide for their peoples, not simply with respect to population growth, but across the board in the policy sphere, from employment and living conditions to education and civil liberties. While virtually all of the governments within the Western Hemisphere have sought to regulate migration to and from their domains, the growing volume of illegal migration demonstrates the inadequacy of institutionalized population management. More dramatically, it demonstrates the inadequacy of domestic policies in both sending and receiving nations.

Thus the political dilemma of illegal migration has two fundamental dimensions: that of providing for the human needs of peoples within the boundaries of the state, and that of fashioning adequate policy responses to the flow of population throughout the Western Hemisphere that preserve the basic rights of the migrant while serving to direct the migratory stream to a rational and beneficial purpose within the hemisphere.

To the extent that there is a fundamental pattern of illegal migration within the Western Hemisphere, it is the recognition by individual migrants of the inadequacy of the sending country in relation to their needs and expectations. Although it is true that expectations have risen dramatically in this century, migrants frequently seek international alternatives out of necessity rather than preference. It could be argued, for instance, that Haitian illegals in the Dominican Republic, working for subsistence wages under even the best of circumstances, undertook their ordeal not solely because they sought improvements in their standard of living. Rather, they are likely to be there because they faced starvation and persecution in Haiti.[1] Heightened expectations do, of course, underlie migratory dynamics, particularly where migrants are attracted to advanced industrialized countries like Argentina, the United States, and Canada. In such cases both subsistence needs and rising expectations mingle to prompt the act of migration.

However stressful the bite of material necessity, in terms of formal demography economic migrants are generally classified as voluntary, having left the sending nation of their own volition. This distinction is incorporated into U.S. immigration law, which establishes quotas for such migrants. Another category of migrant, however, is the involuntary migrants, who usually are politically motivated. Such migrants traditionally are treated differently by demographers and immigration authorities, being accorded the quasi-legal status of refugees. Legal or illegal, however, political refugees reflect the failure of governments to accommodate the expectations of their citizens in the political realm. The recent history of the Western Hemisphere has shown the very close correlation between economic deprivation and political repression. Where these conditions exist in tandem, as in Haiti, El Salvador, Guatamala, and Paraguay, the difficulty of distinguishing between voluntary and involuntary, economic and political, is obvious.

Along with the inadequacy of domestic political and economic performance implied by illegal migration, migrant trends reflect the chauvinism implicit in population management throughout the Western Hemisphere. Alberdi's expansionist pronatal demography has in the twentieth century exhausted its potential usefulness as an agent of nationalist policies. Nevertheless, few governments within the hemisphere have adopted progressive demographic policies aimed at the rational management of population size. The nationalist ethics of growth interface with the structural necessities of subsistence economies to maintain one of the world's highest indexes of population growth within the Caribbean-Central America-South America setting.[2] That the obligation of the modern state extends to the demographic impasse of the human population is an ideal only gradually being acknowledged at the hemispheric level.

The large economic gap between the hemisphere's sending nations (such as Mexico, Colombia, Paraguay, Bolivia, Haiti, Jamaica, the Dominican Republic, El Salvador, Guatamala, and Ecuador) and the principal receivers of the human stream, such as the United States, Canada, Argentina, Venezuela, and Brazil) underscores Kingsley Davis's assertion that wherever technological differences exist, so does migration. The juxtaposition of industrialized, industrializing, and nonindustrial nations in the Western Hemisphere underpins the dynamics of migration and ties the particulars of domestic policies to the greater hemispheric arena.

Although the basis for much of the migratory stream lies in the gross mismanagement of individual governments and the comparative advantages and dependencies of hemispheric states, it is clear that the nations of the hemisphere have not yet devised adequate strategies for coping with the migratory stream. This relates to the other major political dilemma of hemispheric migration. Even if the performance of domestic governments should improve radically throughout the region, nations will continue to be confronted with migration, some of it illegal, assuming the continuation of prevalent standards of accommodation and response.

Whereas the problems of dealing with the causes of illegal migration devolve mainly upon the sending countries, the problem of fashioning a response rests heavily on the receivers. As the authors of this study observe, there are essentially three patterns of state response to illegal immigration: ignoring the situation and dealing with illegal migrants selectively, through the prosecutorial devices of the state; offering a general amnesty or some other form of accommodation permitting aliens to remain within the country legally; attempting to anticipate and circumvent the problem of illegal aliens by actively promoting migration and settlement programs calculated to provide the greatest feasible benefit to the state. In practice it is evident that some combination of these approaches has been adopted in the major receiver nations. In the United States, for example, the Carter administration proposals of 1977 called, in effect, for a general amnesty coupled with further enforcement of the immigration laws while allowing for the possibility of a resumption of contract labor recruitment.

Each of these approaches has special problems. To the extent that the illegal migration is ignored by the receiving nation, or exclusionary laws are selectively enforced, the migrant influx is unlikely to be modified to a significant degree. Further, the stigma of illegality is likely to encourage abuses of aliens within the host society. Under these circumstances, rightly or wrongly, aliens will be blamed for denying employment to citizens. By the same token, aliens will be denied the reasonable product of their labor as their needs are exploited within the host society by those seeking to maximize their own economic circumstances.

The second alternative, general amnesty, presents innumerable bureaucratic problems and likewise threatens the status of resident economic and ethnic groups seeking to better their place within the social and economic order. There is also the magnet problem, the attraction of an amnesty program for potential migrants. Finally, as the case of Argentina demonstrates, there is the question of the sincerity with which an amnesty program is implemented (from the perspective of the migrant). Critics of the Carter proposals in the United States, for example, have pointed to the exposure and injury that aliens already in the country might suffer at the hands of authorities should they reveal their presence without the protections of a basic bill of rights.[3]

The alternative of official colonization and the designated settlement of migrants is also limited as a coping strategy for illegal migration. While such programs afford the migrant legitimate status, they are both exclusionary and preferential. Colonization discriminates both against potential migrants who are refused admittance and citizens who may have little choice concerning the introduction of ethnically distinct migrants into their midst. Where colonization programs have been most successful, as in Bolivia and Canada, they have been expedients for the rapid population of hitherto underpopulated areas, permitting a buffer zone between the designated settlement and the existing community. Where aliens have not enjoyed the benefits of such a buffer between themselves and the host society — witness the recent arrival of Laotians and Vietnamese in the United States — the potential for tension has been markedly high. Nor is it certain that such programs, limited as they have been, are sufficient to quell the tide of migration.

The U.S. experience with the *bracero* program suggests that legal migration was accompanied by substantial illegal entries.[4] Although such efforts in the nineteenth century attracted waves of immigrants to Argentina, Uruguay, and Brazil, the economics of migration have altered. Today's receiver nations throughout the Western hemisphere are not likely to risk the influx that might be generated by a wholesale open-door policy of directed colonization.

In sum, the options available for coping with the migrant stream remain problematical palliatives for a deeply rooted and intractable problem throughout the Western Hemisphere. Policies conceived solely at the national level, whether directed toward the causes or the consequences of migration, are hardly adequate to deal with a phenomenon that joins sending and receiving nations in a transfer of population. As the present study indicates, such dynamics are partially contingent on predatory monopoly capitalism throughout the hemisphere, on inhumane political policies that lead industrialized nations to patronize ruthless and reactionary dictatorships, and even on decently motivated assistance and development policies run amok. The fact that the industrialized and developed countries, which constitute the principal receivers of the migrant flow, are implicated in its causes as well as its consequences should not displace the evidence of failure on the doorsteps of the major senders. Rather, it should provide incentives at the national and hemispheric levels for concerted action in dealing with the migration problem.

Aside from the very general commitments to human rights by distant entities like the United Nations and the Organization of American States (O.A.S.), there is little consensus on the issue of illegal migration within the Western Hemisphere. The matter remains grounded in inadequate national migration policies. What is patently called for is a reversal of the benign neglect approach to the international phenomenon of illegal migration — a concerted and coordinated approach at the hemispheric level, as Johnson and Williams have recommended.

The development of a Hemispheric Migration Council at the level of one of the standing international bodies — the O.A.S. suggests itself — might well be justified as part of a multilevel approach to the political dilemma of hemispheric migration. A number of arguments may be made in its favor.

First, as argued by the authors of this study, the response to illegal migration on the national level has generally been inadequate throughout the hemisphere. Clearly, some further level of cooperation is needed.

Second, as the authors also indicate, the preponderance of hemispheric migration is within the hemisphere itself, suggesting that the phenomenon might best be faced at this level. Virtually all hemispheric nations are implicated in these trends in some way, and thus could benefit from a hemispheric approach.

Third, regional institutions like the O.A.S. have already become involved in administrative and conflict-management functions related to the problems of illegal immigration – the instance of El Salvador and Honduras is a case in point.

Fourth, though lacking in actual sovereignty, such an institution might usefully provide symbolic guidance in the form of a policy against which national policies could be measured and that well might, in its own right, provide certain useful services for the better management of migrant trends. Though one can only speculate on how such a policy might be structured, the list of objectives below suggests its potential reach.

Based on respect for the human rights of migrants, especially their right to dignified working and living conditions, and the need to introduce a more rational and humane structure into the dynamics of population transfer throughout the region, a hemispheric policy might accomplish the following:

1. Set basic standards for the humane treatment of migrants.

2. Provide standards for the treatment of political and economic refugees.

3. Provide a court of appeals, or some other suitable entity, for the investigation of human-rights violations with respect to migrants throughout the hemisphere.

4. Provide or coordinate international relief for the worst instances of "stranded" or "abused" migrants.

5. Provide a clearinghouse and research service for the collection and dissemination of data on illegal migration, to be used for humane purposes in coping with the migrant phenomenon.

6. Coordinate international relief, trade, and aid programs to address the causes and consequences of illegal migration, thus providing coordination of domestic – national level – migration policies in both sending and receiving nations.

7. Coordinate with international labor organizations and provide information and facilities to enable labor to respond more effectively to a range of alternatives in the international labor market within and outside the hemisphere.

8. Provide a forum for the advocacy of the regional and global rights of migrant labor as a counterweight to strictly nationalist labor policies.

Such a list can merely outline what a region-wide policy might strive for; it reflects the prejudices of the author, and is in no way presumed to be exhaustive. Further, imposing yet another level of administration and bureaucracy while fashioning a solution may well be opposed as redundant, unwieldy, unfeasible, or ideologically unsound.

The intractability of the problem at present, however, and its magnitude and intricacy throughout the Western Hemisphere suggest that migration problems can yield only to a persistent, multilevel response to their causes and consequences. The findings in this study suggest that current national policies tend, at both the sending and the receiving ends of the continuum, to embrace a "lifeboat ethic" of survival detrimental to the millions of people asserting, through their migration, their right to a dignified and productive life. To the extent that "quality of life" is realizable for these millions, and everyone else in the hemisphere, it is attainable not by pitting sending against receiving nations, but through cooperative policies inspired by the hope that viable strategies can be designed to cope with problems stemming from migration, of whatever sort. To think less is to accept the classic Hobbesian fate, with all the human misery that implies.

NOTES

1. Karen DeYoung, "$1.50 a Day and the Ground to Sleep on," *Washington Post*, August 28, 1980, p. 37-A.

2. Population Reference Bureau, *1979 World Population Data Sheet* (Washington, D.C.: Population Reference Bureau, 1979).

3. Vicki Kemper, "Manzo Plan Would Give Amnesty to Undocumented Aliens in U.S.," *Arizona Daily Star*, February 2, 1980, p. 1-B.

4. Julian Samora, *Los Mojados: The Wetback Story* (South Bend, Ind.: University of Notre Dame Press, 1972), pp. 44-45.

APPENDIX

We can study the impact of illegal aliens on U.S. policy makers at the executive level through careful use of presidential archives. The materials in this appendix were excerpted from presidential papers housed at the Truman Library in Independence, Missouri, by Professor Miles Williams during 1978. They are offered here as evidence that illegal aliens have been acknowledged by the White House as critical to the national economy. This is part of a more extensive study of illegal aliens and presidential action that Professor Williams is preparing.

As was noted in Chapter 6, receiver countries in Latin America and North America have generally taken a nondecision-making stance with respect to immigration policy. Quoting Peter Bachrach and Morton Baratz, we noted that non-decision-making develops when "dominant values, the accepted rules of the game, the existing power relations among groups, and the instruments of force . . . effectively prevent grievances from developing into full-fledged issues which call for decisions." In this instance the "dominant values" and "accepted rules of the game" refer to a long-standing tradition of population transfers and implied government consent to the exploitation of the aliens arriving from sender countries. The tradition developed in the United States during periods of severe wartime labor shortages. Some aliens arrived with work permits, while others had no papers. But because of the shortage of workers, immigration laws were generally ignored and there were few influential voices arguing against the practice. Agricultural interests were pleased with the arrangement because it provided an ample supply of industrious laborers who could be paid low wages for long hours of hard, disagreeable work. As an added bonus, the *braceros* could not organize or make demands on their employers.

Under the wartime program (1942-47) more than 200,000 *braceros* entered to work in agriculture, and an additional 130,000 worked on the railroads.[1] The number of illegal aliens entering the country is unknown, but the figure was substantial. Texas was not allowed to participate in the program because of its blatant discriminatory practices. Public Law 45, the wartime *bracero* program, ended on December 31, 1947. During the period agriculture had become dependent on the Mexican labor, and did not find the growing unemployment of the late 1940s a persuasive argument for ending the employment of foreign nationals. A new agreement was worked out on February 21, 1948, but Mexico terminated it in October of that year. The position of the farm interests can be seen clearly in the correspondence that reached the White House during this period. The following letter, from Tom Baker of Trailback Plantation in Essex, Missouri, was obtained from the official file papers of Harry S Truman, available at the Harry S Truman Library.

May 10, 1949

Mr. John Steelman
Presidential Advisor
White House
Washington, D.C.

Dear Mr. Steelman,

As you know negotiations with the Mexican Government regarding a new Farm Labor Agreement have been at a standstill for several months. This has caused a great deal of comment and criticism in the 27 states having a need for additional labor at peak harvesting periods. From the daily correspondence and newspaper clippings I receive as a member of the Mexican Labor Sub-Committee of the Special Farm Labor Board, I gather that the general concensus [sic] of opinion is that the needs of the labor users are being sacrificed in favor of oil interests in this country and others which would benefit from the Mexicans receiving a sizable loan from us. Practically without exception, these letters and newspaper clippings infer that our State Department has not approached the problem from a realistic point of view.

Incidentally, United States Employment Service figures indicate there is a definite need for imported "stoop" labor, even though many of our more skilled laborers are out of work at present. The USES is making a fine effort to affect [sic] importation of Puerto Ricans, but in many cases their small stature prevents their doing heavy work.

I realize yours is an especially sensitive position as regards this matter, but I am convinced it would be best for the President and all concerned if pressure could be brought to bear to affect [sic] enactment of a new Farm Labor Agreement between our country and Mexico without further delay, as matters are getting out of hand at this end.

Please give my regards to the President and tell him when "Byrds" get in our way down here we declare "open season" on them until they are thinned out or stop roosting in our crops.

Cordially yours,

Tom F. Baker

Not everyone agreed with Baker's assessment. The following letter to President Truman, also obtained from the official file papers of Harry S Truman, illustrates this.

October 10, 1949

My dear Mr. President:

The National Association for the Advancement of Colored People is gravely concerned about the importation of Mexican citizens who are being used to break a strike of cotton pickers in California. Mexicans, Anglo-Americans, and colored people have stopped work because they are fighting for better working conditions. The use of citizens of another country to wreck the economic hopes of Americans is a practice which our government must actively oppose.

Mr. H. L. Mitchell, president of the Farm Labor Union, A.F. of L., has sent us a copy of his letter to you dated September 28. We have worked with Mr. Mitchell on numerous occasions. He has a deep and patriotic interest in bettering the lot of our agricultural workers who are so vital to our welfare, but so neglected in our legislation.

We join him in urging that a Presidential Commission be set up to investigate conditions among farm workers. Among other things, such a commission would be a valuable aid in focusing public attention on the plight of those who plant and harvest our crops.

Very Sincerely Yours,

Roy Wilkins,
Acting Secretary

In the period following the expiration of Public Law 45, the White House received a number of letters and telegrams from influential agricultural groups, labor organizations, and interest groups representing minorities. The general acquiescence to the wartime agreement with Mexico did not carry over into the postwar period of unemployment. An agreement was reached on August 1, 1949, but there was one significant difference: "On the international level the contractor was no longer the United States government, but the individual farmer or his representative. No longer was the government legally responsible for contract fulfillment. The responsibility lay with the farmer."[2] The U.S. government assumed a position of nondecision-making.

The following letters between the White House and various interested parties, taken together, illustrate how the contradictions of past policies and mobilized interests can bring about nondecision-making. All the material was obtained from Harry S Truman's official file papers, Harry S Truman Library.

May 26, 1949

The President
The White House
Washington, D.C.

My dear Mr. President:

You will remember that I talked to you last Saturday about the labor situation in the Rio Grande Valley of Texas and New Mexico and also in California.

I pointed out that the State Department was not getting anywhere with its negotiations with Mexico and particularly urged that the Immigration Service at El Paso should be reminded that they are not administering this nation and that they should not do as they tried to do last summer — override the President of the United States.

The El Paso boy is still busy. Yesterday I had a call from Fort Stockton, Texas telling me how they had gone to Simmons' farm and pulled off all the Old Mexico Mexicans. The man who did it said they were under instructions to get them all back to Mexico. It happened that Simmons had lost his planting due to a storm and was replanting and now he is completely without labor.

If you a [*sic*] referring the matter to Tom Clark here is a concrete example of the way they are messing things up.

Sincerely yours,

Clinton P. Anderson
[U.S. Senator, New Mexico]

This example of a U.S. senator expressing his indignation at the enforcement of immigration law to the president of the United States received the following response:

June 2, 1949

Dear Clint:

I talked to Tom Clark about the situation on the Mexican border, with regard to the Immigration Service, and he assured me that he would straighten it out at once.

Sincerely yours,

Harry S Truman

At the same time that Anderson and Truman were exchanging messages, a Mexican-American interest group was complaining about the influx of illegal aliens. The following telegram was sent by R. A. Cortez, national president of the League of United Latin American Citizens (LULAC) to David Niles, administrative assistant to President Truman, on June 2, 1949:

I HAVE WIRED COMMISSIONER OF IMMIGRATION WATSON B MILLER AS FOLLOWS QUOTE LOCAL PRESS REPORTS THAT ASSISTANT COMMISSIONER WILLARD F KELLEY [*sic*] HAS PROMISED CONGRESSMAN KEN REGAN THAT WETBACKS IN WEST TEXAS WILL BE RECRUITED FOR URGENT LABOR IN KEEPING WITH SYSTEM NOW USED IN CALIFORNIA AND MONTANA STOP NEWS STORY FURTHER STATES REPRESENTATIVE

REGAN TOOK MATTER UP WITH YOUR DEPARTMENT BECAUSE LARGE SCALE ARRESTS OF WETBACKS WAS [*sic*] DEPRIVING WEST TEXAS EMPLOYERS OF FARM AND RANCH HANDS STOP OUR ORGANIZATION DESIRES TO KNOW IF NEWSPAPER REPORT IS CORRECT AND IF SO WHETHER YOU ARE ENDORS-ING THIS AVOWED POLICY CALLING FOR VIOLATION OF OATH OF OFFICE OF YOUR DEPARTMENT EMPLOYEES TO ENFORCE US IMMIGRATION LAWS STOP REFER YOU TO YOUR FILE 56263/393 AND OUR ANSWER THERETO STOP OUR ORGANIZATION HOLDING NATIONAL CONVENTION HERE NEXT WEEK AND DESIRES TO INFORM THREE MILLION MEX-ICAN-AMERICANS IN SOUTHWEST OF YOUR STAND IN THIS MATTER STOP UNQUOTE HAVING HEARD NOTHING FROM YOU OR MR STOWE SINCE OUR PERSONAL VISIT TO YOU LAST JANUARY AND HAVING RECEIVED AN INCREASING NUMBER OF REPORTS OF COLLUSION BETWEEN IMMIGRATION AUTHORITIES AND EMPLOYERS WE WILL ASSUME UNLESS WE HEAR FROM YOU TO THE CONTRARY THAT THE POLICY ALLEGEDLY ANNOUNCED BY WILLARD F KELLEY [*sic*] HAS THE ENDORSEMENT OF THE EXECUTIVE DEPARTMENT OF OUR NATIONAL GOVERNMENT STOP

The telegram sent to the commissioner of immigration received an immed-iate response, although the charges were not answered. The telegram to Niles also led to a memorandum to Truman, one that may be more revealing about the emerging policy of nondecision-making. These two communications follow.

WASHINGTON DC   JUNE 3 1949   56265/333

MR R A CORTEZ
NATIONAL PRESIDENT
LEAGUE OF UNITED LATIN AMERICAN CITIZENS
214 BROADWAY
SAN ANTONIO

REURTELS YESTERDAY TO ATTORNEY GENERAL AND UNDER-SIGNED CONCERNING PRESS REPORTS THAT ASSISTANT COMMISSIONER KELLY HAS GIVEN ASSURANCES THAT WET-BACKS IN WEST TEXAS WILL BE RECRUITED TO FILL FARM LABOR SHORTAGES YOU ARE ADVISED THAT FOLLOWING RECEIPT OF INQUIRIES BY MEMBERS OF TEXAS DELEGATION BASED UPON COMPLAINTS OF FARM LABOR SHORTAGES KELLY INFORMED INTERESTED PARTIES THAT HE WOULD REQUEST UNITED STATES EMPLOYMENT SERVICE TO INVESTI-GATE TO DETERMINE WHETHER SHORTAGE ACTUALLY EXISTS AND THAT IF CERTIFICATE OF SUCH NEED WERE FURNISHED STATE DEPARTMENT WOULD BE REQUESTED TO PRESENT TO MEXICAN GOVERNMENT FOR ITS CONSIDERATION

THE MATTER OF INTERIM RECRUITMENT OF WETS UNDER CONDITIONS PRESCRIBED IN LAST INTERNATIONAL AGREEMENT PENDING THE COMPLETION OF NEGOTIATIONS FOR NEW AGREEMENT STOP UNITED STATES EMPLOYMENT SERVICE HAS NOT YET REPORTED CONCERNING NEED STOP STATE DEPARTMENT HAS EXPRESSED WILLINGNESS PRESENT MATTER TO MEXICAN GOVERNMENT UPON CERTIFICATE OF NEED BEING ISSUED STOP

WATSON B MILLER
COMMISSIONER OF IMMIGRATION AND NATURALIZATION
[copy was sent to David H. Stowe, administrative assistant to the president]

June 8, 1949

MEMORANDUM FOR THE PRESIDENT:

The attached telegram from Mr. R. A. Cortez, National President of the League of United Latin American Citizens, has brought up an acute problem in connection with Mexican-Americans in the Southwestern states.

The number of illegal immigrants coming across the border each year from Mexico is said to exceed our regular immigration quota for all countries. Of course, the size of this number is made possible by the difficulties of protecting such an extensive border. But in addition to that, employers in the Southwest bring a great deal of pressure to bear on all branches of the Federal government to meet their demand for cheap labor, and a custom has grown up by which these illegal migrants are not deported during a time when the demand for labor is high.

The established citizens and residents of Mexican origin are objecting to this arrangement, and it appears that we are going to go ahead and do it again this summer — under an international agreement if possible, and one is now being negotiated — but I surmise it will be done without an agreement if the negotiations are not successful.

I question the wisdom of these arrangements coming at a time when extensive publicity is being given to the rise in unemployment.

There are two problems which ought to be considered together.

1. The question of illegal migration across the Mexican border.
2. The welfare of the three million Spanish-speaking Americans in the Southwest and Mountain states.

The difficulty, which arose last Fall when 7,000 wetbacks were permitted to cross the border and were immediately put to work, was handled by Dr. Steelman and Dave Stowe.

I am wondering whether it would not be advisable to ask Dr. Steel-man to call in representatives from Justice, Federal Security, State and Labor, with a view toward developing a more consistent policy, and perhaps, opening up the question of the welfare of Mexican-Americans in the Southwest.

David K. Niles

The *bracero* program agreed to by Mexico and the United States on Febru-ary 21, 1948, was terminated in October of that year. A new agreement, which placed responsibility for administering the program on the farmers, was nego-tiated and became effective on August 1, 1949. A little over three weeks later Senator Anderson wrote to President Truman to complain about the continued enforcement of immigration laws. That letter and Truman's response follow:

August 24, 1949

The President
The White House

Dear Mr. President:

I got today the following telegram from one of the biggest farmers in my state:

"This morning's paper states that 150 wetbacks are to come before Judge Thomason in El Paso for deportation. Instructions have been issued by the Immigration Service to pick up all wetbacks who have entered the United States since August 1 [the effective date of the new agreement]. Some cotton has been ginned here already. Farmers are desperate. The labor contract negotiated by the State Department and Mexico is so absurd and unworkable that no farmers will sign it. We do not know whether you can get us relief or not, but unless we can use Mexican wetbacks farmers will lose hundreds of thousands of dollars by deterioration of cotton in the fields."

This just shows how difficult they are making the situation. They gave us an unworkable contract and then start picking up wetbacks so that we can't have any type of labor.

Sincerely yours,

Clinton P. Anderson

August 26, 1949

Dear Clint:

I appreciated your letter of the twenty-fourth in regard to the situation on the border. I have suggested the he* immediately go to

---

*In the context of previous correspondence, the "he" apparently refers to Truman's representative in the Bracero Pact negotiations.

work to try and get that contract written on a sensible basis. It certainly was written by someone without much sense of practical approach.

Sincerely yours,

Harry S Truman

NOTES

1. Richard B. Craig, *The Bracero Program: Interest Groups and Foreign Policy* (Austin: University of Texas Press, 1971), p. 50.

2. Ibid., p. 53.

SELECTED BIBLIOGRAPHY

Abrams, Elliott, and Franklin S. Abrams. "Immigration Policy – Who Gets in and Why." *The Public Interest* 38 (Winter 1975): 3-29.

Alvarado, Manuel de Jesús. "Slaves or Workers? Dilemmas Affecting Undocumented Mexican Farm Workers in the U.S." Tucson, Ariz., 1978. Unpublished research paper. (Mimeographed.)

Amin, Samir, ed. *Modern Migrations in Western Africa.* London: Oxford University Press, 1974.

Antezona, Fernando. "The 'Braceros' of Bolivia: The Human Tragedy of Thousands of Bolivian Migrant Workers in Argentina." *Migration Today* no. 7 (November 1966): 14-18.

Arango Cano, Jesús. *Inmigrantes para Colombia.* Bogotá: n.p., 1953.

Arbeláez C., Alfonso. "El éxodo de colombianos en el período 1963-1973." *Boletín mensual de estadística* no. 310 (May 1977): 7-43.

Armstrong, John A. "Mobilized and Proletarian Diasporas." *American Political Science Review* 70, no. 2 (June 1976): 393-408.

Ayres, Robert L. "Development Policy and the Possibility of a 'Livable' Future for Latin America." *American Political Science Review* 69, no. 2 (June 1975): 507-25.

Bach, Robert L. "Mexican Immigration and the United States." *International Migration Review* 12, no. 4 (1978): 536-58.

Barchfield, J. W. *Agrarian Policy and the National Development of Mexico.* New Brunswick, N.J.: Rutgers University Press/Transaction Books, 1978.

Bastos de Avila, F. B., and S. J. *La inmigración en América Latina.* Washington, D.C.: Pan American Union, 1964.

Bates, M., ed. *The Migration of Peoples to Latin American.* Washington, D.C.: Catholic University of America Press, 1957.

Beegle, J. Allan, et al. "Demographic Characteristics of the United States-Mexico Border." *Rural Sociology* 25 (1960): 107-62.

Bennett, Marion T. *American Immigration Policies: A History.* Washington, D.C.: Public Affairs Press, 1963.

Berger, John. *A Seventh Man: Migrant Workers in Europe.* New York: Viking Press, 1975.

Bermúdez, S. D. "La migración del campesino a Venezuela: Estudio socio-económico en dos comunidades de la costa atlántica: Guacamayal y Manati." Senior thesis, Department of Anthropology, Universidad de los Andes, 1976.

Bouscaren, Anthony T. *International Migrations Since 1945.* New York: Praeger, 1963.

Bouvier, Leon F., Henry S. Shryock, and Harry W. Henderson. "International Migration: Yesterday, Today, and Tomorrow." *Population Bulletin* 32, no. 4 (1977): 3-42.

Briggs, Vernon M., Jr. *Mexican Migration and the U.S. Labor Market, a Mounting Issue for the Seventies.* Austin: University of Texas, Center for the Study of Human Resources, 1974.

———. "Illegal Aliens: The Need for a Restrictive Border Policy." *Social Science Quarterly* 56, no. 3 (December 1975): 447-84.

———. "Illegal Immigration and the American Labor Force." *American Behavioral Scientist* 19, no. 3 (January/February 1976): 351-63.

Bryce-Laporte, Ray S. *The New Migrants: Their Origin, Visibility and Challenge to the American Public – Impact of the Immigration Act of 1965.* Washington, D.C.: Smithsonian Institution, Research Institute on Immigration and Ethnic Studies, 1976.

Bustamante, Jorge A. "The Historical Context of Undocumented Mexican Migration to the United States." *Aztlan, Chicano Journal of the Social Sciences and Arts* 3, no. 2 (Fall 1972): 257-81.

———. *So-called Wetback: The Social, Economic and Political Meaning of Immigration to the U.S.* Mexico City: Universidad Nacional de Mexico, 1972.

———. *Espaldas mojadas: Materia prima para la expansión del Capital norteamericano.* Mexico City: Colegio de Mexico, 1976.

———. "Structural and Ideological Conditions of the Mexican Undocumented Immigration to the United States." *American Behavioral Scientist* 19, no. 3 (January/February 1976): 364-76.

———. "Emigración indocumentada a los Estados Unidos." *Foro internacional* 18, no. 3 (January-March 1978): 430-63.

Cardona, Ramiro, ed. *América latina: Distribución espacial de la población.* Bogotá: Editorial Canal Ramírez, 1975.

Carías, Marco Virgilio. *Análisis sobre el conflicto entre Honduras y El Salvador.* Tegucigalpa: Universidad Nacional Autónoma de Honduras, Facultad de Ciencias Económicas, 1969.

Carliner, David. *The Rights of Aliens.* New York: Avon Books, 1977.

Carrón, Juan M. "Shifting Patterns in Migration from Bordering Countries to Argentina: 1914-1970." *International Migration Review* 13, no. 3 (Fall 1979): 475-87.

Chaney, Elsa M. "Colombian Migration to the United States: Part II." In Interdisciplinary Communications Program, Smithsonian Institution, *The Dynamics of Migration: International Migration,* pp. 87-141. Washington, D.C.: ICP Occasional Monograph Series, vol. 2, no. 5. ICP, 1976.

Chaney, E. M., and C. L. Sutton, eds. "Caribbean Migration to the U.S." *International Migration Review* 13, no. 2 (Summer 1979). Special issue of *Review.*

Chaparro O., Fernando, and Eduardo O. Arias. *Emigración de profesionales y técnicos colombianos y latinamericanos 1960-1970.* Bogotá: Fondo Colombiano de Investigaciones Científicas, 1970.

Chiswick, Barry R., ed. *Conference on U.S. Immigration Issues and Policies, Report.* Chicago: University of Illinois at Chicago Circle, 1980.

Cornelius, Wayne A. *Mexican Migration to the United States: Cause, Consequences, and U.S. Responses.* Cambridge, Mass.: Massachusetts Institute of Technology, Center for International Studies, 1978.

_____. "La migración illegal mexicana a los Estados Unidos: Conclusiones de investigaciones recientes, implicaciones políticas y prioridades de investigación." *Foro internacional* 18, no. 3 (January-March 1978): 399-429.

Cornelius, Wayne A., and Juan Díaz Canedo. "Rural Change and Emigration: Impact on Mexico and the U.S." Paper presented at American University, Washington, D.C., March 18, 1976.

Corwin, Authur F. "Mexican Emigration History, 1880-1970: Literature and Research." *Latin American Research Review* 8 (1973): 3-24.

_____, ed. *Immigrants and Immigrants: Perspectives on Mexican Labor Migration to the United States.* Westport, Conn.: Greenwood Press, 1978.

Craig, Richard B. *The Bracero Program: Interest Groups and Foreign Policy.* Austin: University of Texas Press, 1971.

Crist, Raymond E., and Charles M. Nissly. *East from the Andes.* Gainesville: University of Florida Press, 1973.

Cruz, Carmen Inés, and Juanita Castaño. "Colombian Migration to the United States: Part I." In Interdisciplinary Communications Program, Smithsonian Institution, *The Dynamics of Migration: International Migration,* pp. 41-86. ICP Occasional Monograph Series, vol. 2, no. 5. Washington, D.C.: ICP, 1976.

Davie, Maurice. *World Immigration (with Special Reference to the United States).* New York: Macmillan, 1939.

Davis, Kingsley. "The Migrations of Human Populations." In *The Human Population.* San Francisco: W. H. Freeman, 1974, pp. 55-65.

Departamento Administrativo Nacional de Estadística. "La migración interna y el proceso de concentración de la población de los departamentos." *Boletín mensual de estadística* no. 314 (September 1977): 9-48.

Díaz, Azuero, Agustín. "Régimen legal de emigrantes e inmigraciones en Colombia." Tesis de grado, Bogotá: Universidad Nacional, 1962.

Divine, Robert A. *American Immigration Policy, 1924-1952.* New York: DaCapo, 1972.

Domestic Council, Committee on Illegal Aliens. *Preliminary Report of the Domestic Council.* Washington, D.C.: Department of Justice, 1976.

Domínguez, Virginia R. *From Neighbor to Stranger: The Dilemma of Caribbean Peoples in the United States.* New Haven: Yale University, Antilles Research Program, 1975.

Ehrlich, Paul R., et al. *The Golden Door: International Migration, Mexico and the United States.* New York: Ballantine Books, 1979.

Farrell, James. *Give Us Your Poor (The Immigration Bomb).* San Francisco: Fulton-Hall, 1976.

Fox, Robert W., and Jerrold W. Huguet. *Population and Urban Trends in Central America and Panama.* Washington, D.C.: Inter-American Development Bank, 1977.

Fragomen, Austin T. *The Illegal Alien: Criminal or Economic Refugee.* Staten Island, N.Y.: Center for Migration Studies, 1973.

_____. "Alien Employment." *International Migration Review* 13, no. 3 (Fall 1979): 527-31.

Frisbie, Parker. "Illegal Migration from Mexico to the United States: A Longitudinal Analysis." *International Migration Review* 9, no. 1 (Spring 1975): 3-13.

Galarza, Ernesto. *Merchants of Labor: The Mexican Bracero Story.* Charlotte, N.C. and Santa Barbara, Calif.: McNally and Loftin, 1964.

Gall, Norman, "Los indocumentados colombianos." *American Universities Field Staff Reports* 16, no. 2 (December 1972).

Gamio, Manuel. *Mexican Immigrant: His Life Story.* Chicago: University of Chicago Press, 1931.

Gordon, Wendell. "A Case for a Less Restrictive Border Policy." *Social Science Quarterly* 56, no. 3 (December 1975): 485-91.

Grebler, Lew. *Mexican Immigration to the United States: The Record and Its Implications.* Los Angeles: University of California, Mexican American Study Project, 1966.

Halsell, Grace. *The Illegals.* New York: Stein and Day, 1978.

Hancock, Richard H. *The Role of the Bracero in the Economic and Cultural Dynamics of Mexico: A Case Study of Chihuahua.* Stanford: Stanford University Press, 1959.

Handelman, Howard. "Scarcity Amidst Plenty: Food Problems in Oil Rich Venezuela." *American Universities Field Staff Reports* no. 42 (September 1978).

Hawkins, Freda. *Canada and Immigration.* Montreal: McGill-Queen's University Press, 1972.

_____. "Canada's Green Paper on Immigration Policy." *International Migration Review* 9, no. 2 (Summer 1975): 237-50.

Herrera-Sobel, María. *The Bracero Experience: Elitelore Versus Folklore.* Los Angeles: UCLA, Latin American Center Publications, 1979.

Hoffman, Abraham. *Unwanted Mexican Americans in the Great Depression: Repatriation Pressures, 1929-1939.* Tucson: University of Arizona Press, 1974.

House Committee on the Judiciary. *Illegal Aliens: Analysis and Background, Report of Committee on the Judiciary.* Washington, D.C.: U.S. Government Printing Office, 1977.

House Select Committee on Population. *Immigration to the United States, Hearings Before the Select Committee on Population.* Washington, D.C.: U.S. Government Printing Office, 1975.

——. *Legal and Illegal Immigration to the United States, Report of Select Committee on Population.* Washington, D.C.: U.S. Government Printing Office, 1978.

House Subcommittee on Inter-American Affairs. *Undocumented Workers: Implications for U.S. Policy in the Western Hemisphere.* Washington, D.C.: U.S. Government Printing Office, 1978.

Jamail, Milton H. *The United States-Mexican Border: A Guide to Institutions, Organizations, and Scholars.* Tucson: University of Arizona, Latin American Center, 1980.

Jenkins, Craig. "Push/Pull in Illegal Mexican Migration to the U.S." *International Migration Review* 11, no. 2 (Summer 1977): 178-89.

Jenness, R. A. "Canadian Migration and Immigration Patterns and Government Policy." *International Migration Review* 8, no. 1 (Spring 1974): 5-22.

Johnson, Kenneth F. *Mexican Democracy: A Critical View.* Rev. ed. New York: Praeger, 1978.

——. "Stranded Mexican Aliens in Missouri and Illinois: A Spectrum of Livability and Human Rights Issues." Paper presented to the annual convention of the Rocky Mountain Council on Latin American Studies, El Paso, May 5, 1979.

Johnson, Kenneth F., and Nina M. Ogle. *Illegal Mexican Aliens in the United States: A Teaching Manual in Impact Dimensions and Alternative Futures.* Washington, D.C.: University Press of America, 1978.

Jones, Robert C. *Mexican War Workers in the United States: The Mexico-United States Manpower Recruiting Program, 1942-1944.* Washington, D.C.: Pan American Union, 1945.

Kane, Thomas T. "Social Problems and Ethnic Change: Europe's Guest Workers." *Intercom* (Population Reference Bureau) 6, no. 1 (January 1978): 1.

Kayser, Bernard. "European Migration: The New Pattern." *International Migration Review* 11, no. 2 (Summer 1977): 232-40.

Keely, Charles B. "Counting the Uncountable: Estimates of Undocumented Aliens in the United States." *Population and Development Review* 3, no. 4 (December 1977): 473-81.

Krauter, Joseph F., and Morris Davis. *Minority Canadians: Ethnic Groups.* Toronto: Methuen, 1978.

Kritz, Mary M. "The Impact of International Migration on Venezuelan Demographic and Social Structure." *International Migration Review* 9, no. 4 (Winter 1975): 513-43.

Lee, Everett S. "A Theory of Migration." *Demography* 3 (1966): 47-57.

Lewis, Sasha G. *Slave Trade Today: American Exploitation of Illegal Aliens.* Boston: Beacon Press, 1979.

Lohrmann, Reinhard. "European Migration: Recent Developments and Future Prospects." *International Migration* 14, no. 3 (1976): 229-40.

Mármora, Lelio. "Labor Migration Policy in Colombia." *International Migration Review* 13, no. 3 (Fall 1979): 440-54.

Marshall, Adriana. "Immigrant Workers in Buenos Aires Labor Market." *International Migration Review* 13, no. 3 (Fall 1979): 488-501.

Marshall, Dawn. "The International Politics of Caribbean Migration." In *The Restless Caribbean*, Richard Millett and W. Marvin Will, eds., New York: Praeger, 1979, pp. 42-50.

Martínez, Oscar J. *Border Boom Town: Ciudad Juárez Since 1848.* Austin: University of Texas Press, 1975.

Martínez, Vilma S. "Illegal Immigration and the Labor Force." *American Behavioral Scientist* 19, no. 3 (January/February 1976): 335-50.

Maselli, G. "Immigration as an Essential Element for the Development of Latin America." *International Migration* 2 (1967): 108-26.

Mayer, Kurt B. "Intra-European Migration During the Past Twenty Years." *International Migration Review* 9, no. 4 (Winter 1975): 441-48.

McWilliams, Carey. *North from Mexico: The Spanish-Speaking People in the United States.* New York: Lippincott, 1949.

Morales Vergara, Julio. "Latin Americans in Europe: Demographic Aspects Considered in the Light of Statistics of Several Selected Countries." *International Migration* 12, no. 1-2 (1968): 84-101.

Navotny, Ann. *Strangers at the Door.* Riverside, Conn.: Chatham Press, 1972.

Norquest, Carroll. *Rio Grande Wetbacks.* Albuquerque: University of New Mexico Press, 1972.

North, David S. *The Border Crossers*. Washington, D.C.: Trans-Century, 1970.

———. *Alien Workers: A Study of the Labor Certification Programs*. Washington, D.C.: Trans-Century, 1971.

North, David S., and Marion F. Houston. *The Characteristics and Role of Illegal Aliens in the U.S. Labor Market: An Exploratory Study*. Washington, D.C.: Linton and Company, 1976.

North, Robert C. *The World That Could Be*. New York: Norton, 1976.

Parai, Louis. "Canada's Immigration Policy, 1962-1974." *International Migration Review* 9, no. 4 (Winter 1975): 449-78.

Piore, Michael J. "Illegal Immigration in the United States: Some Observations and Policy Suggestions." In National Council on Employment Policy, *Illegal Aliens: An Assessment of the Issues*, pp. 25-35. Washington, D.C.: National Council on Employment Policy, 1976.

———. *Birds of Passage: Migrant Labor and Industrial Societies*. New York: Cambridge University Press, 1979.

Poitras, Guy, ed. *Immigration and the Mexican National: Proceedings*. San Antonio: Trinity University, Border Research Institute, 1978.

Portes, Alejandra. "Labor Functions of Illegal Aliens." *Society* 14 (September/October 1977): 31-37.

———, ed. "Illegal Mexican Immigration to the United States." *International Migration Review* 12, no. 4 (1978). Special issue.

———. "Toward A Structural Analysis of Illegal (Undocumented) Immigrants." *International Migration Review* 12 (Winter 1978): 469-84.

Richmond, Anthony H. *Aspects of the Absorption and Adaptation of Immigrants*. Ottawa: Information Canada, 1974.

Ríos-Bustamante, A. J., ed. *Immigration and Public Policy. Human Rights for Undocumented Workers and Their Families*. Los Angeles: University of California, Chicano Studies Center, 1977.

Rodino, Peter W., Jr. "The Impact of Immigration on the American Labor Market." *Rutgers Law Review* 27 (Winter 1974): 245-74.

Rodríguez, José Luis. *Los indocumentados*. Barranquilla: Tipografía Dovel, n.d.

Ross, Stanley R., ed. *Views Across the Border: The United States and Mexico.* Albuquerque: University of New Mexico Press, 1978.

Samora, Julian. *Los Mojados: The Wetback Story.* South Bend, Ind.: University of Notre Dame Press, 1971.

Sassen-Koob, Saskia. "Economic Growth and Immigration in Venezuela." *International Migration Review* 13, no. 3 (Fall 1979): 455-74.

Secretariado Nacional de Pastoral Social, Colombia. "Estudio sobre deportados colombianos desde Venezuela: 1973-1975." (Mimeographed.)

Segal, Aaron Lee, ed. *Population Policies in the Caribbean.* Lexington, Mass.: D. C. Heath and Company, 1975.

Stoddard, Ellwyn R. "A Conceptual Analysis of the 'Alien Invasion': Institutionalized Support of Illegal Mexican Aliens in the U.S." *International Migration Review* 10 (Summer 1976): 157-89.

_____ . "Selected Impacts of Mexican Migration on the U.S. Mexican Border." Paper presented to the U.S. Department of State Select Panel on U.S.-Mexican Border Issues, Washington, D.C., October 23, 1978.

Stoddard, Ellwyn R., Oscar J. Martínez, and Miguel Angel Martínez Lasso. *El Paso-Ciudad Juárez Relations and the "Tortilla Curtain."* El Paso: El Paso Council on the Arts and Humanities, 1979.

Storer, Desmond, Freda Hawkins, and S. M. Tomasi. *Amnesty for Undocumented Migrants: The Experience of Australia, Canada, and Argentina.* Staten Island, N.Y.: Center for Migration Studies, 1977.

Tanton, John. *Rethinking Immigration Policy.* Washington, D.C.: FAIR, 1979.

Thomas, Frinley. *Economics of International Migration.* London: Macmillan, 1958.

Torrado, Susana. "International Migration Policies in Latin America." *International Migration Review* 13, no. 3 (Fall 1979): 428-39.

Villalpando, M., et al. *A Study of the Socioeconomic Impact of Illegal Aliens on the County of San Diego.* San Diego, Calif.: County of San Diego, Human Resources Agency, 1977.

Villegas, A. "Migrations and Economic Integration in Latin America: The Andean Group." *International Migration Review* 11 (Spring 1977): 59-76.

Villegas, Jorge, "Condiciones del trabajador migrante, documentos de trabajo." Bogotá: OAS, 1974. (Mimeographed.)

_____. "Migraciones fronterizas de mano de obra colombiano hacia los países del grupo andino." Bogotá: Ministerio de Trabajo, 1975. (Mimeographed.)

Weaver, Thomas, and Theodore E. Downing, eds. *Mexican Migration*. Tucson: University of Arizona, Bureau of Ethnic Research, 1976.

Wilcox, Walter F. *International Migrations*, vol. II, *Interpretations*. New York: National Bureau of Economic Research, 1931. (Authorized copy by University Microfilms, Ann Arbor, Mich.)

Zero Population Growth, Immigration Committee. *ZPG and Immigration: A Discussion Paper*. Washington, D.C.: ZPG, 1974.

Ziegler, Benjamin, ed. *Immigration: An American Dilemma*. Lexington, Mass.: D. C. Heath, 1953.

INDEX

ABOUT THE AUTHORS

KENNETH F. JOHNSON has studied the allegiance-alienation continuum in Latin American politics since the 1960s. Currently he is professor of political science at the University of Missouri-St. Louis, and is conducting research in collaboration with the Hoover Institution at Stanford University. Since receiving the Ph.D. from UCLA in 1963, he has done comparative political research in the American Southwest, Argentina, Bolivia, Guatemala, Nicaragua, and Uruguay. He is perhaps best known for his *Mexican Democracy: A Critical View*. Professor Johnson's most recent inquiries have focused on Canadian studies, the political psychology of Peronism, and inter-American migration. He is also Adjunct Professor of Political Science at Emporia State University of Kansas.

MILES W. WILLIAMS is associate professor of political science at Central Missouri State University, Warrensburg, Missouri. He was visiting professor and investigator at Universidad de los Andes, Bogotá, Colombia, in the academic year 1970 and in the summers of 1974 and 1978. Over the past several years he has carried out extensive research on illegal migration in the American Southwest and Mexico.

Dr. Williams was coauthor of *Democracy, Power and Intervention in Latin American Political Life: A Study of Scholarly Images* with Kenneth F. Johnson, and has written several articles on Colombian politics. He holds B.A. and M.S. degrees from Kansas State College, Pittsburg, and received the Ph.D. from Vanderbilt University.